Desirable Literacies

Approaches to Language and Literacy in the Early Years

Second Edition

Edited by
Jackie Marsh and Elaine Hallet

SAGE

Los Angeles • London • New Delhi • Singapore • Washington DC

SAGE Publications Ltd
1 Oliver's Yard
55 City Road
London EC1Y 1SP

SAGE Publications Inc.
2455 Teller Road
Thousand Oaks, California 91320

SAGE Publications India Pvt Ltd
B 1/I 1 Mohan Cooperative Industrial Area
Mathura Road
New Delhi 110 044

SAGE Publications Asia-Pacific Pte Ltd
33 Pekin Street #02-01
Far East Square
Singapore 048763

Dewey no.	Subject headings
372 .6 MAR	Literacy Early years education
Location H+H	Abstract
3 Week 1 Week ✓ LUO Reference	Order details PO 34348 R 2205 CW

Library of Congress Control Number: 2008923547

British Library Cataloguing in Publication data

A catalogue record for this book is available from the British Library

ISBN 978-1-84787-281-4
ISBN 978-1-84787-282-1 (pbk)

Typeset by C&M Digitals (P) Ltd, Chennai, India
Printed in India at Replika Press Pvt Ltd
Printed on paper from sustainable resources

Contents

Acknowledgements

We would like to thank all of the contributors to this volume for their wonderful contributions and professional approach to the task. We are also indebted to Helen Fairlie and Rachel Hendrick at Sage Publications for making the editorial process so smooth for us. Thanks also to those friends and colleagues who have supported us along the way: we very much appreciate your ongoing encouragement. Finally, we express our gratitude to all of those early years practitioners whose work informs this book; your good practice deserves to be widely disseminated in these pages.

Notes on contributors

Viv Bird is an experienced adult and family literacy practitioner and former editor of *Literacy Today* magazine. Viv is also the author of several literacy guides and many articles. In 2002, she became director of the Literacy and Social Inclusion Project, a three-year Basic Skills Agency national support project delivered by the National Literacy Trust, UK, and was responsible for setting up a website (www.literacytrust org.uk/socialinclusion). With Rodie Akerman, she wrote a position paper, 'Every which way we can' launched at the Institute of Education in London in February 2005. *Literacy and Social Inclusion: The Handbook*, published in November 2005 by the National Literacy Trust Basic Skills Agency, describes how, working in partnership, policy makers can develop a community literacy strategy with positive outcomes for individuals, families and communities. Viv was Director of Reading Is Fundamental, UK, from 2005 to 2007, and was recently appointed as Director of Booktrust, an independent national charity that encourages people of all ages and cultures to discover and enjoy reading.

Ann Browne works on the primary PGCE programme at the University of East Anglia. Her teaching and research interests are largely related to language and literacy learning in the Foundation Stage and Key Stage 1. She has written a number of books of which the most recent is *Teaching and Learning Communication, Language and Literacy* which is published by Sage (2007).

Julie Dunn is a senior lecturer within the Faculty of Education, Griffith University, Brisbane, Australia, where she has responsibility for a range of undergraduate and postgraduate teacher education and applied theatre programmes. Her research interests are diverse, but mostly focus on play and drama within real and virtual spaces. Julie's awarding winning text, *Pretending to Learn* (co-authored with John O'Toole) has been translated into both Mandarin and Danish, and is a major resource in supporting teachers' education in primary drama. Julie was also the winner of the American Alliance for Theatre and Education Distinguished Dissertation Award in 2005 for her research that examined the dramatic play of pre-adolescent girls.

Rosie Flewitt is a researcher in the Education Dialogue Research Unit, Centre for Research in Education and Educational Technology, the Open University. She is engaged in a range of research projects relating to early years communication and learning in home and educational settings. She has a particular interest in literacy skills and practices in the early years, and in how different modes (such as text, images, layout, music and sounds), available in new and more traditional media, offer different learning potentials, reshaping young children's social and learning practices.

Naomi Flynn is a senior lecturer in education at the University of Winchester. She works with student teachers on undergraduate and postgraduate initial teacher education programmes, and manages the part-time PGCE route into teaching. Prior to her career in higher education she was a primary school teacher for 18 years. She taught mostly in multi-ethnic and culturally diverse settings, and for four years she served as head teacher of an inner-city primary school. Her experiences with children from ethnic minorities and for whom English is an additional language gave her a fascination with and a practical understanding of support for second language acquisition; this has developed into her main research interest. She is also interested in effective pedagogy for literacy and in how secure teachers' subject knowledge underpins positive classroom experiences for all children. This is explored in her book *The Learning and Teaching Reading and Writing* which she co-authored with Rhona Stainthorp (John Wiley, 2006.)

Julia Gillen is a senior lecturer in Digital Literacies at the Literacy Research Centre, Lancaster University. She researches aspects of children's learning mainly in relation to new technologies in both formal and informal settings. She is also co-director (with Ann Cameron at the University of British Columbia) of the 'A Day in the Life' project investigating aspects of culture in the lives of two-year-old girls in diverse global communities. Her publications include, *The Language of Children* (Routledge, 2003) and she has written many journal articles and chapters on topics including the use of interactive whiteboards in primary classrooms and children's telephone talk. Julia is a co-editor of the *Journal of Early Childhood Literacy*.

Elaine Hallet is a senior lecturer in Early Years and the Teaching Fellow for Foundation degrees within the Faculty of Education, Health and Sciences at the University of Derby. She teaches on a range of undergraduate and professional early years programmes. Her particular interest is work-based learning, Foundation degrees, the professional development of early years practitioners and early literacy development. She has a wide range of early years experience, having taught in nursery, infant, primary settings, the advisory service, and further and higher education settings. She has carried out research in early literacy and gender issues. Her current doctoral concerns the Early Years Foundation degrees as a professional higher education qualification. She has published in the field of Early Years and early literacy and has presented at local, regional, national and international conferences about early literacy development, early years, work-based learning and Foundation degrees.

Jackie Marsh is Professor of Education at the University of Sheffield, where she directs the EdD programme. She also teaches on the MA New Literacies and MA Early Childhood Education programmes. Jackie is involved in research that examines the role and nature of popular culture, media and new technologies in early childhood literacy, both in- and out-of school contexts. Publications include *Literacy and Social Inclusion: Closing the Gap* (Trentham, 2007, co-edited with Eve Bearne) and *Making Literacy Real* (Sage, 2005, with Joanne Larson). She is a co-editor of the *Journal of Early Childhood Literacy*.

Jim McDonagh is a senior lecturer in the Division of Education at Sheffield Hallam University where he teaches language and literacy on ITE routes. His current interests include English as an additional language and teachers' subject knowledge.

Sue McDonagh has worked extensively in nursery and primary settings and is currently a specialist early years inclusion teacher, working with staff in nursery and reception classes in Sheffield to support children with additional needs and their families.

Guy Merchant is a principal lecturer at Sheffield Hallam University, where he coordinates the work of the Language and Literacy Research Group. He has published numerous articles and book chapters on digital literacy, and is co-editor of the *Journal of Early Childhood Literacy*. His current research focuses on young children's uses of on-screen writing and how this can be incorporated into school curricula.

Fran Paffard is a senior lecturer in early years at the University of Cumbria, based at the Tower Hamlets site in London. She has worked as a primary and early years teacher for many years, and more recently as an advisory teacher and Foundation Stage consultant with the National Primary Strategy. She also works as a freelance consultant with particular interests in bilingualism, birth to threes, schemas and early literacy.

Kate Pahl is a senior lecturer in education at the University of Sheffield. She currently directs the EdD course in Literacy and Language and the Working with Communities masters programme. She also works on the Online MA in New Literacies at Sheffield. Kate is co-author, with Jennifer Rowsell, of *Literacy and Education: The New Literacy Studies in the Classroom* (Paul Chapman, 2005), and co-editor, with Jennifer Rowsell, of *Travel Notes from the New Literacy Studies: Instances of Practice* (Multilingual Matters, 2006). She is currently doing a project that explores ways in which museums can enhance social inclusion and create family learning opportunities. She is also involved in a research project, funded by the Arts Council, with two artists who are using artefacts to look at identity narratives with teachers in schools in Leeds.

Liz Stone began her teaching career almost ten years ago and has taught in Foundation Stage, Key Stage 1 and Key Stage 2. Although she has enjoyed working with all age groups, she feels her real talent lies in teaching and nurturing the very young. She has always enjoyed 'playing with words', writing her own stories, poems and songs for use in the classroom. Liz's classroom-based research has led to publications on topics including improving boys' attitudes to writing through design technology, and the use of spelling journals.

Tim Waller is a reader in early years education at the University of Wolverhampton. He was formerly director of postgraduate studies in the Department of Childhood Studies at Swansea University. Previously, he taught in nursery, infant and primary schools in London and has also worked in the United States. His research interests include ICT and social justice, outdoor learning and equality. He has been investigating the use of computers by young children for over eight years and completed his doctoral thesis on scaffolding young children's learning and ICT. Since September 2003 he has been coordinating a research project designed to investigate the promotion of children's well-being through outdoor play. He has also helped to establish the Men in Childcare Network in Wales. Tim has recently edited a book with Margaret Clark entitled *Early Childhood Education and Care: Policy and Practice*, published by Sage in 2007.

Introduction

Jackie Marsh and Elaine Hallet

It is nine years since the first edition of this book was published and so this second edition is both timely and necessary. In the intervening years, there have been many developments in the teaching and learning of language and literacy in the early years, and this edition, therefore, has been completely revised in order to reflect these changes. In this introduction, we offer an overview of the continuities and changes. Perhaps the first continuity we should attend to is the title of the book itself. Originally, the title was created to relate to the curriculum framework relevant in England at the time of the publication of *Desirable Outcomes for Children's Learning on Entering Compulsory Education* (DfEE/SCAA 1996). Whilst that framework is no longer in place, we decided to retain the title of *Desirable Literacies* because it does signal that what we hope to achieve in this book are reflections on and guidance for a language and literacy curriculum that is engaging and meaningful to learners, practitioners and families alike; truly desirable, in other words.

The aim of this second edition remains the same as the first in that it is intended to be an introductory text on different aspects of the teaching and learning of literacy for both students on early years courses and newly qualified practitioners. However, there may be aspects of the book that will interest more experienced early years educators. In addition, the book continues to offer guidance on practice that will be applicable to a range of settings including schools, maintained and non-maintained nurseries, children's centres, and voluntary settings, although it is expected that readers will adapt the material and guidelines to meet the needs of their specific contexts.

This second edition of *Desirable Literacies* remains concerned with the same issues that dominated the first edition: the need to offer a broad and rich language and literacy curriculum to young children, the importance of recognising literacy as a social and cultural practice, and, thus, ensure curricular links to the wider world, and the need to engage children as active participants in their learning. This is placed within a context in which it is recognised that successive rounds of neo-liberal policy-making across the globe over the last decade has led to an increasing emphasis on accountability and performance-management in many countries. This edition, like the first, stresses the need to ensure that all early years practitioners have the freedom to make informed decisions about children's language and literacy learning based on broad and deep subject knowledge and familiarity with how children learn. The emphasis, therefore, is on an incisive, research-informed review of best practice in a range of key areas. The subject matter of the majority of the chapters remains the same – you will find chapters here on oracy, reading, environmental print, writing, poetry, drama and planning and assessment, as in the first edition. In that edition, we were keen to emphasise the changing nature of literacy in a world in which technological changes were leading to profound social and cultural changes, and to explore the implications for early childhood educators. Again, this remains central to the work of the present volume. We continue to recognise the way in which the literacy curriculum needs to include multimodal texts and practices and to embrace the digital technologies which surround children from birth.

So, what has changed? Well, firstly, the chapters have been revised and updated to ensure that they reflect recent research, theory, policy and practice. Whilst many of the chapters have the same subject matter as the first edition, you will find that some of the authors have changed, which has meant complete rewrites of those chapters. We hope that you agree that this brings refreshingly new perspectives to long-standing issues and debates. Secondly, we have added chapters in areas that have developed in significance since the first issue. For example, we have included chapters on multimodality, media literacy and creativity; all of which issues have dominated the early literacy agenda in recent years. As a result, the book reflects up-to-the-minute research and theory in key aspects of early literacy language and learning.

In Chapter 1, Jim McDonagh and Sue McDonagh offer a succinct overview of language acquisition, exploring the key concepts, outlining the main theories in the field and offering guidance on practical ways of approaching the teaching and learning of oracy in early years settings. In Chapter 2, Naomi Flynn considers the needs of bilingual children and suggests ways in which we can value and build successfully upon children's linguistic repertoire. Both of these chapters recognise the value of a focus on language play in the early years, a theme which is extended in Liz Stone and Julia Gillen's chapter on the teaching and learning of poetry (Chapter 3). They consider a range of stimulating ideas that practitioners can use in their quest for promoting and extending children's language and literacy skills.

In Chapter 4, Elaine Hallet moves on to consider the role that environmental print has to play in children's reading development and analyses the role of the adult in this process. The adult role is not specifically defined as there is a recognition that all of the adults a child encounters in the early years have a crucial role to play and are all, in their different ways, educators and collaborators in the process of acquiring reading skills, knowledge and understanding. In Chapter 5, Guy Merchant presents a helpful overview of the wide-ranging research into early reading development and brings us up to date with recent initiatives. His chapter provides an introduction to ways of developing children as readers in the early years, and stresses the need to provide children with rich and stimulating literacy environments.

Children's reading and writing skills are inextricably linked and, in Chapter 6, Ann Browne presents a comprehensive overview of the nature of writing in the early years. She outlines a range of ideas for stimulating children's writing development in early years settings, nurseries and classrooms, and suggests ways in which we can support children's emergence as successful writers. In recent years, there has been a burgeoning of research in the area of multimodality, which has developed our understanding of how children's meaning-making encompasses a range of modes, not just alphabetic print. In Chapter 7, Rosie Flewitt offers an overview of this research and provides insights, through the use of engaging vignettes, into how early years practitioners can ensure that their curricula facilitate children's multimodal practices.

Creativity has been high on the educational agenda for some time and early years settings have always been keen to ensure that they embrace creative approaches to teaching and learning, despite increasing pressure from government bodies in some countries to formalise the curriculum in the early years. Such pressure can be robustly resisted by recourse to theory and research that illustrates how children are able to develop the necessary skills, knowledge and understanding to become successful communicators through creative, child-centred approaches. In Chapter 8, Kate Pahl outlines a Creative Partnerships funded project in which a creative approach to learning was highly effective for all involved. Creativity is a fundamental aspect of role play and drama, and in Chapter 9, Julie Dunn outlines approaches to drama that are both creative and purposeful. She suggests that adults need to carefully scaffold dramatic play at appropriate points if children are to maximise the literate potential of this kind of play.

In the nine years since the first edition, much has changed in the world of technology. In that edition, we included a chapter focused on the use of the computer, but the chapter that now replaces it, Chapter 10, written by Tim Waller, is focused on a much wider range of technologies. Tim reviews research in this field and offers insights into how children's digital literacy skills and knowledge, developed in the home from birth, can be extended in early years settings. In their interactions with digital technologies, children encounter media texts and there has been much interest in recent years in the concept of 'media literacy', the ability to access, use, analyse and create a range of media. In Chapter 11, Jackie Marsh outlines a range of practical approaches to the development of children's understanding of media texts, focusing in depth on moving image media.

The recognition of the role of families in children's language and literacy development is crucial if we are to forge genuine partnerships and value the different strengths that each party brings to the task of facilitating children's oracy and literacy development. Partnerships with parents have been strengthened through some of the exciting work which has been carried out in family literacy projects. Chapter 12 outlines some exciting approaches to working with families and Viv Bird provides the reader with an overview of key developments in this field over the last decade. During this period, there has been increasing interest in how we can involve parents and families in the assessment of children, and in Chapter 13, Fran Paffard offers suggestions about how this can be achieved. The chapter outlines key principles which should underpin assessment and planning for language and literacy in the early years, and emphasises the need to build a holistic picture of a child's attainment.

All of the authors in this volume acknowledge explicitly or implicitly the need to keep the vision of the child as a motivated individual, engaged in purposeful literacy practices, at the heart of our teaching. There is an implicit assumption in these pages that the language and literacy experiences and activities offered, negotiated with and initiated by children, need to be guided by educators who have a clear understanding of the very nature of oracy and literacy in current cultural landscapes. Here, authors have offered their road maps for this exciting and ever-changing terrain on the understanding that readers will want to venture into new pastures and unchartered territory. We hope that you will find in this second edition of *Desirable Literacies* inspiring material that will help you to chart your own path through the early language and literacy educational environment.

Reference

Department for Education and Employment (DfEE)/School Curriculum and Assessment Authority (SCAA) (1996) *Desirable Outcomes for Children's Learning on Entering Compulsory Education*. London: DfEE/SCAA.

1

Learning to talk, talking to learn

Jim McDonagh and Sue McDonagh

We can take it for granted that by the time a child enters nursery he or she will have acquired much of the grammatical system of his or her native language, much of the sound system and a substantial vocabulary. Although there will be individual differences between children, all will have used language to express meanings, to communicate with others and to make sense of the world in which they are growing up. In using language they also learn about language, their own and the language of others.

This chapter focuses on the important role speaking and listening activities have in the life of the young child. It begins with an overview of the child's early language acquisition and the different perspectives offered by those researching language, and goes on to discuss the role of the adult in developing a child's spoken language. The complexity of the acquisition process can only be lightly sketched here, the emphasis being on the importance of interaction in learning and learning to talk. This is followed by suggestions for classroom- or home-based activities.

Language acquisition – differing perspectives

Until the late 1950s the prevailing views on language acquisition were largely influenced by behaviourism until the work of Noam Chomsky marked a turning point in theories about the nature of language and the nature of language acquisition. The behaviourists' claim that language is learned through the acquisition of linguistic habits and that imitation of adults' speech plays an important role in learning is strongly countered by Chomsky's assertion that language is 'creative', that is, human beings produce novel utterances when they speak, rather than imitations of what they have heard before:

> The normal use of language is innovative in the sense that much of what we say in the course of normal language use is entirely new, not a repetition of anything that we have heard before, and not even similar in pattern – in any useful sense of the terms 'similar' and 'pattern' – to sentences or discourse that we have heard in the past. (Chomsky, 1972: 12)

To account for this ability to produce and understand novel utterances Chomsky claims that human beings possess an innate capacity to acquire language through the Language Acquisition Device (LAD), a mental mechanism specifically concerned with language. According to Chomsky, the adult utterances a child is exposed to are often too ill-formed and incomplete to serve as a suitable model to imitate. A child learning his or her first language will abstract rules from this rather shapeless language he or she encounters and incorporate these into his or her production/understanding of language, and will do so in a relatively short space of time.

It appears that we recognise a new utterance as a sentence not because it matches some familiar pattern in any simple way, but because it is generated by the grammar that each individual has somehow and in some form internalised. Chomsky asserts that natural languages are governed by complex rules that are not apparent in 'surface structure', the actual utterances of a language. If a child acquiring a language had to rely solely on the snatches of language heard in his or her environment he or she would not be able to abstract, and so acquire, the rules. Evidence that children do not acquire language through imitation of adults can be seen from the 'overgeneralisations' evident in their speech; for example, 'It got broked', 'She putted it on the carpet'. In one experiment McNeill (1966: 61) effectively demonstrated that if a child is not ready he or she will not be able to imitate an adult's utterance:

Child: Nobody don't like me.

Mother: No, say 'Nobody likes me'.

Child: Nobody don't like me.
           [Eight repetitions of this exchange]

Mother: No, now listen carefully: say *Nobody likes me*.

Child: Oh! Nobody don't likes me.

If anything, an adult will imitate a child's utterance, although few sober adults would ever say 'All-gone milk' or 'I sawed two mouses'.

Chomsky's ideas on language led to important studies of children's acquisition of language in the 1960s. Evidence was provided that a child's language develops through hypothesis-testing, that is, the child is actively involved in acquiring the mother tongue, and not just a passive recipient, as some behaviourists would claim. Through testing out hypotheses the child's language develops, 'by successive approximations passing through several steps that are not yet English' (McNeill, 1966: 61). The aim of first language acquisition studies was to describe these successive approximations or interim grammars.

Research, such as that of Brown (1973) and deVilliers and deVilliers (1973), demonstrates that children follow a natural sequence of development in their acquisition of language. Although the rate of development might vary between children, the order in which language is acquired remains invariant. If we look at just one area that has been extensively studied, that of sentence structure, we can see that by the age of three or three and a half years, the child is acquiring complex sentence structure with the use of coordinating conjunctions such as 'but' and 'and' as well as subordinating conjunctions like 'because'. Comparative forms emerge ('this is *bigger*'; 'this is *more better*') and we see the beginnings of relative clauses: 'This is one *what* Mummy got'. Over the next year or so the child will acquire many of the irregular forms of verbs and nouns and make fewer overgeneralisations in their speech. However, many overgeneralisations will persist until much later in a child's development. It is not uncommon for eight year olds to say 'I hurted my knee', for instance. Pronouns are largely acquired during this stage, auxiliary verbs such as 'can', 'will' and so on, and the beginnings of passive forms of the verb: 'I got smacked'. The creativity Chomsky mentioned as characteristic of human language is very much in evidence during this period with children producing unique utterances (Pinker, 1994).

Communicative competence

In his writings Chomsky is concerned with discovering the mental reality behind actual behaviour, arriving at an understanding of a native speaker's *competence*. In Chomsky's view a grammar of a language is a model of the linguistic abilities of a native speaker of that language, which allow him or her to speak/understand that particular language. This is the speaker–hearer's *competence*; the speaker–hearer's knowledge of her or his language which is distinguished from Chomsky's notion of *performance;* the actual use of language in concrete situations (Chomsky, 1965: 4).

For Chomsky, the actual use of language in concrete situations is rather untidy and not deemed worth of serious study. Others have argued, however, that language is dependent on the social context and that interaction plays an important role in language acquisition. Micheal Halliday (1976) has proposed a 'functional' view of children's language development and contends that:

> Learning language is learning the uses of language and the meaning potential associated with them; the structures, the words and the sounds are the realisation of this meaning potential. Learning language is learning to mean. (in Kress, 1976: 8)

Halliday's 'meaning potential' is akin to Hymes's (1972) notion of 'communicative competence', but differs from Hymes's in that Halliday is not interested in 'the artificial concept' of competence, that is, what the speaker–hearer *knows*. His concern is with what the speaker–hearer *does* with language in sociolinguistic or functional terms.

Hymes (1972) and Campbell and Wales (1970) both recognise the limitations of Chomsky's definition of 'competence', and propose the notion of *communicative competence* as encompassing a range of ability broader than just grammatical knowledge. Campbell and Wales (1970), in a discussion of developments in language acquisition theory, define competence as:

> The ability to produce or understand utterances which are not so much grammatical but, more important, appropriate to the context in which they are made. (Campbell and Wales, 1970: 247)

'Competence' then is extended beyond exclusive grammatical knowledge to include contextual or sociolingual competence, knowledge of the rules of language use.

The importance of interaction

Chomsky's claim that the linguistic input children received from adults was 'degenerate' and not worthy of analysis, and that the only interface between input and output was located in the child's mind, has been challenged by those researchers who have examined the interactions children have with their 'caretakers'. Those who have studied first language acquisition from an 'interactionist' perspective, like Jean Berko Gleason (1977; 2004), emphasise the contribution of external as well as internal factors to language acquisition. She argues that children do not acquire language all by themselves:

> They are not simply miniature grammarians working on a corpus composed of snatches and fragments of adult discourse. (Gleason, 1977: 199)

By examining interactions between children and their mothers (or other 'caretakers') researchers have established the existence of 'motherese', speech that is produced by an adult (or older child) in interaction with a child whose linguistic competence and cognitive development are perceived as limited. Mother's, caretaker's or child-directed speech is simple and redundant; it contains many questions, many imperatives, few past tenses, few coordinating or subordinating conjunctions, few disfluencies; and is pitched higher with an exaggerated intonation (Snow, 1995; Snow and Ferguson, 1977).

Motherese varies according to the communicative demands of the situation, and even experienced caretakers cannot produce adequate motherese if the child is not present to cue him or her. Landes (1975) highlights that parents and other caretakers modify their speech in various ways until the child is at least 10 years old. From the research into motherese we find claims that the best input for a child is one step beyond the stage the child is at (Gleitman, Newport and Gleitman, 1984).

In addition to the presence of the LAD (Language Acquisition Device) proposed by Chomsky, Jerome Bruner (1983) suggests that there is also a LASS (Language Acquisition Support System). According to Bruner, adults provide a framework of 'scaffolding' which enables the child to learn. In contexts that are familiar and routinised, the adult, one step ahead of the child, cues the child's responses. By providing ritualised dialogue and constraints through questioning and feedback to the child, the adult prepares the cognitive base on which language is acquired. Cazden (1983) also uses the term 'scaffolding' to refer to the adult's role but makes a distinction between vertical and sequential scaffolding. Vertical scaffolding involves the adult extending the child's language by, for instance, asking further questions. Sequential scaffolding occurs in the routinised activities adults and children share, for example during games, bath time, meals, etc. The predictability of the language used in routinised situations provides a framework for language to develop. Cazden also claims that adults support children through providing language models, often in response to children's utterances. If a child, for instance, says 'She taked my crayon' the adult's response might be: 'She *took* your crayon, did she?' To these two aspects of the adult's role, Cazden adds a third, direct instruction. This is mostly seen in contexts where the rules of social convention apply where the child is expected to repeat a word or phrase, for example, 'Say "Bye bye"'.

Evelyn Hatch (1978a) takes the view that the need to converse precedes the acquisition of specific language features. She writes:

> One learns how to do conversation, one learns how to act verbally, and out of this interaction syntactic structures are developed. (Hatch, 1978a: 404)

There is a number of stages in this process, beginning with attention-getting, either verbally or non-verbally. Once attention has been gained, the next task is to nominate a topic. Hatch (1978b: 407) provides an example of the two stages from the conversation of a five-year-old Taiwanese boy, Paul, with an adult:

Paul: Oh-oh!

A: What?

Paul: This [points to ant]

A: It's an ant

Paul: Ant

Paul: This

A: A pencil

Paul: Pencil

Once a topic has been nominated the conversational partner is constrained by the rules of conversation to make an appropriate response. Conversations are then built up ('vertical structures') which serve as the prototypes for the syntactic structures ('horizontal structures') which develop from them (Scollon, 1976). It would appear though, that these structures evident in the exchange between the adult and child above are not typical of child–child speech. One notable difference between adult–child conversation and child–child discourse is in the use of 'functions' (Ochs Keenan, 1983) by children. According to Ochs Keenan, 'functions' are ways of making a relevant response in conversation through repeating, modifying or recombining elements of what the other child has said. In her study of two- and three-year-old children she found that the children made great use of sound play, songs and nursery rhymes. For instance, a child might repeat the whole of a previous turn:

Child 1:   You know why?

Child 2:   You know why? [or substitute a part of the other's utterance]

Child 1:   You know why?

Child 2:   You know what?

By the late 1970s we can see that the prevailing model of the language development process can be seen as a combination of *social* and *cognitive* characteristics which recognises, and goes beyond, the Chomskyan perspective on language. In the early stages we can see caretaker and child involved in interactions that provide a framework on which language is built. We now turn our attention briefly to some further social issues.

Deficit or difference?

In the English-speaking world there has been a tradition of negative views towards other languages and dialects, and amongst teachers, a history of prejudice towards working class non-standard speakers of English. In a study of reception teachers and headteachers Hughes and Cousins (1990) found that the vast majority held 'deficit' views of their pupils' language. These teachers made assumptions about the language spoken in the home and felt that children were arriving at school suffering from linguistic deprivation. In the 1970s language deficit views, through the work of Basil Bernstein (1960) and Joan Tough (1977) amongst others, were extremely influential and lent academic weight to language enrichment programmes such Headstart in the United States. It was in the US that language deficit models came under attack from linguists such as Labov (1972), who argued that the language of the black working class children he studied was not deficient but 'different' from that used by their middle class peers. Unlike the work of Bernstein and Tough, which did not collect evidence of children's language in the home, research which actually examined language in the homes of children tended to support Labov's views. In a longitudinal study which charted children's language development in the home and at school, Gordon Wells concluded that:

> There is no justification for continuing to hold the stereotyped belief that there are strongly class-associated differences in the ways in which parents talk with their children. Nor is there justification for forming expectations about children's oral language abilities on entry to school that are based solely on their parent's membership in a certain social class. (Wells, 1986: 140)

Where there was a difference it was not in relation to their experience in oral language, but in literacy practices that did not match those of school. Wells goes on to argue that schools may perpetuate the disadvantage experienced by administering assessment procedures that emphasise literacy skills, rather than speaking and listening. In their study of four year olds at home and at nursery Tizard and Hughes (1984) lend weight to the argument that children receive rich linguistic experiences regardless of their social background. In their research they found that:

> The conversations in the working class homes were just as prolific as those in the middle class homes. There was no question of these children 'not being talked to at home', and few signs of the language deprivation that has so often been described [...] the working class children were clearly growing up in a rich linguistic environment. (Tizard and Hughes, 1984: 8)

Tizard and Hughes also found that children had few encounters with adults in the nursery school and staff had different expectations from the children's mothers. In the United States, Shirley Brice Heath's (1983) intensive study of three communities also found that there was a mismatch between the language of the home and that of school, and that what was valued in the community was not readily valued by teachers. Heath was interested in how children acquire language and literacy as part of their socialisation into the norms and values of their community. Differing ways of using language based on the different world views of social groups meant that continuity in children's socialisation was broken once they entered school.

Talk in the early years

The ability to participate as a speaker and listener is essential to a child's linguistic, social, emotional and cognitive development in their early years at school. Vygotsky (1962) suggests that talk plays an important part in laying the foundations for a child's intellectual ability in later life. The practice of speaking enables a child to become an active learner and to be able to explore his or her experiences and relationships. Talking is also a means by which learning across the curriculum can be developed into understanding. The introduction of the National Literacy Strategy (DfEE, 1998) and the emphasis on the raising of standards in literacy meant that the role of speaking and listening became marginalised. There was little official emphasis on the value of talk in the classroom until more recent changes have once again placed talk at the heart of the literacy curriculum (DfES 2006; DfES 2007). The teacher's role in finding ways of planning for and valuing talk is essential if children are to grow confidently as learners and thinkers.

The National Oracy Project (Norman, 1990; 1992) outlined three important aspects of speaking and listening:

1   social – how we use language to interact with others
2   communicative – how we transfer meaning
3   cognitive – how we learn through talk.

Children need to have opportunities to talk in a variety of settings in order to support their language development in these three dimensions. These opportunities for talk need to be planned for and resourced by schools and nurseries and the adult's role in valuing talk is essential if it is not to be sidelined (Anning and Edwards,1999).

Role of the adult

If we are to enable young children to develop as speakers and listeners we need to consider our role in the process and how we act as speakers and listeners ourselves. We model the forms and functions of language in our dealings with children, their parents and other adults. If we expect children to listen to others with respect we need to model this behaviour also. This means listening to what children have to say and responding to what interests them, without interrupting or hurrying them on. As early years practitioners, we need to be wary of asking too many questions and ensure we allow children time to process information and respond. An important aspect of the adult's role is to 'scaffold' what children offer, to extend and expand on their utterances. When we question children we need to include 'open' questions, which invite children to think (for example, 'What do you think about ...?'; 'How do you feel about ...?'), in addition to 'closed' questions which enable us to check children's knowledge and understanding (for example, 'Which of these is blue?').

Good early years practice encompasses the idea of adults being participants, not just supervisors, in activities; for instance, taking on a role, in the café or home corner. In this way we can provide children with appropriate vocabulary in the different contexts in which they talk and help them to develop their metalinguistic awareness through talking about talk and drawing their attention to how we use language.

We need to plan speaking and listening activities to make the most of the opportunities for meaningful talk, and we need to monitor and assess the talk that takes place. In assessing children's speaking and listening, the purposes, contexts and audiences for talk have to be considered. Because talk is transient (unless we record it) it is useful to keep notes of children's talk based on our observations. For this purpose, a notebook or talk diary, in which observations are recorded, should be close at hand. In addition, occasional planned observations using a format (DfES, 2003) or a 'talk audit' (Godwin and Perkins, 1998) which specifies the purpose, context and audience, will supplement incidental observations. The following section suggests ways in which talk can be valued.

Story as a focus for talk

Interactive storytelling plays an important part in helping children to develop their expressive and receptive language in the early years. Storybooks, 'story sacks' and props provide essential visual support for children who are learning English as an additional language or who have additional needs. They also provide opportunities for children to hear, process, and practise models of language in a non-threatening way. Children learn to discuss, retell, describe and give opinions on events and characters in their favourite stories. They also learn to use the language structures in well-known stories as a foundation for their own use of language.

Story sacks

'Story sacks' contain a storybook with objects and props for retelling the story. These can be used by adults to encourage children's language development around the story. The sacks can also contain a game around the theme of the story and a non-fiction book connected to the story. For example, a story sack based on Eric Carle's book *The Very Hungry Caterpillar* might contain, in addition to the book itself:

- a toy caterpillar
- a selection of plastic fruit that the caterpillar eats
- a big green leaf with holes in it
- a butterfly
- food from the story (scanned and laminated so children can handle them)
- a board game about the foods the caterpillar eats
- a book about caterpillars and butterflies.

Language/story packs

Cut out, laminated pictures from well-known stories can be used to put on a story board or white board in order to tell the story. Children are invited to use these props to retell the story or make comments on characters. For example, using the book *Rosie's Walk* (Hutchins, 1968) children can make Rosie the hen walk across the yard, around the pond, over the haystack, past the mill, through the fence and under the beehives, talking through each step as they go. Using animals from the book *Brown Bear, Brown Bear, What do You See?* (Martin, 1983) figures of all the animals can be put on the board and the children ask each animal 'What do you see?' and decide which animal comes next in the book.

Show and tell/news time

Children are asked to talk about something they have brought to show the rest of their class or group, or to describe something that has happened to them. The other children are invited to ask questions and make comments. Spoken news can be recorded in a 'news book' as a way of valuing the child's talk. News and comments can also be recorded into a tape recorder and played back. As a variation on this theme, a 'talking television' can be made from a box large enough to fit over a child's head. When it is 'switched on', the person on television can tell the news.

Songs and rhymes

Songs and rhymes regularly sung and spoken can encourage children's language development and their understanding of rhythm and rhyme. This is a particularly useful activity when accompanied by actions as these give extra visual support to those children whose first language is not English or who have additional needs. Songs and rhymes can be used with props such as pictures and puppets to encourage understanding and discussion. For instance, for 'Little Mousie Brown' ('Up the tall white candlestick crept Little Mousie Brown') a finger puppet of Mousie can be made to go up the candlestick. 'Song boxes' or 'song bags' with objects or pictures relating to songs or rhymes can also be used as visual prompts to help children choose which song/rhyme they want to sing. For example, a spider for the 'Incy Wincy Spider' rhyme or a potato for the 'One Potato, Two Potato' rhyme.

Games and play

Turn-taking games encourage listening, copying, vocabulary-building, social interaction, and confidence-building. These games need adult support so that the language can be modelled and children have opportunities to practise following verbal and non-verbal cues. For example, a 'feely bag' with objects inside can be passed around a small group of children. Each child takes a turn to take something out of the bag. Depending on the level of language, the object can simply be named or commented upon. Similarly, bags of objects around a theme can be useful for building vocabulary and for stimulating talk. For example a 'baby bag' could contain a baby's bottle, nappy, dummy, teddy, rattle and so on. The objects can be handled, named and discussed at each child's level of language development.

Imaginative play with 'small world' toys, construction equipment and natural materials such as sand and water, can stimulate a great deal of talk and interaction between children. This play is particularly useful when supported by an adult who can provide a model of language for the children. For example, using wild animals in a jungle setting with logs, trees and sand, talk can centre on finding the young animals and matching them to their parents, on discussing which is the biggest or smallest animal, what animals like to eat, and so on. Adults can also simply provide a running commentary on what the child is doing for example, 'You're hiding the elephant in the sand' and allowing the child time to respond.

Magic microphone

Children sit in a circle and an object such as a stone or a microphone is passed around. The person who has the microphone or object can speak; the others must listen without interrupting. The adult might provide the topic for discussion or the children might talk about things that have happened to them.

Shared story writing/telling

Using props such as puppets or small world figures, children can contribute to telling a story. This is recorded in their words by an adult and made into a book which can be kept in the book corner. Children can also tell a story by speaking into a tape recorder. At the end of the story it is played back and children are invited to make comments. Tapes of stories told by other adults, including other languages if the children are bilingual, can be made and used in the classroom.

Making books

Books can be made using digital photographs taken of the children engaged in various activities. A collection of these books in the book corner is always very popular with children and stimulates a lot of talk. These books are especially useful for children who have difficulties with speech and language because single words or phrases can be modelled and elicited in the books, for example, 'Qasim eating', 'Shazia running', 'Ryan painting'. Books can also be made using the children's own drawing and mark-making. For example, a book based upon a simple version of a favourite story, such as Rod Campbell's *My Presents* (1988), where the children have to lift a flap to see the present drawn by them underneath. Books made around the children's own heritage experiences such as Eid, a new baby or a trip to the post office can stimulate lots of talk in the classroom and nursery.

Speaker's chair

Like the 'author's chair' or 'storyteller's chair' in many classrooms, the speaker's chair allows a child to address the rest of the group about some work, a story, an opinion, news, etc. This can provide an opportunity for children to develop confidence about speaking in a group. The less vocal child is able simply to present their work and listen to others commenting. Comments can be recorded by an adult, in the child's words, and displayed on a 'talk board' or alongside the piece of work.

Hotseating

Older children can take turns to adopt the role of a character from a book, song or rhyme and face questioning from their classmates. For example, playing Humpty Dumpty who is questioned or interviewed about his accident with questions such as 'How did you feel?', 'What happened after you fell off the wall?' and so on.

Role play

Imaginative settings like a dark cave or realistic settings such as a café or post office provide a stimulus for a lot of child–child talk. Children learn to re-enact situations in which they have seen adults, and add their own contributions. Use of pairs of telephones can encourage conversations between children. Adult models of language within the role play area can be important at the outset for a short time. For instance, a doctor's surgery might include talk about appointments, times, illnesses, medicine, etc. A 'talk corner' with a telephone box, a sofa with a table containing stimuli and so on serves a similar function.

Props for talk

Objects like hats, jewellery, a cloak, can stimulate imaginative talk as children take on different roles. Adults can support children's developing language skills by commenting upon the props; for example, 'My hat's got a feather', 'Holly's shoes are shiny'. Likewise, a 'treasure box' of interesting objects like shells, small teddies, keys, Russian dolls, feathers, and so on can engage children who often find it difficult to take part in shared attention activities by providing opportunities for talk about the 'treasure' objects. Puppets also provide a lot of stimulation for talk for even very shy children who are often prepared to talk to or through a puppet.

Other people speaking

Visitors and parents/carers can be invited in to speak to the children or tell them stories. The use of other voices, dialects and languages can enrich the language environment in the early years setting.

Using the outdoors

The importance and impact of outdoor play and experiences outside of the early years setting upon children's development cannot be overestimated. These experiences are particularly important for the development of their social interaction skills and their understanding of their place in the world. Outdoor play offers opportunities to practise the vocabulary of movement and position. It also encourages children to develop the language of negotiation and turn-taking in their interaction with other children. Outdoors, children have opportunities to build upon their social and communication skills in a very practical way. Taking part in activities, such as ring games, throwing and catching or rolling a ball, waiting for their turn to climb up the ladder, contributes greatly to their active learning of language. Outside trips to see other environments, such as the seaside, a farm, an art gallery, offer wonderful opportunities for extending children's vocabulary and to make connections between new information and their own experiences.

Listening centre

Taped stories and rhymes can be used in a listening centre where several children can listen at the same time. The listening centre area also needs to have visual props such as the storybook to accompany the tape, puppets or small world figures to bring alive the story being listened to.

Conclusion

The activities listed above cover a range of purposes, contexts and audiences for children's talk. In planning these we need to consider these three aspects and what opportunities there might be to observe and record children's speaking and listening. We cannot assume that because children like talking and appear to us to be competent speakers that this aspect of their education can be left to develop without support. Speaking and listening skills underpin children's ability to understand the whole curriculum. As Browne suggests:

> Perhaps the most important reason for developing children's oral language is that all learning depends on the ability to question, reason, formulate ideas, pose hypotheses and exchange ideas with others. These are not just oral language skills, they are thinking skills. (2001: 7)

As early years educators we need to ensure that all children have opportunities to develop this essential tool for learning.

Suggestions for further reading 📖

Makin, L. and Whitehead, M. (2003) *How to Develop Children's Early Literacy: A Guide for Professional Carers and Educators*. London: Paul Chapman.

Peccei, J. (2006) *Child Language: A Resource Book for Students*. London: Routledge.

Weitzman, E. and Greenberg, J. (2002) *Learning Language and Loving it: A Guide to Promoting Children's Social, Language and Literacy Development in Early Childhood Settings*. Toronto: Haden Centre.

Whitehead, M. (2007) *Developing Language and Literacy with Young Children*. London: Paul Chapman.

References

Anning, A. and Edwards, A. (1999) *Promoting Children's Learning from Birth to Five: Developing the New Early Years Professional*. Buckingham: Open University Press.

Bernstein, B. (1960) 'Language and social class', *British Journal of Sociology* 11: 271–6.

Brown, R. (1973) *A First Language*. London: George Allen and Unwin.

Browne, A. (2001) *Developing Language and Literacy 3–8*. London: Paul Chapman.

Bruner, J. (1983) *Child's Talk: Learning to use Language*. New York: Norton.

Campbell, R. (1988) *My Presents*. London: Campbell Books.

Campbell, R. and Wales, R. (1970) 'The study of language acquisition', in J. Lyon (ed.) *New Horizons in Linguistics*. Harmondsworth: Penguin.

Carle, E. (1994) *The very Hungry Caterpiller*. Harmondsworth: Puffin.

Cazden, C.B. (1983) 'Contexts for literacy: in the mind and in the classroom', *Journal of Reading Behaviours* 14(4): 413–27.

Chomsky, N. (1965) *Aspects of the Theory of Syntax*. Cambridge, MA: MIT Press.

Chomsky, N. (1972) *Language and Mind*. New York: Harcourt Brace Jovanovich.

deVilliers, J. and deVilliers, P. (1973) 'A cross-sectional study of the acquisition of grammatical morphemes in child speech', *Journal of Psycholinguistic Research* 2: 267–78.

DfEE (Department for Education and Employment) (1998) *National Literacy Strategy*. London: DfEE Publications.

DfES (Department for Education and Skills) (2003) *Speaking, Listening, Learning: Working with Children in Key Stage1 and Key Stage 2*. Nottingham: DfES Publications.

DfES (Department for Education and Skills) (2006) *Primary Framework for Literacy and Mathematics*. Nottingham: DfES Publications.

DfES (Department for Education and Skills) (2007) *Statutory Framework for the Early Years Foundation Stage*. Nottingham: DfES Publications.

Gleason, J.B. (1977) 'Talking to children: some notes on feedback', in C.E. Snow and C.A. Ferguson (eds) *Talking to Children: Language Input and Acquisition*. Cambridge: Cambridge University Press. pp. 199–206.

Gleason, J.B. (2004) *The Development of Language.* Needham, MA: Allyn and Bacon.

Gleitman, L.R., Newport, E.L. and Gleitman, H. (1984) 'The current status of the motherese hypothesis', *Journal of Child Language* 11: 43–79.

Godwin, D. and Perkins, M. (1998) *Teaching Language and Literacy in the Early Years.* London: David Fulton.

Hatch, E.M. (1978a) *Second Language Acquisition.* Rowley, MA: Newbury House.

Hatch, E.M. (1978b) 'Discourse analysis and second language acquisition', in E.M. Hatch (ed.) *Second Language Acquisition: A Book of Readings.* Rowley, MA: Newbury House. pp. 401–35.

Heath, S.B. (1983) *Ways with Words.* Cambridge: Cambridge University Press.

Hughes, M. and Cousins, J. (1990) 'Teachers' perceptions of children's language', in D. Wray (ed.) *Emerging Partnerships: Current Research in Language and Literacy.* Clevedon: Multilingual Matters. pp. 33–46.

Hutchins, P. (1968) *Rosie's Walk.* New York: Macmillan.

Hymes, D. (1972) 'On communicative competence', in J.B. Pride and J. Holmes (eds) *Sociolinguistics.* Harmondsworth: Penguin.

Kress, G.R. (1976) *Halliday: System and Function in Language.* London: Oxford University Press.

Labov, W. (1972) *Language in the Inner City.* Philadelphia: University of Pennsylvania Press.

Landes, J. (1975) 'Speech addressed to children: issues and characteristics of parental input', *Language Learning* 25: 355–79.

McNeill, D. (1966) 'Developmental psycholinguistics', in F. Smith and G.A. Miller (eds) *The Genesis of Language: A Psycholinguistic Approach.* Cambridge, MA: MIT Press.

Martin, B. (1983) *Brown Bear, Brown Bear, What Do You See?* New York: Henry Holt and Co.

Norman, K. (1990) *Teaching Talking and Learning in Key Stage One.* London: National Curriculum Council/National Oracy Project.

Norman, K. (1992) *Thinking Voices.* London: Hodder and Stoughton.

Ochs Keenan, E. (1983) 'Conversational competence in children', in E. Ochs Keenan and B.B. Schieffelin (eds) *Acquiring Conversational Competence.* London: Routledge and Kegan Paul.

Pinker, S. (1994) *The Language Instinct.* London: Penguin.

Scollon, R. (1976) *Conversations with a One Year Old.* Honolulu: University of Hawaii.

Snow, C.E. (1995) 'Issues in the study of input: fine-tuning, universality, individual and developmental differences, and necessary causes', in P. Fletcher and B. MacWhinney (eds) *Handbook of Child Language.* London: Blackwell.

Snow, C.E. and Ferguson, C.A. (1977) *Talking to Children: Language Input and Acquisition.* Cambridge: Cambridge University Press.

Tizard, B. and Hughes, M. (1984) *Young Children Learning: Talking and Thinking at Home and at School.* London: Fontana.

Tough, J. (1977) *The Development of Meaning.* London: Allen and Unwin.

Vygotsky, L. (1962) *Thought and Language.* Cambridge, MA: MIT Press.

Wells, G. (1986) *The Meaning Makers.* London: Hodder and Stoughton.

2

Living in two worlds: the language and literacy development of young bilinguals

Naomi Flynn

Britain is a country rich in its linguistic, ethnic and cultural diversity. Teachers, even in comparatively rural settings, can expect to have children for whom English is an additional language (EAL) in their classes. There is evidence that children who operate regularly in more than one language are likely to develop a linguistic metacognition that enhances their literacy skills. Yet, the teaching of children whose home language is not English is perhaps seen as something specialised and something that is done by 'someone else'. When someone else isn't there, practitioners might feel unsupported and under-skilled so that the child's needs are perceived as a problem rather than a normal part of provision in an inclusive setting. This chapter explores the experiences of children developing a new spoken language and of children reading and writing in a new language. It tracks the research evidence relating to language and literacy development in young bilinguals and it considers issues of individual difference. It offers examples of good practice in early years settings and demonstrates how much the pedagogy that might support EAL pupils in their language and literacy development is in fact good practice for all pupils.

Defining bilingualism

Throughout this chapter we refer to children who are 'bilingual' and those who are developing a 'second' language. It should be noted, however, that many children learning English as an additional language are already exposed to two or more languages before they reach English. This would be true, for example, for Muslim children who will be learning Arabic for their study of the Quran. For this reason the terms 'bilingual' and 'EAL' should be interpreted quite generally to mean children operating in two or more languages where the home language is not English.

Understanding that bilingualism is not one thing is important for practitioners teaching children who come to them with a range of language backgrounds. Children will develop the languages that they eventually use in a range of different ways and from different influences at different times. In those children born to parents who each have a different first language, bilingualism starts from birth. These children grow up learning two languages simultaneously so that neither is a 'second' language; in other words they are 'bilingual-monolingual'. This type of language development is referred to by researchers as Bilingual First Language Acquisition (BFLA) and presents a different developmental path from those children who are exposed to one language at birth (Genesee, 2006). Children who acquire their second language later are subject to differences in their experiences which will be governed by the age at which they encounter their new language, the environment in which they try to learn it and the attitudes of those adults around them to both their first language and to their second language acquisition.

The development of an additional spoken language

Perhaps the most common experience for an early years practitioner, is the need to support English language acquisition in children who are fluent in one home language. Before considering how children whose home language is not English might develop their new language, it is helpful to look briefly again at the processes involved in developing a first language (see Chapter 1). Children developing their home language are most likely to do so in an environment that is built for nurturing spoken communication. They will hear and use this language all the time with parents, carers and siblings; they will receive constant praise and encouragement from the older siblings and adults around them who will also tirelessly provide models of pronunciation, appropriate language use and response in a given context. Thus, the meanings of new words and concepts will be situated in relevant practical examples.

There is evidence indicating that even newborns have a remarkable capacity to discriminate between languages, and are sensitive to the sounds and rhythms of their mother's speech patterns when just two to three months old (Mehler et al. 2000). Research has also shown that the nurturing of first language takes place before children are able to articulate words for objects. Sensitivity to the meanings inherent in their babies' gestures has been observed in the mothers of one- and two-year-old Spanish children As a child points to something, the mother is likely to name the object and look at both the object and her child's face in turn. By doing this she collaborates with the child in identifying and naming, and she creates the potential for naming and describing actions towards the object (Rodrigo et al., 2004).

When developing a second or subsequent language, it is most likely that this will not be in the familiar and nurturing environment of the home. In a nursery or school, children will hear words out of context and thus devoid of meaning; they must vie for attention with other children who are confident in the language of the setting; and they might suffer loss of confidence as a result of their inability to communicate or establish their identity. It is widely accepted that our first language is mapped closely to our sense of self. In addition to the normal stresses of dealing with transition away from the home, young children without spoken English must grapple with the potentially crushing insecurity of not being understood.

Siraj-Blatchford and Clarke (2000) discuss a sequence of phases through which children might commonly go when developing spoken English. These are: an initial continued use of the home language in the new context; followed by use of non-verbal communication such as gesture and expression; then a period of silence is very common, sometimes for as long as six months, during which children listen to others' use of the new language; they may then start to use spoken English through a process of repetition and language play; this progresses to the use of single words, formulaic common phrases and routines; finally they will begin to move to confidence with more complex English. It is crucial for teachers/practitioners to be sensitive to these phases if beginner bilinguals are to develop as confident operators with their new language.

Practitioners may, for example, become concerned by initial silence and interpret this as an unwillingness to take part in activities, or as underdeveloped social skills, stubbornness of character or lack of intelligence. This might in turn lead to low expectations, ready acceptance of solitary play and the provision of low level activities that don't support language acquisition in a meaningful context. Furthermore, not all practitioners will recognise the value of allowing children to operate in their home languages. There is evidence that some languages are regarded as holding higher status than others (Cummins, 2000), and that children's own attitude to their first language and its use outside the home may influence both their capacity to develop a new language and their self-esteem (Parke and Drury, 2001).

One practical way of ensuring a proactive response to children's developing bilingualism is through assessment. There are several scales which can be used to support assessment of language use effectively. One of these, the Hilary Hester Stages of English Learning (CLPE, 1990) identifies the features of children's capacity to use English in four stages of fluency. Used alongside the new arrival and developing bilingual child, they provide a framework from which practitioners can identify learning needs and ways of adapting the learning environment. Their focus on what the child can do in English, rather than what they can't, requires a positive response from the practitioner that will support both social integration and the development of skills in the new language.

Individual difference

Several studies of children operating in English as an additional language (EAL) reveal a need for early years practitioners and school teachers to take careful account of individual difference. While we might not question our obligation to do this for monolingual children with whom we share a language, we may perhaps identify the child with EAL only by their non-use of English. We may consider that the needs of children developing spoken English are somehow the same and that they supersede other differences, such as those related to confidence and social development.

Let's take the example of the practitioner who perceives a three-year-old's silence as problematic. Parke and Drury (2001) discovered that the differing personalities of three nursery-aged girls with EAL had a significant impact on the way in which they were nurtured in their preschool setting. Two of the three were confident risk-takers with good social skills. They chatted in both their home language, Pahari, and in English, and were able to participate quickly in the normal activities of a Foundation Stage setting. The third child, Nazma, lacked confidence and felt very anxious about the transition to nursery. Her teacher commented that she was 'self-sufficient' and 'stubborn' while regarding the child's lively interaction with her bilingual support assistant as confirmation of this, rather than seeing a child whose anxiety was preventing her from wanting to speak in English.

Non-verbal communication

A better informed practitioner might have understood that Nazma's silence was a normal part of the process children go through when acquiring a new language. She might also have chosen to assess Nazma's understanding of English in ways that took account of children's capacity for non-verbal communication. Staff interviewed recently in a Foundation Stage setting in the south of England spoke of this in relation to a three-year-old Nepalese girl, Kanti, who had attended their nursery for just three months. This little girl had been silent, verbally, since arrival, but had a range of ways in which she was able to communicate. For example, she established eye contact with any child or adult speaking to her and would show intense interest in what was being said; she successfully engaged in the same playful activities as the other children – wrapping a parcel for a post office role play area or sharing tools in the sand tray; in response to questions she would nod or shake her head to show she had understood; she engaged mostly in solitary play but would smile and gesture silently to other children who came up to play alongside her.

Rather than interpreting Kanti's separation and silence as problematic, practitioners responded by involving her in talk wherever appropriate and by continuing dialogue with her which allowed her to respond non-verbally. I watched a parent helper skilfully include her in post office role play by animatedly talking to her about what she was doing, praising her for her efforts and questioning her in ways that could elicit a successful response that was non-verbal. The response of adults in this setting fostered a virtuous circle for this child because it acted as a positive role model for the children. Watching Kanti playing at the sand alongside monolingual English children, they smiled with her, copied what she was doing and turned excitedly to comment to the adult practitioners that Kanti had laughed out loud; something they obviously saw as a breakthrough and in which they took pleasure. It is worthy of note that these observations were made in a setting which had only 15 per cent of its children with EAL. Thus, the good practice we may see portrayed in research, which commonly focuses on majority EAL settings, is not restricted to inner-city schools.

The role of other adults and peers in second language acquisition

Staying with the example of Nazma (Parke and Drury, 2001) we might also question the response of her teacher to the child's interaction with the bilingual assistant. While many schools are unable to provide support for children in their home language, there is evidence to suggest that children respond very positively to adults and peers who use their home language in the unfamiliar setting of the nursery or classroom. This does not seem unreasonable if we consider the general need that young children have to feel secure and comfortable in their surroundings. Rather than being seen as part of a 'stubborn' approach to developing a new language, it should be seen as a necessary scaffold to protect both self-esteem and the child's first language as they make their way with acquiring a new language. This comment comes from a leading advisory teacher explaining why her department, which manages EAL provision in a region where there are many isolated bilingual learners, chooses to place bilingual assistants in schools with new arrivals:

> A child who's just landed at the school has got so many changes to face, that what they need is a kind of social/emotional support if you like. That can come from somebody who shares the same language; they feel a sense of security. If you haven't got at least that sense of security then you can't really take in the learning that's going on around you. So this kind of settling-in time, I don't think you can underestimate how valuable that is. I think having someone around who speaks the same language has a tremendous impact on that. I've seen children, for example, who will not speak at all in their new environment, and that's actually a stage of language that children go through, particularly young children. But you bring in a bilingual assistant and it's like a magic effect. You'll see suddenly their facial expression changes, they're talking, and the teacher will see a different side of them that hadn't existed previously. (Interview, June 2007.)

Perhaps the most powerful message here lies in the last sentence; that the practitioner will see a different side to the child once s/he is able to operate in his or her home language. It gives further weight to my earlier comment, that we should question whether we are looking beyond language difference and to the needs of the individual when we support children with EAL. It also underpins the importance of maintaining the children's first language for the dual purposes of supporting their self-esteem and of ensuring that they have a secure grounding in their home language. They will draw intuitively on their first language to help them understand the workings of their new language (Paradis, 1981).

Not all settings will be lucky enough to have access to a bilingual assistant who shares the home languages of its children. Observations of an effective setting later in this chapter explore how a talk- and print-rich environment secures the literacy development of both monolingual and bilingual speakers. However, there is also research which identifies the potential role of siblings in supporting second language acquisition. Gregory (2001) observed Bangladeshi families in East London and noted that older siblings, involved in role play with their younger bothers and sisters, both encouraged their use of spoken English and introduced them to culturally-specific routines that helped them understand school. She described this relationship as having a synergy, where younger siblings act as pupils for older brothers and sisters who in turn have the opportunity to practise their own developing language and literacy in English.

Metalinguistic awareness

Practitioners with experience of children with EAL will recognise that, while their bilingual speakers may not know much about the English language, they probably know plenty about their first language. Children operating in more than one language are known to have what is referred to as metalinguistic knowledge. This means that their understanding of how language operates, how it is structured, is heightened and enhanced by their having to understand the workings of two or more languages. Monolingual speakers will not have the advantage of comparison that working in two languages brings with it.

A clear example of this advantage comes from a newly arrived Polish child in a Foundation Stage class. This little boy was socially outgoing and confident, and was talking with some adult visitors to his classroom using his rapidly developing spoken English. He told the visitors that his car was a Vauxhall Corsa, but added, 'Surname, Vauxhall. First name, Corsa'. This seemingly eccentric aside demonstrates that this five-year-old has grasped the generic concepts of language related to naming in British culture. Had he not been learning two languages it is unlikely that this knowledge would have become so explicit in his understanding at such a young age. Furthermore, he showed evidence of adaptation to different cultural norms relating both to language use and the naming of cars by their manufacturers. His need to learn a new language was embedded in a wider need to explore and understand cultural differences following his family's decision to live away from their home country. For him these differences will simply have been a new set of experiences which he had to assimilate, but we must not underestimate the range of stresses surrounding children when they arrive in a new country; language difference is only one part of this.

Providing a literacy-rich environment for developing bilinguals

The research identified above illustrates how an early years setting might unwittingly raise barriers to language development. These barriers are most likely to stem from lack of subject knowledge and from limitations in the organisation of adult support, rather than from any lack of desire to support children for whom English is not a home language. There are some key features of effective early years settings that will support second language acquisition. These include:

- maintenance of the children's first language
- an ethos that builds self-esteem and celebrates the individual
- reflection of cultural/ethnic and religious difference in activities, stories, resources and pictures
- a strong partnership with parents
- planned opportunities for talk with and between the children
- provision of good models of standard spoken and written English
- recognition and understanding of the stages of second language acquisition
- introduction to new vocabulary in meaningful contexts
- the use of rhyme, rhythm and repetition in stories and songs
- the use of regular, repeated routines throughout the day to foster a sense of security about the nature and purpose of activities.

The following observations (Figure 2.1) were made in an inner-city early years setting where the majority of children do not have English as a first language, and they provide an insight into the range of ways that the learning environment for young bilinguals can be set up to scaffold language acquisition. In this setting there were some staff who shared some of the home languages of the children, but other staff who were monolingual English speakers and children who had home languages other than those offered by the bilingual assistants. Practitioners worked alongside children, communicating

Welcome

As children and their families come into the nursery they see the following:

- 'Hello' is written in a wide range of languages and includes drawings of people saying 'Hello' to support understanding of the meaning of the written words.
- Staff names are displayed with their photos and written in the three main community languages for parents.
- The data projector displays rolling images of the children taken on a recent trip to the farm. This provides an instant visual and engaging set of pictures for discussion, and fosters children's sense of belonging.
- An activity board is set up for the children to plan the activities they want to take part in. This is entirely pictorial.
- Children take their names and place them on an arrivals board. A bilingual assistant speaks animatedly in Punjabi to several children and their parents.
- A poster with two girls dressed in saris says 'The only way to have a friend is to be one'.

Figure 2.1   Welcome in a multilingual nursery

Starting the day

- 'Hello' is said in seven languages.
- Children take part in familiar routines, such as a welcome song and looking at a message board.
- The visitor is introduced in English and Urdu by two members of staff.
- As children move to their 'teams' they sing a simple, repetitive rhyme.
- In groups, children plan what they will do with their team leader; those with less confidence in spoken English are encouraged in making non-verbal responses; staff engage in dialogue that is actively supported with props, hand actions and gestures to support understanding; all children are expected to listen to each other.

Figure 2.2   Setting up in a multilingual nursery

both verbally and non-verbally with them to encourage learning, use of standard English and to develop problem-solving and conflict-resolution skills.

This warm and welcoming environment protects the children's sense of self-esteem, allows the parent–school partnership to flourish and provides print-based scaffolds for the children's eventual journey into using written English. Pictures reflect the wide range of ethnic and cultural backgrounds of the children, and the use of first language is openly encouraged. In fact, it is clear that home languages share equal status with English. Observe how the ethos apparent at the start of the day continues as the children move into choosing their activities in Figure 2.2.

Apart from the presence of the bilingual assistant to support the introduction, the observations above would not be unusual in any good early years setting. Practitioners who are confident with teaching children whose home language is not English will often comment that they do not consider their practice to be far removed from what they would organise in a monolingual setting. A curriculum that is principally oral and operates on practical play-based experiences is what we would recognise as common good practice for all young children. One important thing to note about this particular setting is the use of props and gesture to support understanding of spoken English, and the continuous engagement of the practitioners with the children in order to scaffold effective communication.

Once taking part in their chosen activities, children played in an environment where staff engaged them constantly in talk, where staff and children moved seamlessly between their home languages and English, where routines were familiar and well-established, where picture and sound cues were used wherever possible and where individuals felt valued. This value was demonstrated through the use of pictures of the children themselves as talking points – for example, in the discussion of the farm trip photos, in the pictures displayed in the home corner of one little boy dressed up in his special clothes for Eid, and in the Birthday Book which had pictures taken of each child on their fourth birthday in the nursery. Furthermore, props, such as clothes and cooking utensils in the home corner, reflected the cultural norms from the children's homes.

Evidence of the important role of older peers in developing the English of young bilinguals (Gregory, 2001) became obvious when a six-year-old Punjabi-speaking girl came in to read to the three- and four-year-olds. She read to the younger children in English, of which they had limited understanding, but she held them captivated with her rendition of the traditional story 'The Gingerbread Man'. Staff commented on the importance of this shared reading time both for the six-year-old, in terms of the maintenance of her self-confidence and use of her increasingly fluent English, and for the younger children who experienced a role-model peer speaking fluently in their second language.

Planning

Planning for children whose home language is not English does not have to look very different from planning for monolingual learners, but is does require subject-knowledge relating to second language acquisition in order to be most effective (Flynn and Stainthorp, 2006). Taking the example of the multilingual nursery featured above, much of the planning would have centred on

	The Post Office
Prior learning	• Role play area is set up as a post office • Language of letters and posting has been introduced • Children have written letters addressed to themselves and walked to the post box to post them
Structure of the session	**Introduction** • Introductory circle time in which practitioner asks children how she might send something bigger than a letter • Ensuing discussion about parcels and comparison of parcels of different weights; introduction of words – parcel, heavier, lighter • Revision of language related to letters when introducing the address on the parcel **Adult-led activities** • Wrapping parcels • Weighing parcels • Role play in the post office with an adult alongside **Letter arrival** • At snack time, the postman comes into the nursery to deliver the newly arrived letters that the children have sent to themselves • Discussion about the post mark and what might have happened to those that haven't arrived **Group time** • Children look at pictures of themselves on their trip to the post box and discuss them with an adult

Figure 2.3   Planning meaningful literacy experiences

activities that promoted talk and presented new vocabulary to the children in meaningful contexts. The example of planning for one session in Figure 2.3 is taken from an early years setting with a small number of EAL learners. The teacher here commented that everything that happened in the nursery was, 'visual, oral and practical, because that supports the language development of all of our children'.

The plan above does not represent the full range of activities on offer for the children in this session, but it shows a coherent strand nurturing spoken language development tied to a central theme. Children operating in a second or subsequent language would be supported in accessing new understanding because of the repeated reference to new vocabulary and because of the relevance of the activities to their prior experiences (Long, 2002).

Reading in a new language

The need for spoken language that will inform the reading process becomes even more crucial when children are reading in a language that is not their home language. Earlier in this chapter we considered the differences between children learning to speak in a first and a second or subsequent language. Some of those challenges persist when a child learns to read in a new language. The differences relate mainly to children who already have some familiarity with printed text in their own language or in English; for example, some phonemes will have different graphemic representations, some vocabulary will be unknown and the content may be culturally specific. These differences can present challenges even in young children who are not yet decoding print. For example, a three-year-old may be familiar with stories read at home. These stories may be written in a code that is based around characters rather than the letters of the English alphabet; they may be read from right to left and the book may start at what an English-reading child would consider the back. In addition to this, the story in school may present the child with images and objects that are unfamiliar. The answer for the practitioner lies not in trying to establish a set of norms for reading based around English texts, but in allowing the children to see the differences for themselves and make sense of them by allowing access to books written in a range of scripts. In the same way that children are able to explore language structure through operating in two or more spoken languages, they will be able to accept and understand differences in the printed word if presented with the two together.

It is perhaps a common misconception that children will be confused if they have to learn to read more than one language at a time. It is possible that they may take longer to assimilate both, but the long-term benefits in terms of both cognitive development and the maintenance of identity and self-esteem will outweigh any early disadvantages that are experienced in settings that do not support bilingual development. Research by Bialystock revealed that bilingual children, even Chinese-English children who were learning two different writing systems, had the potential to develop phonological awareness faster than monolingual children when developing early reading (Bialystock, 2006).

When English-speaking children start to read in English, their main barrier to reading might be that they have insufficient phonic knowledge to decode unknown words. In bilingual learners, this will be further compounded by the fact that they may be unfamiliar with the plot line or with some of the language used in the story. Practitioners can go some way to countering this issue by taking time to talk through the main events of the story and any difficult language before the child tries to read the book (Gregory, 1996). In terms of maintaining the status of the home language and raising the profile of the range of nationalities in a setting, it perhaps goes without saying that schools need to invest in dual-language texts and in books that present positive images of children from a range of families and ethnic backgrounds. Even where children are too young to read these books themselves, the presence of a familiar-looking script and the potential for taking home books that can be shared with the family, will foster good home–school links and a sense of belonging to the nursery and school community.

There is a need for some sensitivity in selecting books that do not contain images that may reinforce cultural stereotypes, or story lines that may offend some parts of the community. For example, practitioners may want to consider how appropriate a story with pigs is for children who are Muslim or Jewish. Similarly, always using African or Indian stories that portray only the exotic and the rural, might fuel an image of families living in mud huts, rather than supporting social cohesion in urban communities where African and Indian children are British, and live in houses and flats just like their monolingual friends. However, it is also unhelpful to become so anxious about the selection of texts that children are denied access to what is good or traditional children's literature. Open dialogue with parents and community leaders, and regular monitoring of the range of literature available in the setting, is the most effective way to ensuring that stories are enjoyable for everyone.

Just as with monolingual speakers, the use of rhyme and rhythm in books is helpful in developing phonemic awareness and sensitivity to patterns in English for bilingual children. Rhyme in story and in song gives children access to sound patterns in a context, which is likely to be much more useful than the isolated learning of letter–sound correspondence (Gibbons, 2002). The children listening to 'The Gingerbread Man' story will have been engaged at least in part by the regular repetition of the rhyme associated with the central character running away. The multiethnic setting featured in the observations earlier in this chapter used rhyme and song all the time as a way of engaging the children with spoken English and with routines (see Figure 2.4).

- Welcome song to start the day.
- Song as children move to their activities – 'Who is going to the puzzle area? [x3]. It's Mrs Jones's team'.
- Music plays in the home corner – songs in Asian languages.
- Children sitting in a rocker are encouraged to sing 'Row, row, row your boat, gently down the stream'.
- Music is played during tidy-up time.
- As children are told to come to the carpet, a sequence of three rhymes is used to encourage them to come, to sit down and to be quiet and listen.
- Children sing traditional nursery rhymes together and choose whether to sing in English or Punjabi. Staff and children know the words in both languages.
- At transition to group time, adults sing 'Is everybody sitting at the table? Can everybody find a space?'
- A hoop and a rhyme are used to give children time to talk in groups. The hoop, with a marker, is edged around the group until the marker stops at one child: 'Pass the hoop around, pass the hoop around. What did you do today?'

Figure 2.4   Using rhyme and song in a multiethnic nursery

Writing in a new language

The issues for EAL children learning to write in a new language are related closely to those raised during the discussion of spoken English and reading in English. The crucial role of talk becomes paramount if children are to understand the context of what they are writing about, the vocabulary they need to use, and specific features related to genre and audience. Also fundamental is motivation for writing. In many ways, this list of issues for the EAL child writing is no different from that for a monolingual speaker struggling with what is, after all, a very difficult task.

Kenner (2000) worked with children in an inner-city nursery class on a project to develop their writing. This involved her in working with the children's families who she asked to bring in examples of the sort of written language the children were familiar with from home. One successful example of the development of curriculum materials that are placed in a meaningful context could be seen in the writing of Meera who developed a travel brochure for her forthcoming trip to India. This grew from play and talk in a 'travel agency', and from this child's full engagement with a literacy experience that celebrated her home experiences, her identity and which gave her a clear purpose for communication. Commentary in other chapters in this volume underscores the crucial place of both play and oracy in developing both thinking and writing; this is perhaps even more the case for bilingual than it is for monolingual learners.

Some research identifies that EAL pupils fare less well than their peers when compared by national testing at eleven years old (Cameron and Besser, 2004). However, it could be argued that EAL pupils are tested too early in their second language development for a culturally specific test in English to present a fair assessment of their ability. Cummins (1979) identified that immigrant children develop oral fluency quickly in a way that masks the fact that it takes between five and seven years to develop academic English. Thus, the outcomes of national testing are not necessarily an accurate representation of the success of children learning English as a second language. Furthermore, there is evidence that the metalinguistic awareness of bilingual children can enhance their understanding of writing.

Kenner and Kress (2003) studied children who were between five and six years old in both their primary schools and in the community language schools they attended in addition to mainstream schooling. The home languages spoken by the children were Chinese, Arabic and Spanish. Each was chosen because of salient features of its written form. Observations took place in the children's language schools, but they also elected to watch these children peer tutoring their monolingual friends in writing their home language script. Through this they were able to observe that the children understood a great deal about the written form of their own language because they had to teach its features to another child. Their findings cross-matched the children's experience in their community schools with their peer tutoring and each setting provided an interesting insight into the advantages of bilingual children's linguistic metacognition.

The Chinese pupil showed that she took particular care with line length and formation in her writing, as, in Chinese, the accuracy of the symbols is so crucial to meaning. This attention to detail spilled over into her writing in her primary school, and she found the crossing out of errors at first a frustrating process that detracted from the aesthetic appearance of her handwriting. She was, however, quickly able to operate in both the very different Roman script and with a very different set of cultural expectations related to the English classroom.

The pupil taught in Arabic was writing his home language from right to left. However, his community language teacher supported him in understanding that English script is written in the opposite direction. She continually reinforced this difference in order to support all her pupils when they returned to their English lessons in school. This observation challenges the assumption made by some that the preservation of a home language hinders progress in English

Section focus	Activity
Pre-lesson activity	Thinking of words to describe a lion's movement, teeth and eyes.
Word-level introduction	Review words from pre-lesson activity. Discussion related to appropriate adjectives – fitness for purpose.
Shared text E.g., *If You Want to See an Alligator* by Grace Nicholls	Reading the poem, discussing its features, rhyme pattern, stanza length, the language of poetry, etc. Looking for key adjectives describing the alligator.
Independent work and guided writing	Identifying adjectives for the alligator's movement, jaws and eyes. Creating one new stanza for the poem using these adjectives.
Plenary	Performance of the poem with the addition of the stanza composed by three children in the guided writing group.

Figure 2.5 Poetry composition with young bilinguals

and may be a sign of unwillingness to integrate. On the contrary, this child's Arabic teacher was equipping him to operate successfully in either language and clearly understood the importance of his developing biliterate skills.

Support for writing in the developing bilingual

This final observation was made in an inner-city classroom of six- and seven-years-olds where 70 per cent of the children had English as an additional language. It shows how a skilled practitioner, Bridget, used her understanding of how children develop a new language, and her knowledge of what has gone on in their early years setting, to create a classroom experience that drew together word, sentence and text-level work and scaffolded their use of both spoken and written English (see Figure 2.5).

The outline of this poetry lesson reflects the coherence apparent in the nursery plan for the post office. The aim of the lesson was to explore the language of poetry but to limit the amount of written output the children had to create. The emphasis was on understanding how to write good poetry and on how to use language appropriately in context. Children worked for some considerable time on discussion of words that might describe fierce creatures, and then wrote one short verse in groups that could fit into the existing poem. This lesson might look typical of a well-constructed lesson for all learners, but it supported the bilingual children specifically by having a clear aim which was tied closely to the content and which drove the teacher's dialogue with her children; building up vocabulary in context and using it in context to give it meaning; requiring limited but high-quality written output that allowed for success at the task and the reinforcement of the conventions of well-written poetry in English. High expectations paired with thorough and targeted support, and the teacher's detailed subject knowledge, fostered these carefully composed lines from one group of Bengali-speaking seven year olds:

The alligator's eyes are wicked and sinful,

The alligator's jaws are savagely powerful,

He moves, blundering and awkward.

Summary

The recurring theme throughout this chapter has been that of talk; the need for children to use spoken English before they can be expected to read or write it. To summarise the main points of this chapter:

- Children learning a new language will continue to operate in their home language. This maintains their sense of identity, their self-esteem, and supports development of their new language.
- Children learning a new language should be provided with opportunities to listen, speak and write in meaningful contexts where the purpose of activities is clearly related to their own experiences.
- Teachers can relax about silence, and accept that listening is a normal part of learning a new language.
- Teacher-talk should be clearly articulated, present good standard English, and be supported by visual aids related to the messages being conveyed.
- Children learning a new language need explicit introduction to new vocabulary and the opportunity to use their new words in an environment where they are freed from the risk of failure.
- Children learning a new language need to see explicit modelling of the ways in which text is written and presented in a range of genres.
- Children learning a new language have the same range of individual needs as their monolingual peers.

Suggestions for further reading 📖

Drury, R. (2006) *Young Bilingual Children Learning at Home and at School.* Staffordshire: Trentham Books.

Gregory, E. (2008) *Learning to read in a New Language: Making Sense of Words and Worlds.* London: Sage.

Kenner, C. (2004) *Becoming Biliterate: Young Children Learning Different Writing Systems.* Staffordshire: Trentham Books.

Resources

CLPE (1990) *The Hilary Hester Stages of Learning English.* http://www.clpe.co.uk/pdf/StagesofEnglishLearning.pdf (accessed November 2007).

Mantra Lingua – bilingual books and CDs for children http://www.mantralingua.com (accessed November 2007).

References

Bialystock, F. (2006) 'Bilingualism at school: effect on the acquisition of literacy' in P. McCardle and E. Hoff (eds), *Childhood Bilingualism: Research on Infancy through School Age.* Clevedon: Multilingual Matters. pp. 107–24.

Cameron, L. and Besser, S. (2004) *Writing in English as an Additional Language at Key Stage 2: DfES RR 586.* London: DfES Publications.

CLPE (1990) *The Hilary Hester Stages of Learning English.* http://www.clpe.co.uk/pdf/StagesofEnglishLearning.pdf

Cummins, J. (1979) 'Cognitive/academic language proficiency, linguistic interdependence, the optimum age question and some other matters', *Working Papers on Bilingualism,* 19: 121–9.

Cummins, J. (2000) *Language, Power and Pedagogy: Bilingual Children in the Crossfire.* Clevedon: Multilingual Matters.

Flynn, N. and Stainthorp, R. (2006) *The Learning and Teaching of Reading and Writing.* Chichester: Wiley.

Genesse, F. (2006) 'Bilingual first language acquisition in perspective', in P. McCardle and E. Hoff (eds) *Childhood Bilingualism: Research on Infancy through School Age.* Clevedon: Multilingual Matters. pp. 45–67.

Gibbons, P. (2002) *Scaffolding Language: Scaffolding Learning.* New Hampshire: Heinemann.

Gregory, E. (1996) *Making Sense of a New World: Learning to Read in a Second Language.* London: Paul Chapman.

Gregory, E. (2001) 'Sisters and brothers as language and literacy teachers: synergy between siblings playing and working together', *Journal of Early Childhood Literacy,* 1 (3): 301–22.

Kenner, C. (2000) *Home Pages: Literacy Links for Bilingual Children*. Staffordshire: Trentham Books.

Kenner, C. and Kress, G. (2003) 'The multisemiotic resources of biliterate children', *Journal of Early Childhood Literacy*, 3 (2): 179–202.

Long, S. (2002) 'Tuning in to teacher-talk: a second language learner struggles to comprehend', *Reading*, 36 (3): 113–18.

McCardle, P. and Hoff, E. (eds) (2006) *Childhood Bilingualism: Research on Infancy through School Age*. Clevedon: Multilingual Matters.

Mehler, J., Christophe, A. and Ramus, F. (2000) 'What we know about initial state for language', in A. Marantz, Y. Miyashite and W. O'Neill (eds) *Image, Language, Brain: Papers from the first Mind-Articulation Project Symposium*. Cambridge, MA: MIT Press. pp. 166–78.

Paradis, M. (1981) 'Neurolinguistic organisation of bilingual's two languages', in J. Copeland (ed.) *The seventh LACUS Forum*. Columbia: Hornbeam Press.

Parke, T. and Drury, R. (2001) 'Language development at home and school: gains and losses in young bilinguals', *Early Years*, 21 (2): 117–27.

Rodrigo, M.J., Gonzalez, A., De Vega, M., Muneton-Ayala, M. and Rodriguez, G. (2004) 'From gestural to verbal deixis: a longitudinal study with Spanish infants and toddlers', *First Language*, 24 (1): 71–90.

Siraj-Blatchford, I. and Clarke, P. (2000) *Supporting Identity, Diversity and Language in the Early Years*. Maidenhead: Open University Press.

3

White cars like mice with little legs: poetry in the early years

Liz Stone and Julia Gillen

Introduction

Four children, on the cusp of four to five years old, stand on a simple wooden boat in their school playground, accompanied by their teacher and a researcher acting as scribe. In the rain they gaze out at a mostly urban scene in north-west England. It is a hilly environment, so they can see quite a distance across the valley. Prompted by their teacher, the following poem is authored by the children:

> Can't wait!
> Don't know what's there
> Going on a boat trip!
> Big drops of rain
> One in my eye
> One on my pocket
> One on my tights
> Like drops from a tap.
>
> I can see a massive tree
> Bending in the wind
> I can see a church spire
> Pointing like a finger
> I can hear the wind

Whoosh!
I can't see the hills
They are covered in clouds
I can see white cars
Like mice with little legs.

To introduce ourselves: the first author, Liz, is an experienced practising teacher; the second author, Julia, a supportive researcher. I (Liz) would describe myself as having a love for poetry in my professional and personal life. When I think back to my childhood, as one of seven children, I remember my parents, perhaps unconsciously, fostering within us a love of wordplay, poetry and rhyme in the games they played with us and the rhymes and songs they sang to us. An introduction to poetry and rhyme is a part of the nurturing process for some children, but not for others:

> Poetry matters. In the way we name our children, in the way we sing them to sleep, in the way we survive a car journey. (Wilson, 1998: 3)

The second author (Julia) has drawn on understandings of poetry in her research into child language development (Gillen, 1997; 2006; 2007). The first of those was inspired in part by reflections on sharing nursery rhymes with young children on a car journey – clearly a rite of passage for many of us! An early years teacher's task is to either begin or continue that nurturing process by 'immersing' children in words, rhymes and poems with which they can play and enjoy. Ultimately, they in turn will use them to extend and enrich their vocabulary and enhance their ability to describe their experiences of the world around them.

This chapter will contain ideas, suggestions and justifications for the use of poetry in the early years that we hope many readers in diverse settings will find useful to draw upon. However, we also situate these in the context of the specific space and time at which the events we draw upon happened – the school year was 2006–07 in a particular reception classroom in north-west England. We explain how the school and, at a micro level, the classroom, has chosen to embed poetry within an approach to early years literacy that is in transition – from the *National Literacy Strategy Framework for Teaching* (DfEE, 1998) to an approach that includes a rich, multimodal approach to language and inputs from a popular synthetic phonics programme. We relate this to current policy in Scotland, Northern Ireland, Wales, as well as England where the Early Years Foundation

Stage policy documents (DfES, 2007a) were published as we worked on the drafts of this chapter. However, notwithstanding interest in policy, a principle aim here is to convey the sense in which policy need not be experienced as overly deterministic. It is vital for the classroom teacher/s and their teams to have the experience, knowledge and confidence to reflexively shape their curriculum and pedagogic practices to include what they know 'to work' while being ever alert for ideas that can lead to further improvements in a classroom that is, after all, an ever-changing environment. Some commentators such as Cook (2007) raise the question as to whether it is this aspect of professional practice, rather than any notion of centralised curriculum decisions, that should drive the decisions as to what happens in the early years classroom (for the purposes of this chapter we mean to refer broadly to the age range up to eight years old).

In Liz's classroom, poetry is a tremendous factor in language and literacy experiences. Staff make use of their own experiences to also suggest ideas that will apply to younger, and older, children. Central to this approach is advocacy of a multimodal approach to poetry; one of our purposes here is to trace the various ways in which we mean this.

Authoring the poem quoted above was a multisensory experience. The children manifestly enjoyed concentrating on the scene in front of them – not merely *seen* as an externally visible reality but *experienced* by themselves as embodied beings in a specific setting. The teacher, well known to them, encouraged them to verbalise this experience, to express with some degree of precision their thoughts and feelings. The poem records their thoughts as they move from the socio-dramatic play location of the playground 'boat' to an instantaneous preservation of sensations, to the final unexpected simile. But, of course, it does more than capture thoughts that might be non-verbal and fleeting; it externalises and verbalises these thoughts. Language is important as providing both a means for expressing our understanding of experiences and for deepening, indeed shaping, our understandings of the world.

Language is experienced by children (indeed by all of us, but meriting special emphasis in childhood as we shall discuss below) as part of a holistic experience. 'Multimodality' is an in-vogue term for a phenomenon that has long been clear to many practitioners who work most sensitively in the early years. We all interact with the world through multiple means, using channels available to us, including all or some, of sight, vision, touch, smell, hearing and so forth, but this is especially true of young children (Anning and

Edwards, 1999; see also Chapter 7, this volume). In authoring the poem above, the children were engaging with the following five domains.

Visual
Poetry offers a 'new look' at items in the world and their characteristics. Authoring poetry requires looking closely at the world – how does this tree differ from the next? What makes this view different from the last time I looked at it?

Touch and smell
Poetry often expresses how senses of touch and smell can be used to experience the essence of an object or experience. As the children gazed up and out of the 'boat', the feel of the rain became the primary sensation.

Sound
The power of poetry is often strongly linked to dimensions of sound. These children are learning how to bring sound into their poetry with onomatopoeia. The 'whoosh' was probably introduced through recent memory of the text, *We're Going on a Bear Hunt* by Michael Rosen and Helen Oxenbury (a poem with associated dramatic, artistic and language activities that had provided a major theme for the class for a week). As we will explore below, poetry can assist children to consciously build upon their innate capacity to discriminate between the phonemes of a language. Also, rhythm and rhyme are profoundly associated with music, one of our deep-seated cultural systems that can interact so powerfully with the language capacity.

Affect and motivation
Poetry can be very enjoyable. Pleasurable engagements with poetry can cause hearers, readers and writers to feel more motivated, to extend their capacities through memorisation, authoring, writing and so on.

Language and literacy
Many poems and poetry-related activities are particularly well-suited to explorations in the aural/oral domain. We feel that spending a lot of time working with this channel, as opposed to focusing too heavily

on printed text resources, can actually enhance literacy engagements. Benefits of working with spoken poetry include:

- using opportunities to extend vocabulary in immediately mean-ingful ways
- experiencing the spoken in tandem with touch and smell can be more immediate, in certain situations
- combining the spoken with pictures can, as we will show below, be a powerful stimulus for authoring
- training the memory (in ways that are pleasurable, as again we'll explore below).

In the following sections we write more about why we feel poetry is such a rich nexus of practices for working effectively with young children, and suggest how to do this, drawing on examples from Liz's classroom and elsewhere. We then offer a brief description of one particular engagement with poetry, draw some conclusions together and suggest further resources.

Why poetry?

Poetry draws on innate capacities for language. Even before language as such develops, babies have innate capacities for distinguishing between all the phonemes of language; their capacities to discrimi-nate between sounds are in some sense even more fundamental than sight, which on the contrary remains blurred and restricted for the first few months. Nevertheless they are, in this very early stage, very capable of interacting with others in interactions that may be termed 'protoconversations', as explained below:

> In the gentle, intimate, affectionate, and rhythmically regulated play-ful exchanges of protoconversation, 2-month-old infants look at the eyes and mouth of the person addressing them while listening to the voice. In measured and predictable cycles of response to regular time patterns in the adult's behaviour, the infant moves its face, which it cannot see or hear, and reacts with movements of face, hands or vocal system to modified patterns of adult vocal expression that it is inca-pable of mimicking, and that have not been available in that form *in utero* [...] Evidently the responses of the infant are made expressive by internally generated motives and emotions that resemble those carried in the adult expressions. Infant and adult can, for a time, sympathise closely and apparently equally with one another's motive states, using similar melodic or prosodic forms of utterance and similar rhythms of gesture. (Trevarthen and Aitken 2001: 6)

There is a number of interesting points in this explanation by Trevarthen and Aitken:

- Human infants are innately disposed, sometimes people say by analogy 'programmed', to communicate in a dyadic situation (that is, with one other) when extremely young, before much motor control is developed.
- This communication is nonetheless multimodal, especially once the baby is around three months, old with gestures (especially gaze and smiles) as well as vocalisations.
- Interactions are rhythmic, in terms of exchanges between the two parties and within those turns.
- These communications are primarily playful, and clearly bring pleasure to each party.

Wonderful sources for examples of delightful protoconversations can be found in the book and video/DVD from The Social Baby Project (Murray and Andrews [2000] and NSPCC [2004]). You can also read explanations of young children's language development in Peccei (1999) and Gillen (2003).

Research on protoconversations and playful interactions in early language provide support for an argument that it is the exchange of patterned sounds, not the transmission of propositional knowledge, that is at the heart of communication, and that language is intrinsically multimodal and created in dialogue. Vygotsky, the influential Russian psychologist, wrote: 'In the home environment [...] the process through which the child learns speech is social from start to finish' (Vygotsky, 1987: 90). Obviously, discussion of this process is beyond the scope of this chapter, but we can note that for many children listening to and then participating in songs, rhymes and other language routines (that is, where repetition features strongly) is an important element of their language learning (Gillen, 1997; see also Chapter 1, this volume).

Liz's granddaughter, Ruby, was quite slow to begin talking. Her family knew the value of songs and rhymes in developing speech and language, and read and sang to her regularly. At a very early age, Ruby showed pleasure at hearing familiar songs and rhymes and, though reluctant to join in at first, Ruby began prompting the reader/singer to repeat them, with phrases such as 'gain, gain' (meaning 'Sing/say it again'). At about 20 months Ruby could 'fill in the gaps' at the end of each line of the 'potty poem' (see page 50). By 27 months she was singing whole songs or rhymes, making up the words and using some known words as she wandered happily around the place; for example, she would sing 'Twinkle twinkle ittle tar oh why under what ee are' (Twinkle twinkle little star, how I wonder what you are). Ruby also used familiar tunes and sang parts of rhymes to them, for example:

Humpty Dumpty sat on a wall

Humpty Dumpty sat on a wall

Humpty Dumpty sat on a wall

Humpty Dumpty sat on a wall (All sung to the tune of 'Twinkle twinkle little star'!)

Ruby has also attended nursery school for two half-days per week from the age of four months. Her nursery operates within recommendations for good practice in the early years Foundation Stage and its guidance on communication, language and literacy states that 'music, dance, rhymes and songs play a key role in language development' (DfES, 2007b: 39). Ruby's mother talked to her key worker to find out songs and rhymes they used regularly and which ones Ruby particularly enjoyed so that she could say and sing them at home. As soon as Ruby was able to sit up, and before she had any formal vocabulary, she would smile and giggle and make 'rowing and rocking' movements to the song, 'Row, row, row your boat', which they had sung regularly at nursery.

Recent developments in Liz's school and classroom have been in tune with Alexander's (2003) observation that despite policy claims around the end of the twentieth century to prioritise orality in the curriculum, the basics of pedagogy were identified (with various terms) as what has traditionally been known as the '3 Rs' (reading, writing and arithmetic). Drawing on his extensive research abroad, Alexander argued that 'from an international standpoint the educational place of talk in our primary schools seems ambivalent' (Alexander, 2003: 23). More recently, policy in England seems to have taken this view seriously: 'Far more attention needs to be given, right from the start, to promoting speaking and listening skills to make sure that children build a good stock of words, learn to listen attentively and speak clearly and confidently' (DFES, 2006: 3).

Poetry also helps children develop phonological awareness by listening to the sounds in words and phrases. 'Children need first to hear the constituent sounds in words and phrases, and then begin to map out the graphic symbol for them' (Goswami, 1993, cited by Jeni Riley 1996: 10). Poetry facilitates the gradual awakening of phonological awareness through its patterning, its frequent devices of

Figure 3.1 Child acting out 'How much is that doggy in the window?'

employing repetitions in syntactic structures and sounds, with carefully employed variation. So content is 'cast in verbal forms designed to assist the memory by conferring pleasure' (Havelock, 1986, cited by Luce-Kapler, 2003: 85).

Speaking and listening skills can be developed by simple reciting of familiar rhymes and poems. We have found that many children are reluctant to speak in group or class situations, but will happily recite a familiar rhyme or listen to another child reciting a rhyme, and help them with sequence and order if they need it.

In Liz's role play theatre, we provided costumes and written versions of familiar nursery rhymes, such as 'Miss Polly had a dolly', 'How much is that doggy in the window?', 'Little Miss Muffet' and so on. Acting with a considerable degree of independence, the children dressed themselves up, allocated roles and assisted each other in reciting the rhymes and acting out roles (see Figures 3.1 and 3.2).

Other pupils bought tickets for the theatre and sat with ice creams and popcorn as they watched the show. The main objectives and outcomes linked to this activity consisted of showing an awareness of rhyme and speaking clearly, and showing awareness of the listener. On the second time this activity took place, Liz decided that the children were so busy 'reading the texts' that it impaired their ability to speak with volume and expression. As an intervention strategy, staff removed the written versions of the poem and put them in the book corner: this was more effective.

Figure 3.2   Children acting out 'Little Miss Muffet'

At the early, emergently literate stage, children benefit much more from hearing poems than reading them. When the teacher reads, the children are able to access rich and wide-ranging vocabulary. New vocabulary can be explained first, and then the text is heard in its purest form, uninterrupted, there to become immersed in and to enjoy: 'The dissection of the reading process should never be allowed to diminish the pleasure of the text' (Riley, 1996: 86).

Children can also experiment with changing words (led by the teacher) in poems and rhymes, and thinking about how this changes the meaning. Liz led the way with the following example:

Hickory Dickory dock the mouse ran up the clock,

Hickory Dickory din, the mouse is very thin.

The children retorted:

Hickory dickory doo, the mouse went to the loo.

Hickory dickory doo, the mouse just lost his shoe.

Hickory dickory doo, the mouse just had a poo!

Hickory dickory dee, the mouse just came for tea,

Hickory dickory dee, the mouse sat on my knee.

Hickory dickory dee, the mouse just had a wee!

Prediction skills using context and syntax can be developed by learning poems and rhymes by heart. The same skills can be developed by using rhyming poems, read by the teacher, the children using 'oral' cloze procedure to put in rhyming words. The repetition and patterns of poetry make it an excellent resource for the development of early reading skills (Riley, 1996). The patterns can be used as models for children's own writing.

How can we make poetry and rhyme an integral part of the early years curriculum?

In Liz's classroom, poetry is part of the everyday routines and Liz does not limit words and their constituent sounds to a short phonics session. For example, as the children come in, they start the day with a song. Most songs are basically musical poems and the usual prediction skills can be used to help the children to learn the words. Liz does not limit the songs to the usual ones for the very young, but prefers to be relatively ambitious. The repertoire is broadened to include songs from other cultures, pop music, musicals and so on. Julia was charmed to be welcomed on her first visit to the classroom by a rousing rendition of 'Getting to know you' (Rodgers and Hammerstein) from the classic musical *The King and I*. This enables the children access a range of vocabulary, music and styles.

In this Roman Catholic school (which welcomes other faiths, especially Muslims), the morning begins with a sung prayer, sometimes composed by the class, or the teacher. The class sings a 'days of the week' song, an alphabet song and chants the months of the year. The children look at the clock and play a 'What time is it Mr Wolf?' reading time game. They look at the weather and include the day's weather in the 'What is the weather today?' song.

In this short space of time, approximately 20 minutes, the children have experienced a range of music. They have used poetry and song in prayer, used vocabulary related to the weather, experienced vocabulary related to the passing of time (days, months, numbers), read the time on a clock and had a great deal of fun in the process! Liz is part of a job-share, and there are two other members of staff. Both teachers share the same philosophy on the importance of using poetry and rhyme, and support staff are fully informed as to why it is used and are enthusiastic in their own use of it.

Teachers should try to be a poetry role model and we strongly recommend 'having a go' at writing your own poems. Read them to the class and ask children to be your critical friend, or ask them to help you with the last line. The poems can be very simple, for example:

You and Me

You're cold, I'm hot
You're good, I'm not
You're tall, I'm small
You stand, I fall.

You're young, I'm old
You're hairy, I'm bold
You're thin, I'm fat
You're bumpy, I'm flat.

You're generous, I'm mean
You're dirty, I'm clean
You're smooth, I'm rough
You're tender, I'm tough.
But I like you!

Liz Stone, 2005

In Liz's classroom this poem has been recited several times and made into a game. Liz can now start it off, say the first line, then pause after 'You're' and 'I'm' and the children collectively supply the missing words. Their memories have clearly been stimulated through use of the regular structure. Peters and Boggs (1986) emphasise how useful to language development this 'slot and fill' pattern can be.

Teaching staff may play two different versions of the same song and ask children what is similar different about them and which one is their favourite and why. This can also draw their attention to the fact that poetry is not just about what is written, but how it is read. Staff can make taking the register an opportunity for word-play through alliterative names, changing first phoneme in names, rhyming names, saying 'Good Morning' in some of the children's home languages (such as Urdu, Polish, and so on). Initially, these are mostly modelled by the teacher but as the children become more familiar with the activities, they will begin to try them out themselves.

As mentioned, prayer time can also be a poetry opportunity. Here, again, the teacher has modelled a practice of changing words to familiar songs to make them into prayers. The example below is adapted from and sung to the tune of 'Bob the Builder' (Hit Entertainment Ltd):

God's a Builder

Chorus:

God's a builder,
He can fix it,
God's a builder,
Yes he can.

He gives us our food so
good to eat,
Packed lunch and dinners,
fruit so sweet.
We're very lucky
to have a feast,
We pray for those who
have the least.

Chorus

Please help those whose
plates are bare,
Feed them and clothe them
and give them care.

Chorus

As a faith school, it views prayer as of great importance in the school and something which plays a major part in everyday routine and practice. Although it is important to say and value traditional prayers, it is also important to note the changes in children's home life and interests. Using popular culture and involving children in writing or saying prayers which they can relate to can have more meaning and value to them. When asked what their favourite out-of-school interests were, a group of children aged three to thirteen 'all showed popular culture interests evident in each and every one of their choices' (Evans, 2004: 1).

Number songs and rhymes are again familiar to the children and can be used in a cross-curricular way or simply composed for use in mathematical activities. For example, in a subtraction activity the class had a teddy bear shop (linked to the text *We're Going on a Bear Hunt* by Michael Rosen and Helen Oxenbury, 1993), and changed the words to the number rhyme 'Five currant buns in a baker's shop' to:

Five teddy bears in a teddy bear shop
Soft and cuddly with fur on the top
Along came a girl/boy with some money one day
Bought a teddy bear and took it away.

The poem below was written to use in a dance session where the children used ribbon sticks to represent the movements of the wind as described in the poem:

The Wind

Warm, gentle, soothing wind,
Brushing, stroking, cooling wind.
Whirling, whipping,
swirling wind.
Curling high,
Sweeping low.
Buzz off wind!
It's time to go.

Liz Stone, 2006

Action rhymes are used as warm-ups and cool-downs to physical education lessons. If the same rhyme is used over a number of weeks, the children are able to recite it as they move.

Staff try to read at least one poem a day, followed by a discussion of the poem when they have read it, and asking questions such as: 'What did we say this word meant?'; 'Talk to your partner and try to think of another word you could put here which has the same meaning'; 'Can you think of a better word to use here?' In all everyday activities and routines, teachers draw the children's attention to interesting words: 'I think this word sounds really exciting'; 'This word sounds like what it is describing' (onomatopoeia); 'What do you think this word means?'; 'This word makes me laugh'. It is sometimes useful to model using a thesaurus if you are writing together.

Children and staff often learn a new short poem together, preferably one which requires good expression when reading; for example 'Potty'. Over a period of, say, a week, the children take turns in performing the poem, commenting on expression and delivery so as to improve performance as a whole. It is rewarding for staff and children because 'To be able to say a favourite poem to yourself, or quote passages which have meaning to you, can so often bring comfort and satisfaction' (Brownjohn, 1994: 350).

Figure 3.3   The Potty poem

Potty

Don't put that potty on your head, Tim
Don't put that potty on your head
It's not very clean
And you don't know where it's been, so
Don't put that potty on your head!!

In Liz's classroom, just a few readings of this poem (using the obvious prop of a potty!) led to unsuspecting visitors (in this case Mrs Gillen!) having a 'hat' placed on their head whilst the children recited the poem with wonderful expression and intonation (see Figure 3.3).

There then followed a barrage of volunteers wanting to stand with a friend in front of the class and recite the poem alone.

Playground games and rhymes are a valuable element of culture. The best known historical collectors of nursery and playground rhymes are undoubtedly Iona and Peter Opie who published their first collection in 1959 (Opie and Opie, 1997). More recently, researchers in primary school playgrounds such as Elizabeth Grugeon in the UK (Grugeon, 1999; 2001) and Ian Turner and June Factor in Australia (Factor, 2000; Turner, Factor and Lowenstein, 1978) have done much to reveal the extraordinary continuity combined with creative innovation that characterises such language games (Gillen, 2006). They are passed from generation to generation and exemplify the 'part played by children in preserving certain rituals, customs and beliefs on behalf of the community as a whole' (Sealey, 2000: 77).

Children should be first taught, and then encouraged to use, playground rhymes in their play. For example, in the circle game 'Dree, drie, droe, drop it', the children sit in a circle and one child walks around the circle carrying an object such as a beanbag or a toy and the group sing:

> Dree, drie, droe, drop it
> I've got a beanbag [originally 'penny'] in my pocket
> I lost it, I found it
> Dree, drie, droe, drop it, drop it, drop it.

The child then drops the beanbag behind a friend who chases around the circle to try to catch them before they sit in their place. When observing this game in school, Julia noticed how promoting these rhymes in the hall or classroom was followed by creative adaptations in the playground. For example, two girls worked out how to play a version just by themselves.

Planning poetry activities

When writing poems, Liz always uses a model, keeping it simple and repetitive. Rhythms and routines have a strong place in which to anchor language development, aiding processes of segmentation, analysis as well as providing the 'gaps' pregnant with possibilities in which creativity occurs (Gillen, 1997; 2007). In the classroom, staff guide the children through the process, 'feeding' them with words and ideas as necessary to keep them engaged. If they cannot think of their own words, they are given choices and use their word choice so that they have ownership of the finished poem. Pride in the finished result often means that confidence is enhanced, and the degree of scaffolding they have actually received may be forgotten. Then, their expectations as to what they can do next time are actually strengthened, with heartening results.

In the Foundation Stage in particular, it is almost impossible for the teacher alone to deliver planned sessions, therefore detailed plans and enthusiastic and willing support staff are an invaluable resource. Some of Liz's plans are used elsewhere in the school, and adapted as required. Figure 3.4 is an example of the plan used to support the children in writing the poem featured in the introduction to this chapter.

The Boat Trip

Objectives

- to use language to imagine and recreate roles and experiences
- to expand vocabulary, exploring the meaning and sound of new words
- to use talk to organise and clarify thinking, ideas, feelings and events
- to use all their senses to help them describe what they experience

Activities

Tell the children that they are going to go on an imaginary boat trip (explain that imaginary means pretend or not real).

Tell them that together, you are going to write a poem about what you can see on our boat trip and that you are going to ask them some questions which will help them to think of what to include in the poem.

Explain that you will write the words for them, but that it will be their poem and you will be reading it to the rest of the class.

Questions

- How do you feel?
- What is the weather like?
- What is the weather doing to you?
- What does that remind you of?
- What can you see?
- What can you hear?
- What does that remind you of?

Ask each question, listening to or recording children's answers, giving them choices of words if they cannot think of them themselves, and write each line of the poem as it develops, reading it back to the children as you add each new line.

Inside, the children draw a picture of themselves on the boat trip and something that they saw or experienced.

Differentiation by outcome and teacher support

- prompt as necessary
- model multisensory experience, reflection and the selection of appropriate words
- encourage use of similes – accept the unexpected comparison

---

Figure 3.4   An example of planning: guided poetry writing

Incorporating words and pictures in authored texts

Pictorial poetry writing using a multimodal approach is entirely appropriate for, and yet should not be restricted to, the early years. Children's drawings, particularly post-Foundation Stage are too rarely valued as 'texts'. Dyson (2004: x) notes that 'drawing, for example, is often dubbed as "planning for writing" even though it

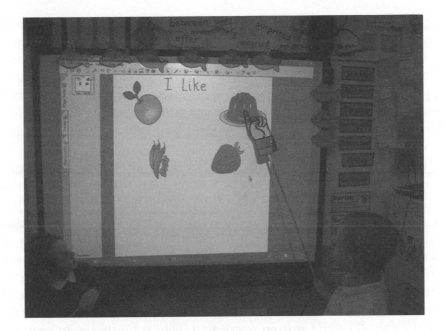

Figure 3.5   Using an interactive whiteboard

may not have been so intended by the child.' We agree strongly with her declaration:

> Given time, materials and space young composers quite readily inter-weave whatever symbolic tools are at their disposal – drawing, singing, gesturing, talking, and, yes, writing. (ibid)

In an early reception class activity, the teacher models a simple poem by manipulating a small set of objects on an interactive white-board. The pupils select from the set of images and repeat the basic template of the poem, while introducing their own adjectives or modifying phrases. Figure 3.5 shows a child selecting images, saying 'I like … ' he points to each picture and authors his poem to the class out loud. This boy said:

> I like crunchy apples,
> I like wobbly jellies.
> I like popping out peas.
> I like soft strawberries.

Liz and colleagues try to make poetry authoring multisensory, authentic and active. The same poetry-writing activity may involve the child painting simple pictures, drawing, collecting objects from the classroom or outdoors, using a digital camera to take pictures and so on. Young children can 'write' poems based on first-hand experience, so if, for example, the poem is about a tree, a multisensory approach is needed. They need to see, touch, hear and smell the tree before and during the writing process. Asking questions such as 'How does it feel?'; 'What does that remind you of?' are useful teacher prompts.

It is not necessary for children to scribe at all during the writing process; taking the physical act of writing away will enable them to concentrate on visual, oral and tactile elements. Research (for example, as discussed by Medwell and Wray, 2007) has demonstrated that giving opportunities to children to dictate texts to adults leads to an increase in quality of their composition. When the poem has been scribed by the teacher, the children can then make a pictorial representation of the poem, sometimes changing the order or sequence of the poem to make it their own and indeed sometimes voluntarily deciding to add some written words to it. Figure 3.6 shows an example of this approach.

From this activity, the children 'wrote' the following poem and presented it pictorially (see Figures 3.7 and 3.8):

> I see a huge, rough tree
> I see swishy, swashy grass
> I see a speeding train
> I see a black, spotty gate.

Figure 3.9 presents an illustration of a similar poem composed by a Year 1 pupil. The poem read:

> I see green grass
> I see speeding cars
> I see the wet boat
> I see the circled logs
> I see the willow tree.

Conclusions

Current national curriculum documents for the UK and beyond make relatively few direct references to poetry. The discerning teacher, recognising the importance and value of poetry within the school curriculum, will find many objectives which can be met

Objectives or steps towards Early Learning Goals (to use language to imagine and recreate experiences, use talk to clarify thinking, ideas, feelings and events, explore and experiment with sounds words and texts)

- to explore the things we see around us in the school grounds, using all our senses
- to think of colours and interesting adjectives to describe the things we see around us in the school grounds
- to experiment with and use describing words to create a group poem based on one we have read, using the things we see around us
- to make pictorial representations so that we can 'write' our own poem based on what we have experienced

Activities (outdoors)

Read the poem 'I see' to the children.

> *I See*
>
> I see golden, gritty sand
>
> I see beautiful blue sea
>
> I see green grass bending on the sand dunes
>
> I see dull, broken shells
>
> I see pink crabs scuttling
>
> I see grey seagulls drifting
>
> I wonder if all these wondrous things
>
> Would want to look at me?

Liz Stone, 2007

Discuss after the first reading, then read it again asking the children to focus on the words used to describe things or to tell them more about them. Draw to their attention the fact that the poem is made more interesting because describing words (adjectives) are used to tell us more about things. The first line tells us that sand is golden in colour and that it feels gritty if we touch it. If the line just said 'I see the sand', we wouldn't know anything about the sand and it wouldn't be as interesting.

Ask the children if they noticed what most lines start with and tell them that many poems have repetition in them. Tell the children that you are going to work in groups to write an 'I see' poem using the things you can see in the playground. They will think about what colour each thing is, how they feel, what they look like, maybe how they smell or sound.

When you are outside, ask the group you are working with to pick something they can see and think of two words to describe it. The children may need lots of prompts here, for example 'What does it feel like?'; 'Can you think of another word for "big"?'; 'Is it rough or smooth?'; 'What can you hear?' For the younger, or less able children, it may be necessary to give them a few alternatives, more powerful adjectives and let them choose so that they still have ownership of the poem; for example 'Instead of "big" we could say "enormous", "massive" or "gigantic", which word do you like?' Write the words on card and either stick them onto the object or ask a child to hold the card whilst another pupil takes a photograph of them. Get the children to pick about five things and keep reading what they have so far using the adjective prompt cards as you do so.

When you have finished, model drawing pictures to represent each line of the poem, saying each line as you do so (for example, 'I see long, wavy grass', etc.).

The children then write their own pictorial representation of their poem and 'read it' in any order so that the poem becomes unique to them.

Figure 3.6   Poetry all around us

Figure 3.7   I see a huge, rough tree

Figure 3.8   I see a black, spotty gate

through listening to, reading, writing and experiencing a range of poetry and rhyme.

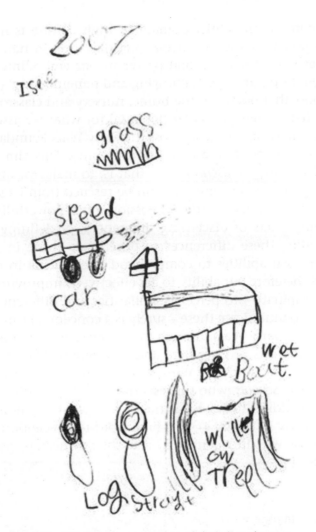

Figure 3.9   A pupil's pictorial representation of their 'I see' poem

It is important that practitioners are aware that not all children are introduced to nursery rhymes, poetry and songs from birth, and that parents should be informed of the value of these in developing children's early language and communication skills. One stance to take with poetry is that it is one of the arts that marks high culture; that it may be at best, pleasant to read with children, at worst irrelevant. This can lead to an ambiguous attitude as to its value:

> Poetry is a pleasure in itself. It can be read for no other reason than its intrinsic value as an art form. As such, it could be regarded as something of a luxury in a busy classroom, intent on raising standards. (Lancashire Schools Effectiveness Service, 2005)

To treat poetry as the elitist domain of high culture is in effect to narrow its potential and, as Luce-Kapler declares, 'In narrowing the role of poetry, we forget its oral power in our embodiment and its ability to develop our ways of knowing and remembering' (2003: 85).

We propose that poetry in the home, nursery and classroom, as we describe it here, offers particular potential for what we assert to be a key aim in education, not just across the Early Years Foundation Stage (as useful as it is) but also a continuing priority. This aim is the fostering of the ability to *discriminate* – that is, to make meaningful distinctions. The word 'discriminate' can be rescued from its sometimes negative connotations to the expression of a powerfully positive human ability. Acts of discerning differences, of defining them, of communicating these differences to others, are those in which we increase our own abilities to comprehend phenomena in the world, and indeed therefore our ability to act effectively. Improving our abilities to discriminate – to perceive similarities and differences, and to express and communicate these – surely is a conceptual thread of education from the early years through to advanced endeavours; whether in the sciences, arts or elsewhere and throughout life. The penultimate word then, to Anthony Wilson in his introduction to *The Poetry Book for Primary Schools*, who suggests that, 'poetry is uniquely placed in allowing children to say what they really want to say in the way they want to say it' (1998: 4). The final word to a reception age pupil from Liz's class, who independently read their own shape poem about a spider as:

Spider

Climbing, climbing walls,

Climbing the ceiling,

Tickly.

Creepy, creeping,

Spider in the web!

Suggestions for further reading 📖

Department of Education, Northern Ireland (2005) *Programme of Study for English at Key Stage 1: Talking and Listening*. Available online at http://www.deni.gov.uk/eng_ks1-2pdf

Learning and Teaching Scotland online service includes poetry; for example, the Edwin Morgan poetry resources, at http://www.ltscotland.org.uk/literacy/index.asp (accessed 4 April 2007).

Rose, J. (2006) *Independent Review of the Teaching of Early Reading*. Nottingham: DfES Publications. Available online at http://www.standards.dfes.gov.uk/phonics/report.pdf (accessed 8 May 2007).

The Poetry Society, http://www.poetrysociety.org.uk (accessed 5 April 2007).

SCEMES Online, www.scemes.net/poetry (accessed 5 April 2007).

Acknowledgement

With thanks to St John Southworth Primary, Nelson, Lancashire, for permission to use the case study material.

References

Alexander, R. (2003) 'Oracy, literacy and pedagogy: international perspectives', in E. Bearne, H. Dombey and T. Grainger (eds) *Classroom Interactions in Literacy*. Buckingham: Open University Press.

Anning, A. and Edwards, A. (1999) *Promoting Children's Learning from Birth to Five: Developing the New Early Years Professional*. Buckingham: Open University Press.

Brownjohn, S. (1994) *To Rhyme Or Not to Rhyme*. London: Hodder and Stoughton.

Cook, M. (2007) 'Learning for life or getting ready for school? Reflections on the proposed Foundation Stage framework', in *English four to eleven*. Leicester: The English Association and the United Kingdom Literacy Association.

DfEE (Department for Education and Employment) (1998) *The National Literacy Strategy: Framework for Teaching*. London: DfEE Publications.

DfES (Department for Education and Skills) (2006) *Primary Framework for Literacy and Mathematics*. Nottingham: DfES Publications.

DfES (Department for Education and Skills) (2006) *The Rose Report: Independent Review of the Teaching of Reading*. London: HMSO.

DfES (Department for Education and Skills) (2007a) *Statutory Framework for the Early Years Foundation Stage*. London: HMSO. Available online at http://publications.teachernet.gov.uk (accessed 8 May 2007).

DfES (Department for Education and Skills) (2007b) *Practice Guidance for the Early Years Foundation Stage*. London: HMSO. Available online at http://www.teachernet.gov.uk (accessed 16 August 2007).

Evans, J. (2004) *Literacy Moves On: Using Popular Culture, New Technologies and Critical Literacy in the Primary Classroom*. London: David Fulton.

Factor, J. (2000) *Kidspeak: A dictionary of Children's Words, Expressions and Games*. Victoria: Melbourne University Press.

Gillen, J. (1997) '"Couldn't put Dumpy together again": the significance of repetition and routine in young children's language development', in L. Abbott and H. Moylett (eds) *Working with the Under-Threes: Responding to Children's Needs. Volume 2*. Buckingham: Open University Press. pp. 90–101.

Gillen, J. (2003) *The Language of Children*. London: Routledge.

Gillen, J. (2006) 'Child's play', in J. Maybin and J. Swann (eds) *The Art of English: Everyday Creativity*. Basingstoke: Palgrave Macmillan.

Gillen, J. (2007) 'Derwent's Doors: Creative Acts', *Mind, Culture and Activity*.

Grugeon, E. (1999) 'The state of play: children's oral culture, literacy and learning', *Reading* 33 (1): 13–16.

Grugeon, E. (2001) '"We like singing the Spice Girl songs ... and we like Tig and Stuck in the Mud": girls' traditional games on two playgrounds', in J.C. Bishop and M. Curtis (eds) *Play Today in the Primary School Playground*. Buckingham: Open University Press.

Dyson, A. Haas (2004) 'Introduction', in J. Evans (ed.) *Literacy Moves On: Using Popular Culture, New Technologies and Critical Literacy in the Primary Classroom*. London: David Fulton.

Lancashire Schools Effectiveness Service (2005) Newsletter Issue 26, October. Available online at http://www.lancsngfl.ac.uk (accessed 26 January 2008).

Luce-Kapler, R. (2003) 'Orality and the poetics of curriculum', *Journal of the Canadian Association for Curriculum Studies* 1 (2): 79–93.

Medwell, J. and Wray, D. (2007) 'Handwriting: what do we know and what do we need to know?' *Literacy* 41 (1): 10–15.

Murray, L. and Andrews, L. (2000) *The Social Baby*. The Children's Project/ NSPCC.

NSPCC (with Lynn Murray) (2004) *The Social Baby DVD/Video*. The Children's Project/NSPCC. Available online at http://www.socialbaby.com (accessed 16 August 2007).

Opie, I. and Opie, P. (1997) *The Oxford Dictionary of Nursery Rhymes. Second Revised Edition*. Oxford: Oxford University Press.

Peccei, J.S. (1999) *Child Language. Second edition*. London: Routledge.

Peters, A.M. and Boggs, S.T. (1986) 'Interactional routines as cultural influences upon language acquisition', in B. Schieffelin and E. Ochs (eds) *Language Socialization Across Cultures*. New York: Cambridge University Press.

Riley, J. (1996) *The Teaching of Reading*. London: Paul Chapman.

Rosen, M. and Oxenbury, H. (1993) *We're Going on a Bear Hunt*. London: Walker Books.

Sealey, A. (2000) *Childly Language: Children, Language and the Social World*. Harlow: Pearson Education.

Sloan, G. (2003) *The Child as Critic: Developing Literacy Through Literature, K-8*. New York: Teachers College Press.

Trevarthen, C. and Aitken, K.J. (2001) 'Infant intersubjectivity: research, theory and clinical applications', *Journal of Child Psychology and Psychiatry* 4 (1): 3–48.

Turner, I., Factor, J. and Lowenstein, W. (1978) *Cinderella Dressed in Yella. Second edition*. Richmond, Australia: Heinemann.

Vygotsky, L.S. (1987) 'Thinking and speech', trans. by N. Minick in R. Rieber and A. Carton (eds) *The Collected Works of L.S. Vygotsky. Vol. I Problems of General Psychology*. New York: Plenum Press. pp. 43–287.

Wilson, A. (1998) *The Poetry Book for Primary Schools*. London: The Poetry Society.

Signs and symbols: children's engagement with environmental print

Elaine Hallet

'That says "McDonalds", I can see the "m".'

We live in an environment that is filled with print. This five-year-old child is engaging with the everyday print she sees, and reads the familiar sign and symbol that advertise her favourite place to eat. The child is at the beginning of her literacy journey through which she develops knowledge, skills and understanding of the written word, becoming a reader and a writer. This chapter discusses the importance of environmental print in children's early literacy development within the home and the early years setting, and highlights the important role of adults in supporting children's engagement with it. Throughout the chapter, activities for providing opportunities for children to engage with a range of environmental print and texts are given.

Wray et al. define literacy as:

> the ability and willingness to exercise mastery over the processes used in contemporary society to encode, decode and evaluate meanings conveyed by printed symbols. (Wray et al., 1989: 169)

This definition of literacy became significantly clear during a study visit to Japan. I was spending time in and around the Tokyo area visiting schools to observe the teaching of literacy. As a monolingual speaker, reader and writer of English, I was surrounded by the printed symbols of a language from which I could not derive any meaning. I needed to make sense of the patterns, signs and symbols around me in order to live within the Japanese society in which I was a temporary resident.

My study visit involved visiting four schools to find out how reading and writing was taught to young children. I was traveling to the schools by public transport. I had arranged for an interpreter to meet me at each school to assist me during my visit. However, my first task was to arrive at the school. At the simplest level, I had to read the train timetable in order to catch an appropriate train to begin my journey to each school and then be able to read the station sign at the end of my journey. I did manage to complete several successful journeys to and from the schools. How did I do this? I developed my own strategies to 'decode and evaluate meaning' from the print in the environment which surrounded me. One strategy I developed to reach my final destination of my journey on the Tokyo underground was to count the number of stations the train stopped at: one, two, three, four, five ... I knew that I had to get off the train at the tenth station, 'Roppongi', the destination of my temporary home. I counted the stations repeatedly during several journeys until I was able to remember visually the pattern of black marks which comprised the station's name – so arriving safely. The stations now have their own individualised musical jingle to herald the station's arrival which would have helped me in this memory game.

The experience of navigating my way around the underground in Tokyo enabled me to develop an awareness of a young child's perception of their world being surrounded by unfamiliar signs and symbols. I had been placed in a similar position to that of a young child or an adult with limited literacy skills. They too, develop individual strategies for decoding the print around them in order to understand and live within the society they reside in, just as I had done. A baby is born into an environment in which he or she is surrounded by patterns, shapes, logos and symbols, all of which represent some aspect of the world in which he or she lives. Each child's understanding of his or her society develops as he or she grows and interacts with the environment and the adults and children within it. This 'social experience' enables a child to live in a 'literate society' (Wray et al., 1989: 1) in which literacy is valued as an essential life skill. For children to become part of this literate culture, it is important for them to talk, read and write using the predominant language of the society in which they live. For some children, this may involve acquiring the language and literacy skills of more than one communication system. As Naomi Flynn explains in her chapter about the language and literacy development of young bilingual children in this volume, many children are competent in developing literacy skills in their community language as well as the host language of the society in which they live.

Environmental print is often the first contextualised and meaningful print which a child encounters. The importance of children understanding that print conveys meaning is recognised as an Early Learning Goal for the Communication, Language and Literacy area of learning and development in the *Statutory Framework for the Early Years Foundation Stage* in England. By the end of the Early Years Foundation Stage children should:

> know that print carries meaning and, in English, is read from left to right and top to bottom. (DfES, 2007: 13)

In the early stages of literacy development, children recognise whole words which they see as a pattern or a shape, not necessarily attending to the individualised letters. This is known as the 'logographic phase' (Frith, 1985). There is a myriad opportunities for developing children's logographic skills at home, in the outdoor environment and in the early years setting. The next section considers the nature and range of environmental print.

Engaging with environmental print around the home

The environment which surrounds us comprises many forms and types of text. Print is visible on everyday objects in the home, in the local environment and in early years settings. We see print on paper and through technology we see it on screen. This print helps us to function in everyday life. Through reading the print around us we are able to, for example, read the map, satellite navigator and road signs to travel on the correct road to our destination; read signs such as 'danger' to avoid accidents; read the television programme schedule to view our favourite programme; set the DVD player; download tunes for our MP3 players; follow instructions for a PlayStation game; shop at the appropriate shop; order and buy items online; bank via the internet; pay for a cinema, bus or train ticket; browse through a catalogue and so on. In a multilingual environment, some of this print will be in scripts other than English. Thus, environmental print is integral to our daily lives and plays a strong functional role within it. If we are confident in our literacy skills, we take for granted the countless literacy transactions that enable us to complete our daily tasks.

There are many more everyday situations that provide opportunities for young children to interact with print in contextualised meaningful ways; for example, a visit to the health clinic; a walk in the park; visiting a relative's or neighbour's house; choosing toys at a toy shop; reading the menu at a café and so on. These encounters are crucial for children's developing awareness of the forms and purposes of print. Developmentally, young children engage in the world in which they live through playful exploration of it. Children are more likely to investigate the print around them and learn about it if, 'the print is genuine and the situation supports play' (Whitehead, 2007: 58). Whitehead defines 'genuine print' as being everywhere, the everyday print that already exists in the environment around us, as the examples above show, and not in prepared materials such as flashcards. For children to be able to actively engage with this print they need to be allowed to explore in a playful way as readers and writers. As they flick the pages of a catalogue, mark-make on a blank form from the post office they interact and engage with print in a range of situations that support literate play (Whitehead, 2007). Through this play their understanding of the written word emerges and develops. Hall (1987) describes this process of early literacy development as 'emergent literacy'. Through contextualised play situations children emerge as literate children able to talk, read and write in the world in which they live.

The home is a significant environment for babies, toddlers and young children as it is the first permanent environment they encounter from birth. A child's home is a rich source of print for them to engage with. As Leitcher points out, 'print does not merely reside in a household but rather flows through it' (Leitcher, 1984 in Hall, 1987: 16). The home is a child's first exposure to the printed word and there are many potential encounters with texts. Take time from reading this to look up and see what words are in your immediate surroundings. The home is a rich source of words, signs and symbols. Figure 4.1 gives some examples of the type and range of printed words and text that can be found. This is not to suggest that all homes will contain this range of print. Inevitably, the types and amount of print will vary from family to family. Yet, all homes will contain some of these or similar items, however small a number. The commonly held deficit model of a home that is 'print free' and that children will have no exposure to print before beginning school is simply not feasible in today's society. Some children will be exposed to an environment of print and oral language of more than one language.

The kitchen

- calendar
- recipe book
- pizza takeaway packaging/menus
- symbols, numbers, letters and logos on appliance dials (fridge, cooker, washer, microwave)
- labels (written and pictorial) on packaging, such as food packets, ready-made meals, washing powder, cleaning products
- cooking instructions on food cans, packets, ready-made meals
- written shopping list
- till receipt from the supermarket
- advertising leaflet
- utility bills
- notice board with reminders pinned on, for example dentist and doctor appointments
- labelled storage jars with the words 'coffee', 'tea', 'sugar'
- words and messages on mugs
- words and pictures on fridge magnets on the fridge
- plastic carrier bags with logos and shop names on
- paper money and coinage
- store and credit cards
- mobile phone
- television

The sitting room or lounge

- television
- DVD player
- newspapers
- magazines
- books
- comics
- catalogues
- blank ordering forms
- television programme schedule
- teletext
- laptop computer
- telephone
- telephone directory
- mobile phone
- address message pad and pencil by telephone
- birthday cards
- written letters and envelopes
- DIY leaflet
- word, symbols and numbers on electric or gas fire

The bathroom

- words on soap and labels on toiletries
- words on towels, flannels and bathmats
- foam letters for bath play
- waterproof book for bath play
- words symbols and numbers on taps and showers

A child's bedroom

- computer
- television

Figure 4.1 Print around the home

(Continued)

- MP3 player
- game packaging
- words and pictures on quilt cover and curtains
- words, logos and pictures on clothing and shoes
- notebooks, pens and pencils
- comics
- books
- calculator
- ruler
- catalogues

Figure 4.1   Print around the home

As Figure 4.1 shows, a child is surrounded by a richness of print and absorbs it as his or her literacy journey begins and progresses. Children need to have access to a range of environmental print opportunities to engage in on a daily basis. We underestimate the potential the environment provides for such experiences for literacy learning. In order to gain an understanding of what the opportunities are, take a look at a fictional child, Jo and the opportunities she has to engage in meaningful ways during her 'environmental print day'. The story of her day is developed from real experiences and has been devised to demonstrate the potential for encountering print within the home, the local environment and a nursery setting. Imagine Jo is three-and-a-half years old and attends a local nursery.

Case study 4.1   Jo's environmental print day

Jo is woken by her mother who draws her curtains, swiftly letting the sun in. These have letters on and momentarily form words in the sunny breeze. As Jo gets up she looks out of her window and notices the paperboy walking down the street carrying a bright orange bag with the word 'News' written on it. She goes downstairs to the breakfast table. The postie has delivered the mail and on her plate there is a postcard for her from her grandma. It reads 'Dear Jo'. There is a picture of a tower on it and her mum helps Jo read the word 'Blackpool' on the front of the postcard and together they read the message on the back. Evidently it is raining in Blackpool as her grandma has drawn an umbrella and a big rain cloud with raindrops falling from it.

Then, her mum asks, 'What cereal do you want Jo? Come and choose.' Jo looks at the three cereal packets on the breakfast table. She recognises the bright yellow packet with a blue 'W' for 'Weetabix' and chooses this. She pours some milk from the green and white carton with a cow on the front and drinks her milk from her favourite cup which has a 'J' printed on the side. Jo looks around the kitchen and can see other things beginning with the sound 'j' that starts her name, like the jar of 'jam' and the carton of 'juice' on the table and of course, 'Jump' her tabby cat.

After breakfast, she goes upstairs to get ready for her morning at the nursery. Jo brushes her teeth and then starts to get dressed. 'What shall I wear today?' she asks herself, looking in her wardrobe and seeing a blue jumper her grandma knitted for her. It has a picture of 'Shaun the Sheep', her favourite character from the television programme of the same name. Her name was sewn into the back collar so she could read it and know which way to put it on. Jo puts on her shoes. They have a bright white 'tick' on them which shines in the dark, and leaves a pattern and the word 'Nike' in mud and wet sand.

Jo picks up her book bag containing the book 'Spot's Birthday Party', which she shared with her mum last night, safely inside. She will be able to exchange it for another from the nursery library today. Her book bag has a house drawn on it with children playing around it and the words 'Nursery House' written on the door. It is just like her nursery.

The short journey to the nursery on the bus is quite busy. Jo knows she is going in the right direction as she recognises some shop, street and road signs along the way. Her mum points out the sign 'Daniel Hairdressing' where she had her hair cut the other day. She notices the green 'BP' letters on the bright yellow sign at the petrol station and the sign 'Time and Plaice' with the smiling fish where she goes with her mum to buy fish and chips for their tea. The black, white and red sign showing a parent and child walking signals that she is near her nursery 'Nursery House' as the sign tells drivers to drive carefully as there are children about.

Jo and her mum go inside the nursery. She finds her coat peg and hangs up her coat . It has got a picture of a tabby cat like her cat Jump and the word 'Jo' underneath. Jo is pleased to be in her nursery and shows her mum her painting on the wall. After she had finished it she told Tracey, the nursery nurse, about it and Tracey had written the caption underneath 'Jo playing at home with her cat Jump'. Jo reads this to her mum.

There are many words and messages for Jo to read in her nursery. These tell her where things belong and tell her what to do. The sign in the toilets, 'Wash your hands', reminds her to do so; the sign in the painting area tells her to 'Hang your apron up here'; the large sign

(Continued)

(Continued)

hanging over the book corner invites her to 'Come and read a book'; the menu by the door tells her that her snack today is a milk and a piece of apple.

Once Jo says 'goodbye' to her mum she starts to find out about the activities on offer in the nursery and some involve print. In the home corner, she can play with resources to read and write with. There are comics, catalogues, newspapers, magazines, recipe books and maps to read. There is a notebook by the telephone to write messages in, paper and envelopes to write letters, a diary and a calendar in which to write appointments. Jo begins reading and writing. Later in the morning, she goes with Tracey and the nursery group to look at the cars in the car park and examine the number plates on them. Tracey points out that some of the black marks are letters and some are numbers. Back in the nursery, after her snack of apple and milk, Tracey reads her group the story 'Mrs Wishy Washy' using a big book for all to see. Jo is able to read the story with Tracey and she likes to join in with the repeating rhyme, 'wishy, washy, wishy, washy', when the animals are washed. Jo chooses the traditional story 'The Gingerbread Man' to borrow from the nursery library as it has another repeating rhyme she can join in, 'Run run as fast as you can, you can't catch me I'm the Gingerbread Man'.

The morning session is soon over for Jo and her mum comes to take her home. On the way home, they stop at the newsagents. Mum buys a newspaper for herself and a 'Postman Pat' comic for Jo. Jo asks for tube of 'Smarties' as she likes to find the hidden letter inside the lid. What letter will it be? The lid reveals the letter 'm' – 'That's what my name begins with', comments her mum.

Jo's afternoon at home is spent doing several activities. She reads her comic, draws a picture and writes a letter to her grandma. Following the instructions from a recipe she makes some biscuits with her mum, she sings along to the songs on her 'Nursery Rhyme Time' DVD and watches CBeebies television programmes before tea. At teatime Jo has great fun playing with the spaghetti letters on her plate. She finds a 'j' for 'Jo' and 'Jump' her cat, as well as 'm' for 'mum'. At bath time, Jo makes her name on the side of the bath by throwing wet sponge letters onto the side of the bath. Out of the bath and once dry, she snuggles down under her quilt which is covered with letters and numbers. She remembers the activity she did with Tracey in the nursery car park that morning and looks for some numbers amongst the alphabet letters on her quilt cover; she finds '5', '3' and '7'.

Her mum comes to read her a story. Jo chooses 'The Gingerbread Man' which she borrowed from the nursery library. Before she drops off to sleep, she has joined in the rhyme several times 'Run, run as fast as you can, you can't catch me I'm the Gingerbread Man!'

Jo has had a print-filled day surrounded by words, letters, logos, signs, pictures and sounds with many opportunities to engage and interact with the print in a meaningful and contextualised way. She listened, watched and played with the print-rich environment, learning about her world and the place literacy as a vital vehicle for communication has within it. Jo's environmental print day is not typical for all children. It is presented to show the potential a print-rich environment has for children to have a range of opportunities to engage in print and gain meaning from it. When surrounded with a literate environment of print and texts, children like Jo will experience:

- receiving personal messages
- following instructions
- gaining information from outdoor signs and symbols
- gaining information from logos
- associating phonetic sounds with symbols
- distinguishing between letters and numbers symbols
- enjoying story
- enjoying the pattern and language of repeated rhyme
- mark-making
- seeing adults as readers and writers.

All children will have some opportunity to interact with print in their everyday life, particularly within their home and local environment. These print-rich environmental experiences should be built upon and extended when children transfer from their home to an early years setting. The next section concerns the development of a literate environment for children's progression on their literacy journey in early years settings.

Engaging with environmental print in the early years setting

Children transfer from their home to an early years setting such as a nursery, preschool playgroup, children's centre or Foundation Stage class or unit. This transition includes a change of environment and introduces new significant adults for children, such as a key worker. A transitional object like the child's favourite toy can be an important link or the bridge between the child's home and their new environment (Winnicott, 2006). Likewise, using some of the print experienced, and talking about those print-rich experiences the child has already had in the home, within the early years setting, will create 'transitional space' and experiences for children, providing a context for the practitioner to observe each child's literacy knowledge and skills, enabling them to build upon and provide appropriate literacy activities for each child to step along their literacy pathway (May et al., 2006).

On entering an early years setting children in England will experience a curriculum delivery based upon the *Statutory Framework for the Early Years Foundation Stage* (DfES, 2007), covering the age range from birth to five years of age. The framework consists of six areas of Learning and Development comprising three elements (DfES, 2007: 11):

1 The early learning goals – the knowledge, skills and understanding which young children should have acquired by the end of the academic year in which they reach the age of five.
2 The educational programmes – the matters, skills and processes which are required to be taught to young children.
3 The assessment arrangements – the arrangements for assessing young children to ascertain their achievements.

Literacy is covered by the Early Learning Goals and educational programme for Communication, Language and Literacy. The overall aim of the educational programme is to develop:

> Children's learning and competence in communicating, speaking and listening, being read to and beginning to read and write must be supported and extended. They must be provided opportunity and encouragement to use their skills in a range of situations and for a range of purposes, and be supported in developing confidence and disposition to do so. (DfES, 2007: 13)

The environment for the Early Years Foundation Stage curriculum to be provided for children in a meaningful and contextualised way is important. Bruce (1997) points out that the environment, the child and the knowledge are key elements within the early years curriculum. Every child consolidates his or her knowledge, skills and understanding through these three key elements. Research in the last 20 years, particularly by Hall (1987), Hannon (1995), Weinberger et al. (2005) has focused on the kind of environment needed for literacy learning within the early years setting and recognises the knowledge and skills that children bring with them to the nursery and school from the home. As we have seen, the acquisition of literacy is developmental and begins early in life. The early years setting needs to build upon the experiences children have before coming to the setting, and to provide an environment which extends and provides further meaningful interactions with print. This example describes a print-rich environment in a day care centre that demonstrates this:

> Much of the environmental print in the Centre is contextualised in that meaning can be derived from the surrounding context. For example, photographs of each child's family members, accompanied by a written caption and each person's name, helps the children make connections between pictures and writing. In the Daycare Centre, we see children learning about literacy through their use of print around the building. They are learning that print can be used to give and organise information, give instructions, denote ownership, send messages, depict a song, tell a story and recount an event. They are learning that print is meaningful and that it serves many different purposes; they are beginning to recognise the functions of print. (Barratt-Pugh, 1997: 62)

As this example suggests, having print around the early years setting is not enough; such print needs to be contextualised. Hall (1988) describes three conditions necessary for the creation of a curriculum which supports literacy knowledge, skills and understanding to emerge with young children in a developmental way through an emergent literacy provision:

1   Children must have access to a literate environment.
2   Children must have access to literate adults.
3   Children must have opportunities to practise literacy. (Hall, 1988: 16)

The establishment of a 'literate environment' is key to facilitating children's literacy development and progress. Adults play an important role in resourcing such an environment, and providing children with literacy contexts and opportunities to develop literacy practices. This is discussed further in this chapter. Research suggests that children begin to make meaning from the print through the context in which text occurs and that they initially read using environmental clues and visual patterns, not attending to the actual structures of words (Frith, 1985). Thus, the context in which literacy activities are provided within the Early Years Foundation Stage is important. Role play and the establishment of reality-based play contexts provide an excellent means of providing meaningful contexts for print (Hall, 1987; Hallet, 2004; Whitehead, 2002; Wray et al., 1989). Structured play situations, such as a dentist, hospital, café, home, shop, post office and so on, in which socio-dramatic play takes place as children take on different roles, enable children to take part in literacy activities which mirror the functional uses of print in society. Language and print from the outside environment can be effectively used within the play area. Environmental print taken directly from the children's local community can be used within the play setting to give play meaning and purpose. Children can collect the print themselves; for example, they can gather forms from the post office, menus from a takeaway, and catalogues from shops, and use them in their play area so that they are involved in recreating the environment they see and experience each day within their early years setting.

In addition to using environmental print within the play area, there are many other opportunities for extending children's engagement with print and texts around them and providing a rich world of literacy experiences. Figure 4.2 'Environmental print activities' on page 73 is a comprehensive list of literacy activities to use in the home and early years settings facilitating children's engagement in environmental print. It is not enough, however, to simply provide a range of print resources for these activities. Adults play a vital role in interacting with children through talk, which helps children access and fully engage with the print and texts surrounding them. The final section of the chapter outlines ways in which adults may successfully do this.

Adults supporting children's engagement with environmental print

As previously indicated, adults significantly contribute to children's literacy development through environmental print. This section explores their role and offers a framework for working. Babies and young children learn about literacy through the literacy encounters in their everyday lives, particularly when there is an active engagement with someone more skilled than themselves. The first adults babies and children interact with are their parent/s or carer/s and it is now recognised these are their first educators (DfEE, 2000). Through verbal and non-verbal interactions they help their baby and then child interact with and gain meaning from the world and culture in which they are born. They are in these early stages, forging the 'roots of literacy' (Hannon et al., 1991: 5). Adults facilitate young children's understanding of the literacy process by talking, listening to and extending their responses and interactions. Babies and young children interact with a range of adults; for example, their parents and carers, childminders, nursery nurses, key workers, health visitors, crèche workers, playgroup and preschool leaders, babysitters, relatives, neighbours, siblings and community workers. All these adults have a role to play in children's language and literacy development by supporting their engagement with environmental print, by talking and asking questions about it, and by using it as a resource for playing. Figure 4.2 shows the range of environmental print.

Alphabet book

The world a child lives in is full of 'children's culture', media and popular culture artefacts such as cartoon, TV and film characters, story characters, comics, advertising and packaging. This is a rich-print source to use in the nursery or classroom. Children can be asked to bring in pieces of print they are familiar with; for example, sweet and food wrappers. These can be put in a book in a sequenced alphabet presentation; for example, 'h' for Hoola Hoops, 'k' for Kit Kat, 'm' for Mickey Mouse, McDonalds, and 'p' for Polo mints as suggested by Ketch (1991). Reading familiar print helps children to read in a contextualised way and may help with phonetic sound association.

Chalking wall/board

A blank wall or board and a basket of chalks are provided for children to draw, mark-make and write upon. This can be inside or outside the setting. A bucket of water and a wet cloth makes this resource reusable.

Community links

A planned visit to the local building, for example, supermarket, shop, takeaway, cafe or factory, in which the staff working there talk with the children about how they use print to package, advertise and sell their products. The visited workplace can be recreated in the school or early years setting by the children who can use print to operate their own workplace.

Community photographs

A collection of photographs showing print and community languages in the local area can be taken; for example, of street names, road signs, shop fronts, door numbers, and a name sign outside their school or early years setting. An adult sharing these photos with a child can stimulate discussion and help children recognise that print is important and informs them about the place in which they live.

Environmental print day

This focuses on household print within the home and how it can be used for literacy development. Parents/carers can be asked to bring examples of print from their home to the early years setting or school class. Print-related activities such as the ones described in this list are set up for parents/carers to take part in with their children. This supports parent/carers in helping their child's literacy development.

Interest literacy workshop

This is a time when parents/carers can work with their child with reading activities. The reading materials can be developed around a specific interest of a child; for example, football, swimming, bugs, snakes, dinosaurs, Disney or television characters. Reading material which includes non-fiction environmental print, for example, football programmes, maps, catalogues, can be used for reading and writing activities such as designing a football poster.

Jigsaws

Photographs, postcards, carrier bags, leaflets, food packages, logos can be cut up and laminated, then made into jigsaws for children to complete. This will help children to read pictures, words and symbols by playing a game.

Literacy packs

These are literacy-related activities in a wallet folder which parents/carers can borrow to use with their child at home. They can include environmental print such as:

- *A shopping pack*, which might include:
  - a handwritten shopping list
  - photographs of shops and their name signs
  - a catalogue
  - a till receipt

Figure 4.2 Environmental print activities

(Continued)

- a non-fiction book about different types of shops
- a storybook about shopping; for example, *The Shopping Basket* by John Burningham
- notes for parents/carers about how to use the pack with their child.

- *A writing pack*, which might include:
  - blank forms
  - a notebook
  - a diary
  - a calendar
  - paper of different sizes, shapes and colours
  - envelopes
  - pens and pencils
  - a story about writing; for example, *The Jolly Postman* by Janet Ahlberg
  - notes for parents with suggestions of how to use the pack with their child are included in the wallet/folder

---

Magnetic letters

These sticky letters can be used to copy words seen in the environment or for children to mark-make and write freely with.

Message board

This is a blank board situated in the nursery or school classroom with paper, pencils and paper by the side. Children, parents and practitioners are able to write messages for information or personal messages to others and pin them onto the message board. The recipients can reply by leaving a message or for it to be read out. This interactive board shows that print communicates messages to others and to particular audiences.

Name labels

One of the Early Years Foundation Stage Early Learning Goals is for children to be able to:

> Write their own names and other such things as labels and captions. (DfES, 2007: 13)

This activity involves children making posters of familiar signs and logos. Cutting out letters of a child's name from the large print found on boxes can produce a name label for their bedroom. This activity will help the child become familiar with the shape and letters of their name.

Newspaper letters, words and sounds

Newspapers and magazines are a source of many different styles of print fonts. Children are asked to look through them and collect a sound, for example, 'th', or a word, for example, 'the', which the child cuts out and glues onto a piece of paper or highlights with a highlighter pen. This helps to develop phonemic and word recognition.

Number plates

In the early stages of literacy development it is difficult for children to distinguish between letters and numbers as they can both look like a pattern or shape to a child. By looking at parked car number plates an adult can talk about the concept of what a number is and what a letter is and the difference in pattern and shape. The child can copy the numbers and letters onto a clipboard in order to feel the difference in shape and form. (The health and safety of children must be considered during this activity.)

Outdoor play

The Early Years Foundation Stage requires all settings to provide an outdoor space in which children can play (DfES, 2007). Children can form their own print to interact with in a

---

Figure 4.2 *(Continued)*

play context, such as a garage. They can write number plates for their bikes and trikes, label the petrol pump with a dial showing the price of petrol, writing road signs, street names and chalk out road markings on the ground.

Print games

The following games use signs, symbols or letters in the environment and can be played at group time in the early years setting or classroom or by parents in the home or on a car journey:

- 'I spy'
- matching and snap game: logos and words from packaging, such as cereal packets, can be cut out and glued onto card and used for visual and word recognition
- track game: a board game where a child stops on a space and picks up a card which could have a sweet wrapper glued onto it or a photograph of some environmental print; for example, a road sign or street name sign. The child has to read the print in order for the game to continue

Print journey

This involves recording print that can be seen on a journey from the top of a bus, from a tram or a train window; for example, shop signs, traffic signs, pedestrian crossings, advertising hoardings.

Print picnic

A picnic is held to celebrate print and this is the theme. An invitation to the picnic is written, a written reply allows a child to attend. Children are asked to wear clothes with letters or words on. The food eaten is made of letters or has writing and words on; for example, a cake with the words 'Happy Birthday' iced on, buns with each child's name written on, the tablecloth and napkins have the alphabet written on. Good games to play are 'pass the parcel', where the forfeit has to be read, word games like 'word snap' and hangman', or magnetic letters, played before 'the alphabet song is sung. Each child receives a party bag with a word search, a storybook, a comic a notepad and pencil in to take home.

Role play

Literacy materials can be included into all role play areas so that children can use print in relevant and purposeful ways for communication; for example, blank forms in a post office, a menu in a café, an appointment book in a doctor's surgery, a recipe book, calendar, notepad and pen in the home corner.

Sand

Plastic letters and words cut out from cardboard packaging can be used in sand for children to write their name, words and sentences. A practitioner can talk about the letters and words as the children play.

Shopping for print

A visit to a shop where a range of logos, packaging and advertising is found. These can be collected, drawn and copied so that the print, text, logos and adverts can be recreated in art and technology activities, such as designing and making food packages and advertisement signs for the play area.

Story sacks/story boxes

Story sacks or story boxes are a cloth bag or box containing a children's fiction book with supporting props and materials to stimulate reading. To help children engage in books, soft toys, artefacts, an audio CD and a language game based upon themes in the storybook are provided. Environmental print like a menu, recipe, ticket, timetable, letters are included if appropriate. A laminated activity card with suggestions for parents to develop listening, reading and writing knowledge skills, and understanding with the story and resources with their child is included in the story sack or box.

Figure 4.2   *(Continued)*

(Continued)

(Travelling) teddy

A named teddy bear becomes the children's teddy bear that goes on adventures. Any child or adult who goes on holiday or day visit takes the teddy bear with them. The teddy writes a postcard about his/her adventure which the children receive. This shows that writing is for a particular audience and has a purpose.

Water

Sponge or plastic letters floating in the bath or water tub can be played with to make words.

Word walk

Parents/carers with their children collect words and print from the local environment, the grounds of the school or early years setting or a specific part of the local area, like the shops. Adults encourage each child to look for words and collect print such as sweet wrappers, crisp packets and bus tickets.

The walk can be structured or unstructured according to the needs of the children. Some suggestions are to:

- walk around the nursery, school, classroom or playground and see how many words you can collect
- collect words beginning with a particular sound; for example, a, b, r, ch, sh
- collect the following print – a road name, shop name, a message, a logo

The words can be recorded by the children on a clipboard; any print can be collected in a carrier bag. The collection is taken back to the setting and is talked about, categorised and developed in activities; for example, the road names can be used in a language game.

Photographs of the walk can be put in a book for children to read in the book corner. (The health and safety of children must be considered during this activity.)

Writing table

A table supplied with a range of resources for writing, such as greeting cards, different colours and sizes of paper and envelopes, notebooks, blank forms and so on, will enable children to express their knowledge of print as a form of communication. Practitioners can act as role model writers by writing letters and messages to children on the writing table for children to read and write back to. This shows that writing communicates meaning, has an audience and is purposeful.

Figure 4.2   Environmental print activities

A child's first interaction with a supportive adult is with their parent/s or carer/s. Research by Brice-Heath (1983), Davie et al. (1992), Hannon (1995), Newson and Newson (1977), and Weinberger (1996) indicates that parents and families are, 'powerful influences on children's literacy development' (Nutbrown and Hannon, 1997: 8). Payton's (1984) research illustrates this point. She recorded in detail her daughter's literacy development before starting school. She found that her daughter, Cecilia, had been actively involved with the printed word long before she was able to read the print. In reflecting upon her role as a parent, Payton found that the contextual talk and conversation she provided helped her child to use her cognitive processes and gain meaning from the print around her. In this extract, Payton analyses the processes which enabled her daughter to gain meaning from environmental print:

> Cecilia has been immersed in an environment full of print (labels on clothes, grocery items, shop signs, street names, etc.) similar to the way in which she has been open to the influence of oral language from infancy. Print is passive, there to be noticed or not. That it is eventually perceived is incontrovertible. The following incident shows Cecilia's achievement and understanding. She and I were queuing at the checkout in the supermarket and as I emptied the contents of the basket onto the counter, Cecilia indicated the writing on the price ticket and correctly remarked, 'That says "Co-op". As far as it was known, Cecilia had neither previously asked nor been told the word, it appeared genuine inference. In many typical everyday conversations it was the day's shopping requirements, where they were to be purchased, how the journey should be made and so forth, which provided contextual information. It is argued therefore that it is these exchanges which prepared and created the necessary climate for the comment to be made, in similar manner to the way in which sense had been constructed in oral situations before. Here also the child hypothesised, analysed and finally formulated a proposal. (Payton, 1984: 27–8)

Once children arrive at an early years setting, they need to be greeted by adults who are mainly early years practitioners who will continue this role of facilitating and supporting children's learning by extending children's encounters with print. Parents and early years practitioners need to interweave their contributions and value the way every adult contributes to their child's individual literacy journey.

There is a number of models available which provide a framework for adults' involvement in children's literacy development. The ORIM Framework comprises four elements for adult's supporting children's literacy development by providing opportunities, recognition, interaction and modelling (Nutbrown and Hannon, 1997). The following introduces a further model for adults supporting children's early literacy development based around seven 'S's. The adult is seen to have a number of roles: supplying, supporting, scaffolding, sharing, showing, saying and seeing (Brailsford et al., 1999). Table 4.1 develops their model in order to suggest how the adult can support children's engagement with environmental print.

Table 4.1 The seven 'S's framework: adults supporting children's engagement with environmental print

Adults help babies and young children by:	
Supplying	Providing opportunities and resources inside and outside the home and early years setting that will enable babies and young children to interact with environmental print.
Supporting	Valuing children's literacy learning, whether it is spoken comments about a sign, a letter, a word or their mark-making. Helping children to interact with environmental print by asking questions about its meaning, intervening to extend learning where appropriate.
Scaffolding	Helping children to achieve tasks that they may or may not be able to do on their own; for example, read signs around them. Talking with children about the signs and symbols they see. Asking questions and talking about the print around them so that children start noticing the print and use the context they see it in to make meaning from it.
Sharing	Sharing photographs, books, etc. which feature environmental print. Sharing experiences of print in the environment; for example, talking to children about interesting signs they have seen in the street at the shops, etc.
Showing	Providing a role model for children. Demonstrating ways of using environmental print; for example, 'Look, this sign tells me that I should wash my hands now'. Showing the importance of using the print around us to fulfill particular tasks; for example, reading recipes when cooking.
Saying	Praising children's efforts for gaining meaning from the print around them.
Seeing	Observing children's development closely in order to plan effectively for their future learning and development and, or early learning goals. What print are they noticing in the early years setting/outside? How can we build on this in planning an appropriate activity?

Conclusion

It is clear that print surrounds babies and young children in a highly visual way both in the home, the local environment and the early years setting. We live in a society in which the nature of printed text is changing rapidly (Kress, 1997) and we are becoming increasingly more sophisticated in our understanding of printed, digital and televisual texts, and environmental print is becoming increasingly more important in our lives. Early years settings need to ensure that they reflect this evolving world and technological culture the child inhabits, and are responsive to providing a range of print and texts that children encounter in their everyday environment (Larson and Marsh, 2006). Supportive adults who provide experiences with texts that children recognise and are familiar with can help them to engage with print in a meaningful way enabling them to feel comfortable and confident in their literacy practices. Environmental print provides an important means of bridging the gap between the home and the early years setting as shown in Figure 4.2. This provides a wide range of activities for practitioners to use in the home and early years settings with babies and young children to help them engage in environmental print on their literacy journey.

Suggestions for further reading 📖

Kay, J. and MacLeod-Brudenell, I. (eds) (2008) *Advanced Early Years*. London: Heinemann.

Williams, J. and McInnes, K. (2005) *Planning and Using Time in the Foundation Stage*. London: David Fulton.

References

Barratt-Pugh, C. (1997) 'This says "Happy New Year", learning to be literate, reading and writing with young children', in L. Abbott and H. Moylett (eds) *Working with Under-Threes: Responding to Children's Needs*. Buckingham: Open University Press.

Brailsford, M., Hetherington, D. and Abram, E. (1999) 'Family literacy: desirable planning for language and literacy', in J. Marsh and E. Hallet (eds) *Desirable Literacies*. First edition. London: Paul Chapman. pp. 195.

Brice-Heath, S. (1983) *Ways with Words: Language, Life and Work in Communities and Classrooms*. Cambridge: Cambridge University Press.

Bruce, T. (1997) *Early Childhood Education*. London: Hodder and Stoughton.

Davie, R., Butler N. and Goldstein, H. (1992) *From Birth to Seven: A Report of the National Child Development Study*. London: Longman/National Children's Bureau.

DfEE (Department for Education and Employment) (2000) *Curriculum Guidance for the Foundation Stage*. London: Qualifications and Curriculum Authority.

DfES (Department for Education and Skills) (2007) *Statutory Framework for the Early Years Foundation Stage*. Nottingham: DfES Publications.

Frith, U. (1985) 'Developmental dyslexia', in J.C. Marshall, M. Coltheart and K.E. Patterson (eds) *Surface Dyslexia*. Hillsdale, NJ: Lawerence Erlbaum Associates.

Hall, N. (1987) *The Emergence of Literacy.* London: Hodder and Stoughton.

Hall, N. (1988) 'Write from the start', *Child Education,* April.

Hallet, E. (2004) 'Planning for early learning: Foundation stage and Key Stage 1', in I. MacLeod-Brudenell (eds), *Advanced Early Years Care and Education.* London: Heinemann. pp. 241–69.

Hannon, P. (1995) *Literacy, Home and School: Research and Practice in Teaching Literacy with Parents.* London: Falmer Press.

Hannon, P., Weinberger, J. and Nutbrown, C. (1991) 'A study of work with parents to promote early literacy development', *Research Papers in Education* 6 (2): 77–97.

Kay, J. and MacLeod-Brudenell, I. (eds), (2004) *Advanced Early Years Care and Education.* London: Heinemann.

Ketch, A. (1991) 'Delicious alphabet', *English in Education* 25(1): 1–4.

Kress, G. (1997) *Before Writing.* London: Routledge.

Larson, J. and Marsh, J. (2006) *Making Literacy Real.* London: Sage.

Leitcher, H.J. (1987) 'The linguistic and social background of emergent literacy', in N. Hall (ed.), *The Emergence of Literacy.* London: Hodder and Stoughton. pp. 11–21.

May, P., Ashford, E. and Bottle, G. (2006) *Sound Beginnings: Learning and Development in the Early Years.* London: David Fulton.

Newson, J. and Newson, E. (1997) *Perspectives on School at Seven Years Old.* London: Allen and Unwin.

Nutbrown, C. and Hannon, P. (eds), (1997) *Preparing for Early Literacy Education with Parents.* Nottingham: REAL Project/NES Arnold.

Payton, S. (1984) 'Developing awareness of print: a young child's first steps towards literacy', *Educational Review* 2. University of Birmingham.

Weinberger, J. (1996) *Literacy Goes to School.* London: Paul Chapman.

Weinberger, J., Pickstoe, C. and Hannon, P. (eds) (2005) *Learning From Sure Start: Working with Children and Families.* Maidenhead: Open University Press.

Whitehead, M. (2007) *Developing Language and Literacy with Young Children.* London: Paul Chapman.

Winnicott, D.W. (2006) 'Relationships', in P. May, E. Ashford and G. Bottle (eds), *Sound Beginnings: Learning and Development in the Early Years.* London: David Fulton. pp. 126–40.

Wray, D., Bloom, W. and Hall, N. (1989) *Literacy in Action.* London: Falmer Press.

Early reading development

Guy Merchant

Understanding reading development is of central importance to early years practitioners. Although the curriculum area of communication, language and literacy is broad in scope, it includes guidance on the development of early reading, setting it in the context of wider language experience. As we shall see, literacy learning begins well before children start their compulsory schooling and builds on early experiences in the home and in daily life. This chapter looks at how reading develops and how those working in under-fives settings can support young children in the early stages. I begin with an overview of the reading process, summarising key themes in research and practice, and then move on to look in more detail at the kinds of understanding and skills that form the foundations of literacy. The area of letter–sound correspondence (phonics) and the part that it plays in reading development receives specific attention. This leads on to a consideration of the changing nature of the reading experience and how this can be used to provide relevant and meaningful learning for young children. Emphasis will be placed on the value of working with a wide range of texts as a vehicle for developing key skills and understandings.

Changing perspectives: from reading readiness to emergent literacy

It is now widely recognised that children growing up in our text-rich society begin their literacy learning well before the start of formal schooling. Written language on labels and clothing, on television computer screens and toys, in public places and in the home surrounds the young from the very earliest stages. Researchers have shown how babies and toddlers respond to written text and begin to display literate behaviour from an early age (Brooker, 2002; Crago and Crago,1983; Marsh, 2004; Wade and Moore, 1996). To build on this experience of literacy, early years workers aim to recognise and value those under-standings that have been developed at home and in the child's primary social networks.

Our thoughts about educational practice in early reading have evolved rapidly in recent years. Learning to read, once the exclusive province of compulsory schooling and formal instruction, is now seen in broader terms as a process that begins with children's earliest encounters with print and the written word, and is supported by adults at home and in educational settings. Current thinking has prompted us to re-evaluate our definition of what reading is and what it means to be literate, as well as the ways in which early learn-ing in literacy can be developed.

Previously, the teaching of reading was seen as an essential ingre-dient of formal learning, strictly controlled by a qualified profes-sional in the school setting. Typically, teaching was associated with structured reading tasks like alphabet learning and memorising 'sight' vocabulary. For many children the difficult transition from home to school coincided with one of the most important and chal-lenging kinds of learning they were to encounter (McNaughton, 2002). Although current practice still emphasises the importance of formal teaching (DfES, 2006b), it is placed in a wider and richer con-text of literacy development.

The traditional view held that success in early reading was based on well-established pre-reading behaviours. So, importance was given to visual and aural discrimination in determining children's 'reading readiness'. An influential text for reading teachers suggested that the child 'must be mentally and physically ready for reading, and physically and emotionally settled at school' (Dean, 1968: 45). It was also suggested that children should have developed a 'fair vocab-ulary' before learning to read. Although precisely what constituted a fair vocabulary, or an acceptable level of language development for beginning reading remained problematic; these ideas are still influ-ential. Even motor skills were seen as an ingredient in reading readi-ness, since 'handling books requires fairly fine muscle control' (Dean, 1968: 45).

The idea of reading readiness was based on a model of psychologi-cal development that suggested that children would not, or could not learn to read successfully until certain prerequisite skills were estab-lished. Further, it was suggested that these skills were governed by a process of physiological maturation, and that adult intervention might not necessarily speed up that process (Moyle, 1976). Children's early experience of literacy was overlooked in the enthusiasm to identify and describe the exact mental and physical prerequisites for the successful learning of decoding skills.

The influential work of Smith (1971) and (Goodman, 1970) drew professional attention to the idea of reading as an active search for meaning. Smith in particular saw the acquisition of literacy in social terms. Meaning making, it was suggested, is constructed through interaction with more competent readers – and adults in particular. Although meaning-based approaches are not without their critics (for example, Beard, 1993), for those working with the under-fives they highlight the importance of early encounters with alphabetic writing. Young children *can* be introduced to the distinctive features of written language and learn how texts that use words and letters can convey meaning. This broader conception of literacy also encouraged professionals to give more value to the richness and variety of literacy experience that children bring to early years settings and formal schooling. The work of Brice-Heath (1983) and Hall (1987) focused on significant preschool 'literacy events'; these and other studies have helped us to reframe our definition of what constitutes early literacy. Summarising this new way of thinking, Stierer et al. (1993) assert that young children:

> Have spent a lot of time studying literacy-based elements in their environment and observing people using literacy, and [...] they will have put some powerful effort into unravelling the phenomena of reading and writing.
>
> (Stierer et al., 1993: 5)

So, we no longer define literacy simply in terms of the formal instruction of decoding skills. Instead we can consider how we build and develop an understanding of how written language works, about the uses of different kinds of texts on page, on screen and in the world about us. For the young child, learning how to act like a reader is the first step in becoming a member of a community of readers. This way of looking at early stages in learning about reading and writing is referred to as 'emergent literacy' (Clay, 1991; Hall, 1987). Emergent literacy, according to Riley (1996) is:

> concerned with the earliest phase of understanding about print that enables the child to generate hypotheses about the nature of reading and writing. (Riley, 1996: 89)

Ideas about emergent literacy have helped adults working in the early years to move towards a clearer conception of their role than that suggested by advocates of reading readiness. The importance of children's participation in literacy events, the need for adults to model the processes of reading and writing, and the significance of drawing on children's experience underpin work in the early years. In this way adults become active participants rather than passive observers of literacy development.

What we know about the reading process

For most of us, the processes involved in making meaning from what we read are so deeply learnt that they seem routine and automatic. For something that appears to come quite naturally to us, it is surprising how hard it is to explain to others. As with driving a car or performing everyday operations on a computer, it is only when you try to instruct others that you realise how habitual these activities have become. From a psychological point of view, this kind of learning is very useful since it releases our attention from the detail of basic functions allowing us to concentrate on the wider picture. In driving, when we have routine control of stopping and starting, steering and changing gears, we can give our fuller attention to the flow of traffic or finding our way through an unfamiliar city. Similarly in reading, our ability to recognise words rapidly and automatically allows us to pay attention to meaning even in unfamiliar texts.

Current theory and research in reading suggest that skilled readers are indeed active in their search for meaning (Stanovich, 1980; Taylor and Pearson, 2002) and that they depend upon rapid whole word recognition, looking at each word in turn as they read continuous text (Rayner and Pollatsek, 1989). Skilled readers are also familiar with different kinds of texts, the purposes they fulfil and the different kinds of reading they entail. So they will not be looking for evocative prose, and lengthy sentences heavy with metaphorical reference in the handbook for the microwave; nor will they expect that reading their favourite artist's *MySpace* site will help them in assembling flat-packed furniture. The skilled reader has quite specific expectations of texts, and uses reading strategies that are appropriate. This may involve reading images or diagrams alongside written text or reading selectively for specific information. Reading, then, is a highly complex process that involves orchestrating knowledge and skills at a number of different levels. So, how do children develop these understandings and how do they become part of the community of readers?

Research and theory about learning to read has generated much heated debate and our attempts to turn ideas into practice have often resulted in an over-simplified view of reading (Taylor and Pearson, 2002). Advocates of meaning-based approaches have been criticised by those who favour a structured skills-based approach, and vice-versa. This debate over methods is reflected in contrasting models of the reading process, commonly referred to as either 'top-down' or 'bottom-up'. Top-down approaches give pride of place to making meaning, suggesting that we should deal with the larger units of context and meaning before directing children's attention to the smaller units (sentences, words and letters). In contrast, bottom-up approaches begin with the smallest units of language, building up from individual letters, to whole words, sentences and so on, to finally arrive at meaning.

Current theory suggests that the top-down and bottom-up models are based on a rather artificial distinction. Skilled readers, as we have seen, operate rapidly and flexibly at a variety of different levels. They may not depend too heavily on the 'sounds' that letters represent, but do use this knowledge when they need to (in using a dictionary or reference material or when reading car number plates). So, skilled reading is typified by the rapid deployment of appropriate strategies. It follows that learning to read must be concerned with practising and perfecting these strategies in the pursuit of gaining meaning from texts (Pressley, 1998). Young children should be introduced to all the aspects and levels of the reading process. In other words they need plenty of experience of the function and meanings of written text on page and on screen, as well as a systematic introduction to the technicalities of the lettered representation of meaning.

So far we have talked in rather general terms about the knowledge and skills involved in reading. I now go on to explore some key aspects of learning to read that help to structure work with young children in the early years. It is important at this stage, however, to re-state the fundamental principle that reading is about the active construction of meaning. In focusing on distinct areas of reading it is always helpful to consider how these can be explored in the context of meaningful literacy activity.

Key aspects of learning to read

In this section, I focus on five key areas of reading, showing how they can be developed and integrated in early years settings. The five areas are: literacy awareness; syntactic awareness; word recognition; orthographic knowledge and phonological awareness. Each area is

Table 5.1 The five aspects of early reading

Literacy awareness	Knowledge about genres, the uses of written text and different media that are used.	• navigating the CBeebies website • reading about Charlie and Lola • following messages and signs
Syntactic awareness	Knowledge about the grammatical structure of different types of text and the differences between spoken and written language.	• repeating a rhyme with expression • predicting how some written text might end
Word recognition	The ability to recognise individual words in their written form.	• recognising own name • identifying the name of a favourite television programme
Orthographic awareness	Knowledge about the spoken language that leads to awareness of similarities and differences in words or parts of words.	• playing the game 'I Spy' • making up rhymes in words • joining in with clapping games
Phonological awareness	Knowledge about the ways in which words are spelt and the correspondence between sounds and letters.	• naming individual letters in own name • noticing shared spelling patterns in written words

described and illustrated below, and Table 5.1 provides a summary of their key features.

The first area, **literacy awareness**, is concerned with the child's understanding and experience of the written word and the role that it plays in everyday life. Such an understanding constitutes the sorts of knowledge about language that are associated with emergent literacy (Hall, 1987). Important learning about the ways in which literacy is used in society is derived through observation and participation in the literacy routines associated with social activity, whether these involve leisure, such as choosing and using a video game, or business, such as following directions and signs to locate a particular building in the city. We live in a world which is richly patterned with written text. From an early age, most children will have learnt how familiar logos and slogans appear on the packaging of their favourite food or drink, on clothing and in the television promotions of these products. They will also be familiar with the curves and lines of the particular letters that represent their own name and will have seen their parents or other adults interacting with text on page and screen. In early years settings we build on this knowledge by using and discussing texts both inside and outside the classroom. Taking children on a 'print walk' provides an opportunity to draw attention to the different signs and notices and the messages they convey to children as Elaine Hallet suggests in Chapter 4, in this volume. You will also be able to point out the variety of scripts used, some of which may represent the different languages spoken by children, their families and their neighbours. Inside the classroom and on visits, you can also focus on the specific uses and features of screen-based technologies and the ways in which the written word is used in such contexts. The ways of talking about literacy that we generate through text-related activities are central to children's early literacy development (Baker et al., 2000).

An important aspect of literacy awareness is the development of concepts about print (Clay, 1985). Clay used this term to describe children's knowledge of print in written text. So this knowledge includes understanding where to begin reading a book, the directional concepts of top to bottom and left to right that are used in the sequential reading of stories, as well as concepts such as 'word' and 'letter'. As Hasset (2006) observes, these concepts of print privilege book reading and do not include the sorts of knowledge needed for making sense of multimodal texts and those that allow different reading paths. It is also worth acknowledging that children's concepts about print will vary according to the nature of their early experience. Bilingual children may well be familiar with scripts that adopt different conventions of directionality or different units of meaning (for example, Urdu or Cantonese). In a similar way, home environments in which children participate in regular use of specific kinds of texts, such as fan material or on-screen texts, are likely to promote different kinds of literacy awareness. Nevertheless the idea of concepts about print does suggest the sorts of understanding that contribute to literacy awareness.

The development of literacy awareness will include:

- understanding the functions of different kinds of texts (for example, labelling, giving directions or providing entertainment)
- understanding that the written word carries meaning
- understanding how writing relates to the spoken word and the ways in which we talk about text
- distinguishing writing from pictures and visual symbols
- understanding directionality and reading paths in different texts

- awareness of the left-to-right directionality of written English
- knowledge of some technical terms associated with reading (for example, text, picture, note, word, link, space, letter and so on).

The second area of early reading is **syntactic awareness** or knowledge of grammatical structure. This knowledge is not about naming the parts, as in the study of grammar, but about becoming familiar with the patterning and sequence of language. Although such an awareness is part and parcel of oral language development it extends beyond it, and this is one reason why spoken language is often included in literacy curricula for the early years (as in Early Years Foundation Stage and the Primary National Strategy). Children will begin to be introduced to the distinctive patterning of written language – often through the repetition of phrases and sentences in their favourite stories. They will get to know about 'the voice' or register associated with the written form, and the grammatical completeness that characterises the more formal structures of most written texts.

To illustrate this idea of the syntactic patterning of written language, you can compare the oral exchanges in a conversation with how they are reported in writing. For example, to write about a conversation we would normally make some changes to make it easier to read. These might include an indication of who is speaking ('she said'; 'he replied'), what they are referring to (the inclusion of specific objects or ideas), and some tidying up of false starts or non-standard grammatical features. Although there are no fixed rules, particularly in creative narrative writing, the point is that an important part of learning to read involves learning about the kind of language that is associated with the written form. A key function of shared reading is to introduce children to the distinctive features of written language.

The third area of early reading is **word recognition**. Through their early encounters with writing, young children will learn that certain combinations of letters are used to represent familiar words. Developing out of the kinds of understanding outlined above, they will begin to recognise the written form of their own name, the title of a favourite video or book, or the brand name of their breakfast cereal. Although this sort of awareness should be encouraged, the emergence of early word recognition does not signal that children should immediately be moved on to learning lists of 'key words'. Research seems to suggest that in early word recognition children are responding to things like context, colour and word shape rather than specific combinations of letters. In experiments, researchers have altered the font style, the alignment or the letter spacing in words and have found that young children do not always recognise familiar words under these conditions. Frith (1985) describes this as *logographic* reading, a stage at which children are responding to more general features rather than spelling sequence. Logographic reading, then, is an important aspect of emergent literacy, but should not be mistaken for the kind of word recognition that skilled readers engage in.

Being attentive to the constituent parts of words involves **orthographic awareness**, which is the next area to consider. Orthographic awareness is concerned with the ways in which letters and letter strings are used to represent words. It is what we use in identifying families of written words (for example, 'wood', 'good' and 'hood') and also in our attempts to spell unfamiliar words. Various studies have shown how an awareness of orthographic patterning is important to early reading. While Riley (1996) suggests that an ability to identify and label letters of the alphabet on entry to school is a good indicator of early reading success, Byrne (1998) highlights the importance of paying attention to letter strings. Collecting and classifying words and letters from magazines and catalogues, advertisements and food packaging can be used to develop early orthographic awareness.

Closely related to orthographic awareness is the final area of early reading, **phonological awareness**. Phonological awareness can be described as knowledge about the sound structures of language and how words can be broken down and built up from individual units of sound (phonemes). A number of studies have shown how an ability to rhyme, alliterate and identify syllables in words contributes to later success in reading in English (Goswami, 1999; Goswami and Bryant, 1990). For most beginning readers, phonological awareness provides a good foundation on which to build later work on sound–symbol correspondence – what most of us refer to as 'phonics teaching', and this is the subject of the next section. But for the moment, it is important to emphasise that using nursery rhymes, chanting jingles and raps, repeating alliterative phrases, playing 'I spy' and clapping games are not only commonplace elements of good early years practice, they actually constitute an important part of the early stages of reading.

The five areas of early reading development described above are not to be seen as a developmental sequence and certainly do not need to be learnt in isolation. In fact, what we know about effective early literacy practice shows that explicit skill teaching works best in the context of authentic and enjoyable engagement with text (Pressley, 1998). The challenge for early years practitioners is to provide this sort of learning context and to support young readers in achieving the early learning goals outlined in the *Statutory Framework for Early Years Foundation Stage* and the National Literacy Strategy.

The question of phonics

Standards in literacy continue to be a political concern both in England and elsewhere. The teaching of reading, and particularly the emphasis given to phonics, has become a major focus for the media with headline reports claiming that phonics teaching is not only 'common sense', but that it has been 'abandoned' or even 'banned' in favour of other methods. There is little factual basis to these claims, and they have tended to turn attention away from the investigation of method and good practice in teaching phonics. Phonics teaching is used to describe classroom routines through which young children learn the particular correspondences between written letters and the sound components of individual words. As such it is an important part of learning to read, but of course, it is not the whole story.

A recent government enquiry, the Rose Review (DfES, 2006a), was tasked to investigate the relative merits of synthetic and analytic approaches to phonics teaching, following renewed concern over reading instruction in the United Kingdom. Specific emphasis was given to deciding on the relative merits of synthetic and analytic approaches. In brief, synthetic approaches involve segmenting and then blending individual sounds in words (for example, c/a/t), whereas analytic approaches involve identifying common sounds in sets of words (for example, cat, cup, card). The Rose Review and a raft of curriculum guidance, training and resource material have now been generated to promote the use of synthetic phonics, despite the fact that it is likely that children, parents and many teachers will continue to use both approaches.

Following similar concerns about phonics teaching in the United States, a review of research findings by the National Reading Panel (2000) concluded that there was little evidence to favour one method over another, and recent work even seems to suggest that a systematic approach, using both synthetic and analytic approaches may be best (Juel and Minden-Cupp, 2001).

Although there are passionate and influential advocates of specific approaches – some aligned with commercial interests – two main principles are clear. Firstly, because of the complexities of English spelling, some systematic phonics teaching needs to be an integral part of reading instruction. Children need to know how letters and letter strings combine to represent the phonic elements of words, both in order to spell and to help in decoding unfamiliar words. Secondly, phonic knowledge, as we have seen in the previous section, is only part of the wider process of reading. Phonics alone would lead to a limited and impoverished kind of literacy and one that is insufficient for that required for full participation in society. After all, phonics teaching is a means to an end, not an end in itself (Adams, 1990).

Developing early reading – the reading experience

Successful work with under-fives will be informed by an understanding of the diversity of early experience and the importance of the five areas as well as an understanding of how progression in this learning feeds into the structures of the formal curriculum at Key Stage 1. Learning experiences that involve interaction around meaningful and appropriate texts are the best starting point. Here, I begin by looking at working with text, and then show how the five areas can be developed through specific activities. The section concludes with a specific focus on the role of story in early years education.

Working from text

The benefits of an early introduction to print are well documented (Butler, 1988). An influential study by Wade and Moore (1996) looked at how introducing books to babies has long-lasting benefits that can be traced through early years provision and later on in school performance. Good books for the very young encourage enjoyment through a rich interplay between visual and print features. These and other kinds of multimodal texts are an important introduction to reading. Advances in book technology have built on the fascination with novelty, prediction and surprise, and encourage children to interact with the text by turning wheels, lifting flaps, and examining pull-outs or pop-ups. For the very young there is an increasing number of 'indestructible' books on the market – made out of cloth, board and synthetic materials. Books for the young can also appeal as simple but memorable stories, sometimes referring to everyday routines (such as mealtimes, washing, etc.), including characters from the media (such as those from popular television series) or introducing children to the realm of the imagination. At this stage children will also experience the intimacy of sharing the text with an adult, a friend or sibling. They will also be learning about the physical characteristics of books and how to handle them. In short, they will learn that books are valued, that they can be both useful and enjoyable.

Whitehead (1996) draws our attention to the ways in which early encounters with books form the foundation for the development of concepts about print:

> Babies and older toddlers respond to pictures and to print in books in a variety of ways; first with eye-gaze, smiles, gurgles and squeals, scratching at the paper, pointing and bouncing with enthusiasm. Eventually this develops into naming, joining in with the words, turning the pages and initiating real discussions about character, motives and plots as well as linguistic talk about letters, sounds and the conventions of print.

> (Whitehead, 1996: 66)

Whitehead provides a clear account of the kinds of learning that can emerge from early book-based interactions. However, it is becoming increasingly apparent that young children enter school with much more varied experiences of literacy than was once imagined. Gregory and Williams (2000) illustrate the diversity of home literacy activities that children participate in, and go on to suggest that only a narrow range of these are officially recognised by the school. Changes in literacy associated with new technologies in the home are also influential as a number of studies show (Hassett, 2006; Marsh, 2004; Merchant, 2005). Nonetheless, this work points to the fact that significant early literacy learning takes place in the context of the home. In order to recognise and build on such learning, strong professional relationships with parents and caregivers are essential. Continuity of experience between home and school is important. Establishing a good relationship in the early years is a strong foundation for the home–school partnership as it develops. The growing recognition of the importance of this partnership to the development of literacy is recognised (Hannon, 1995).

Enriching and broadening children's experience will mean introducing them to new forms of paper- and screen-based texts. Under-fives settings need to be well-resourced with a broad range of materials that reflect children's backgrounds and interests. Materials will need to be updated regularly and should be easy for children to access. Book provision needs to include different kinds of texts (fiction, non-fiction, poetry and rhyme) as well as different formats. In choosing books we need to bear in mind not only the interests of the children but also the ways in which print and illustration provide positive role models of different groups in society. Including dual text material is important, because this can give status and recognition to other kinds of writing, some of which children may already be familiar with. Experience of text in book form will be complemented by an introduction to a broader range of written forms.

Developing an understanding that writing is meaningful must take into account the fact that these meanings are an integral part of social practices. So alongside book-based work, attention can be given to signs, labels and notices. Literacy within children's experience may include food- and toy-packaging, advertisements and catalogues, train tickets, DVD cases, football results, computer games and magazines. These kinds of texts should be strongly represented in early years settings and children should have regular opportunities to talk about and compare different kinds of texts.

Attention should also be given to providing an inviting and stimulating environment for literacy. This will include an attractive and comfortable book corner as well as access to computers and audio material. Display will be an important part of creating this environment. It may be decorated with children's work, or show images of adults and children reading together. When using images of people reading, you should try to include pictures of friends and adults that children know and can identify with. If you are using your own images make sure that you have permission to do so. Those responsible for creating reading areas will also want to take care that images do not give the impression that reading is a female or male activity, or excludes social or ethnic groups.

Favourite books, magazines and games can be featured in reading areas alongside examples of different kinds of print, including texts written in different scripts. Reading areas might also include books and posters made by individuals or groups of children, or photograph albums with simple captions that record everyday events or special occasions, like birthdays or religious festivals. As well as reading areas, early years and nursery settings should make use of all opportunities to create a text-rich environment. Role play areas can provide a useful context for spontaneous literacy activity. They may reflect elements of a story that has been read – a CD-Rom or a video narrative and could include props that will allow for the acting out of various roles and key events. Alternatively, they can draw on children's experience of popular culture (Marsh, 2005) or social settings, such as shops, garages or cafés. In these settings, resources that encourage imaginative play with different kinds of texts can be included.

Although the physical environment is important, this should be accompanied by planned activities for sharing text through talking and reading. Young children should have plenty of opportunities to see adults (including their own parents or caregivers) involved in reading, but there will also be more formal occasions when adults read aloud to children and engage them in talk about the features of a specific text. On such occasions, adults will be reading to children from a range of different texts, modelling the sorts of reading behaviours they use as well as how they construct and interrogate the meaning of the text as a whole. They may use large format books (big books) or interactive whiteboards which allow for discussion of specific features of a shared text. In this shared text work, adults will be building on children's understandings of literacy and drawing children's attention to images and written text. They will also focus on specific features, such as repeated words or phrases, links or navigational devices. At this stage they will be familiarising children with the technical language for talking about text (for example, page, image, screen, line, word or letter).

Developing the five aspects of reading

Working from texts will provide many opportunities for developing the five aspects of early reading referred to above. Although these opportunities may arise quite spontaneously in an early years setting, there is also a need for regular, focused activities, which should be carefully planned. This section provides an overview of the kinds of activities that form an essential part of good early years practice in literacy.

Many of the text-based activities referred to in the previous section provide plenty of scope for **literacy awareness**. As well as listening to adults reading different texts including stories and rhymes, revisiting their favourites and beginning to join in, young children should be introduced to print in different forms. This may involve talking about the written word on screen, on posters, leaflets, in catalogues and on packaging. Collections and displays of these kinds of texts will involve children in actively looking at print in the environment and discussions will begin to introduce the terminology of written language. In working with print, children will be encouraged to point to words as they are read, so that they can begin to understand the one-to-one correspondence between the written and spoken word. They should also be introduced to written text on screen in similar ways – using computer monitors or interactive whiteboards. With continuous text, such as an enlarged nursery rhyme, pointing to each word in turn will demonstrate the left-to-right orientation of written English and the 'return sweep' that takes the reader from the end of one line to the beginning of the next. Here the adult will use prompting questions such as:

- Where do I start to read this rhyme?
- Which word should I read next?
- Where do I read next? (after the end of a line)

Developing **syntactic awareness** will be achieved through focusing on the patterning and sequence of written language. Clark (1988) shows how young children become familiar with the language of books through revisiting favourite texts. She recorded children in a nursery school as they retold these stories. Her observations show how they learned to handle books and, importantly, that, 'book language does not vary with retelling' (Clark, 1988: 48).

She illustrated how young children begin to use vocabulary and grammatical features that are associated with the written form and that in doing so, they begin to use a 'special voice' or register. To promote the sorts of learning that Clark describes, we will need to make sure that children have a rich diet of reading material and that favourite material is available in books and other forms, so that children can consolidate their learning about the language of text. As we shall see in the following section, texts with a predictable, patterned structure are particularly supportive for young learners' early reading development.

In their reading and re-reading of texts, adults will want to draw children's attention to grammatical structure. One way of doing this is to deliberately omit a word as you are reading and ask for suggestions – for example, 'Jack and Jill went up the hill to … a pail of water.' A bell or chime can be used to help focus children's attention on the missing word. A more sophisticated approach to this game is to use a Post-it® or mask to cover the missing word on an enlarged text or big book. You pretend that you don't know the hidden word and ask children to agree on the one that 'fits' or 'makes sense'.

Encouraging early **word recognition** should build on children's interest in text on page and screen. It is important to re-state that this is not, at the earliest stage, about learning to recognise key words out of context through the use of flash cards or other methods. The essential learning is that a commonly occurring word has a familiar shape in the text and that the particular letter combination and sequence is stable. Using labels of children's names to indicate the activities in which they are involved builds on something familiar (their own name) and has an authentic purpose – it has a real function in routine organisation and at the same time encourages word recognition. Talking about children's favourite television characters, food or toys can lead to collecting and displaying posters and other artefacts, advertisements and packaging to draw attention to commonly occurring words. Parents can become actively involved in this sort of project, which can be an excellent way of introducing talk about text at home and in the early years setting. Simple word recognition can also take place in the context of shared reading. For example, matching word cards will help children to recognise the names of characters in the stories they read.

The use of rhyme, song, rap and poetry has particular significance in the development of **phonological awareness**. Here we are helping young learners to identify the sound patterns (phonology) of the English language. In the early stages it is useful to focus on the beginning sounds, and the division of longer words into syllables. Activities that concentrate on identifying and reproducing these sound patterns are beneficial. We are not concerned at this stage with matching spoken sounds to letters of the alphabet. Listening for pairs of words that rhyme – for example, in the counting rhyme *One Smiling Grandma* (Linden, 1996) or in *The Gruffalo's Child* (Donaldson and Scheffler, 2005) – and talking about the alliteration are good starting points. Collections of objects that begin with the same initial sound are also a useful resource that can be used in a variety of different ways (see DfES, 1998 and DfES, 2004). Young children will be keen to play games, like 'I spy', particularly where the game focuses on objects in the immediate environment. Alliteration (words that begin with the same sound) can be discussed by using published rhymes, audio resources or those composed in the nursery setting. Using the children's names to create alliterative phrases is always an enjoyable activity (for example, 'Rihana running round' or 'Sam sitting still'). Songs and raps for young children, clapping and skipping rhymes also help to show how words can be broken down into syllables. Again, these should be a regular feature of the early years curriculum.

As we have seen, research suggests that children who can label the letters of the alphabet on entry to school are likely to make good progress in early reading (Riley, 1996). **Orthographic awareness** will be developed by talking about letter names and how they are sequenced in words with familiar spellings. Children can be introduced to letter names and sounds – working with magnetic letters and alphabet tiles provide a context for systematically introducing the alphabet. These letter naming and recognition skills will be reinforced through the use of alphabet books and through involving children in producing their own as an individual or collaborative task. Alphabet friezes and simple word matching games will also be used to develop orthographic awareness, and children will be encouraged to focus attention on letter sequences as they experiment with their own word-processed and paper-based writing.

The role of story

The work of a number of early years specialists, including that of Meek (1988), has been influential in drawing our attention to the role that narrative texts play in supporting young readers. Story plays a powerful role in personal, linguistic and conceptual development and many studies suggest that storybook reading can lay the foundations for success in early reading. The work of Bus et al. (1995) in summarising research evidence lends strong support to the importance of story. However, Senechal and LeFevre (2002) are more cautious, suggesting that it is the particular nature of interaction around storybooks that is of key significance. Others, such as Gregory and Williams (2000) and Hassett (2006) argue that storybook reading is only significant *because* it is valued in school contexts constituting part of the official literacy curriculum. If this is the case, then best practice should be sensitive to the experiences of young children, the changing nature of literacy and the diverse home literacies in which they have participated.

Narrative, in a variety of forms, does seem to be an enjoyable and social experience for many children. Story introduces young children to carefully chosen vocabulary, distinctive patterns of language and predictable events. So, for example, the language patterning and illustration of *Brown Bear, Brown Bear, What Did You See?'* (Martin, 1995) supports children in memorising and predicting the text to a high degree of accuracy without necessarily depending on word-level decoding. In addition, the question and answer format of the written text helps children to draw on their grammatical understanding (syntactic awareness). In a similar way, the repetitive language of a traditional tale like 'The Gingerbread Man' is simply structured and punctuated with the chorus of 'You can't catch me, I'm the gingerbread man!' which is easily committed to memory. This repetition enables young children to experiment with their own reading as they revisit this story either with an adult or on their own. The ingenuity of the Charlie and Lola story *I am not sleepy and I will not go to bed* (Child, 2002) draws on children's knowledge of these characters from the television and the internet, developing an understanding of how texts in different forms relate to one another.

The cumulative list structure that characterises stories like *A Dark, Dark Tale* (Brown, 1981), *Bringing the Rain to Kapiti Plain* (Aardema, 1981) or the traditional tale of 'The Enormous Turnip' is also a useful device for encouraging participation in oral reading and scaffolds children's early attempts at independent reading. Another popular device in storybooks is the use of rhyme, which again aids prediction and supports recall and also can be used to develop phonological awareness.

Many of the popular children's books produced by the Ahlbergs make use of rhyme and humour in ways that are supportive to the beginning reader (for example, *Peepo*, Ahlberg and Ahlberg, 1985).

The under-fives will enjoy a rich diet of stories. Regular story sessions can be used to introduce children to new stories and to revisit old favourites. As Browne suggests:

> At story time, the teacher's enthusiasm for books is transmitted to children. The teacher is modelling how to read, the way words tell the story, the function of illustrations, and the movement of text across and down the page. (Browne, 1998: 29)

Other adults and older children can sometimes be encouraged to read aloud or talk about what they enjoy reading and this can be built into the early years reading programme. This sort of experience can be particularly enriching if you are able to involve someone who reads and writes a language other than English and can introduce children to stories or other texts from another culture and use their own language for at least some of the time. Becoming familiar with other languages and scripts is important for all children growing up in our multicultural society, but will be particularly significant for children who speak that language.

Shared text sessions can be followed up with a variety of different kinds of activity. It is important to encourage children in responding to what has been read to them. Through the questions they ask both during and after sharing sessions, we are able to monitor and extend children's understandings – not simply of the text itself, but of the ideas, issues and concepts that it contains. Our aim here is to establish the practice of talking about text which Chambers observes is helping children, 'to be articulate about the rest of their lives' (Chambers,1993: 10). On other occasions, the adult may provide a model for oral response by giving his or her own comments on the text and inviting children's views. This should not be seen as a mechanical exercise in assessing children's comprehension, but more as an open-ended discussion arising from reading.

It is also useful to think about other ways of responding to stories and other texts. Painting, printing and modelling are exciting ways to develop work on key themes or characters. Children can also use drawing programmes and digital photographs or collaborate in animation projects. In role play and dressing-up they can re-enact and adapt the stories they have heard. Story can also be used to give structure and purpose to table-top play, as well as small and large construction activity.

It is important to ensure that books that have been read aloud are accessible to children so that they can revisit them in their own time and at their own pace. Versions of stories on video, audio tape and on CD-Rom are useful resources. Work involving story sacks, in which a featured book is presented together with games, relevant objects and soft toys, has been particularly successful in generating enthusiasm and talk around texts.We can see then how the use of story and other texts draws on children's literacy awareness, as well as providing a context for syntactic, phonological and orthographic awareness and supports their early attempts at constructing meaning from the written word.

Conclusion

Adults working with children in the early years have a vital contribution to make to the development of early reading. By creating a supportive and stimulating environment for early literacy learning, by establishing good links with parents and caregivers and by direct teaching they can help to lay the foundations for later success. Effective early years practice will:

- build on children's early literacy experience at home
- recognise the importance of text in the child's immediate environment
- broaden children's experience of the range and function of different kinds of text on page and screen
- introduce children to enjoyable and thought-provoking stories
- introduce children to rhyme and wordplay
- ensure that reading is seen as active meaning-making
- encourage children to enjoy and share texts of different kinds
- develop children's literacy awareness, word recognition, syntactic, phonological and orthographic awareness
- recognise the importance of play in rehearsing and consolidating literacy learning.

Above all, the adult's task is to value the child's early literacy learning and to extend this by creating a stimulating environment for reading development. This introduction to written language takes place at a significant point in a child's life and it is important that fundamental attitudes and understandings are established. Providing this experience is an exciting challenge which, if met with enthusiasm, can provide both child and adult with opportunities for meaningful interactions in early years settings.

Suggestions for further reading 📖

Marsh, J. (ed.) (2005) *Popular Culture, New Media and Digital Literacy in Early Childhood.* London: Routledge Falmer.

Myers, J. and Burnett, C. (2004) *Teaching English 3–11.* London: Continuum.

Whitehead, M. (2004) *Language and Literacy in the Early Years.* Third edition. London: Sage.

References

Adams, M.J. (1990) *Beginning to Read: Thinking and Learning about Print.* Cambridge, MA: MIT Press.

Baker, L., Dreher, M.J. and Guthrie, J.T. (2000) 'Why teachers should promote reading engagement', in L. Baker, M.J. Dreher and J.T. Guthrie (eds) *Engaging Young Readers: Promoting Achievement and Motivation.* New York: Guilford. pp. 1–16.

Beard, R. (ed.) (1993) *Teaching Literacy: Balancing Perspectives.* London: Hodder and Stoughton.

Brice-Heath, S. (1983) *Ways with Words: Language, Life and Work in Communities and Classrooms.* Cambridge: Cambridge University Press.

Brooker, L. (2002) '"Five on the first of December!": What can we learn from case studies of early childhood literacy?', *Journal of Early Childhood Literacy* 2 (3): 291–313.

Browne, A. (1998) 'Enjoying books in the early years', *The Primary English Magazine* 3 (4): 29–31.

Bus, A.G., van Ljzendoorn, M.H. and Pellegrini, A.D. (1995) 'Joint book reading makes for success in learning to read: a meta-analysis on intergenerational transmission of literacy', *Review of Educational Research* 65: 1–21.

Butler, D. (1988) *Babies Need Books.* Harmondsworth: Penguin.

Byrne, B. (1998) *The Foundation of Literacy: The child's acquisition of the Alphabetic Principle.* Hove: Psychology Press.

Chambers, A. (1993) *Tell Me: Children, Reading and Talk: How Adults Help Children Talk Well About Books.* Stroud: Thimble Press.

Clay, M.M. (1985) *The Early Detection of Reading Difficulties: A Diagnostic Survey with Reading Recovery Procedures.* Third edition. London: Heinemann.

Clark, M.M. (1988) *Young Literacy Learners: How We can Help Them.* Leamington Spa: Scholastic.

Clay, M.M. (1991) *Becoming Literate: The Construction of Inner Control.* London: Heinemann.

Crago, M. and Crago, H. (1983) *Prelude to Literacy.* Illinois: Illinois University Press.

Dean, J. (1968) *Reading, Writing and Talking.* London: A & C Black.

DfES (Department for Education and Skills) (1998) *Progression in Phonics.* Nottingham: DfES Publications.

DfES (Department for Education and Skills) (2004) *Playing with Sounds: A Supplement to Progression in Phonics.* Nottingham: DfES Publications.

DfES (Department for Education and Skills) (2006a) *Independent review of the Teaching of Early Reading'. Final Report, Jim Rose* (The Rose Review). London: DfES Publications. Available online at http://www.standards.dfes.gov.uk/phonics/report.pdf (accessed 4 August 2007).

DfES (Department for Education and Skills) (2006b) *Primary Framework for Literacy and Mathematics.* London: DfES Available online at http://www.standards.dfes.gov.uk/primary/frameworks/literacy (accessed 4 August 2007).

Frith, U. (1985) 'Beneath the surface of developmental dyslexia', in K.E. Patterson, M. Coltheart and J. Marshall (eds) *Surface Dyslexia.* Hove: Lawrence Erlbaum.

Goodman, K. (1970) 'Reading: a psycholinguistic guessing game', in H. Singer and R.B. Ruddell (eds) *Theoretical Models and Processes of Reading.* Newark, DE: International Reading Association.

Goswami, U. (1999) 'Causal connections in beginning reading: the importance of rhyme', *Journal of Research in Reading* 22 (3): 217–40.

Goswami, U. and Bryant, P. (1990) *Phonological Skills and Learning to Read.* Hove: Lawrence Earlbaum.

Gregory, E. and Williams, A. (2000) *City Literacies.* London Routledge.

Hall, N. (1987) *The Emergence of Literacy.* Sevenoaks: Edward Arnold.

Hannon, P. (1995) *Literacy, Home and School: Research and Practice in Teaching Literacy with Parents.* London: Falmer Press.

Hassett, D.D. (2006) 'Signs of the times: the governance of alphabetic print over "appropriate" and "natural" reading development', *Journal of Early Childhood Literacy* 6 (1). 77–103.

Juel, C. and Minden-Cupp, C. (2001) 'Learning to read words: linguistic cues and reading strategies', *Reading Research Quarterly* 35 (4): 458–93.

McNaughton, S. (2002) *Meeting of Minds.* Wellington: Learning Media.

Marsh, J. (2004) 'The technoliteracy practices of young children', *Journal of Early Childhood Research* 2 (1): 51–66.

Marsh, J. (ed.) (2005) *Popular Culture, New Media and Digital Literacy in Early Childhood.* London: Routledge Falmer.

Meek, M. (1988) *How Texts Teach What Readers Learn.* Stroud: Thimble Press.

Merchant, G. (2005) 'Barbie meets Bob the Builder at the workstation', in J. Marsh (ed.) *Popular Culture, New Media and Digital Literacy in Early Childhood.* London: Routledge Falmer.

Moyle, D. (1976) *The Teaching of Reading.* Fourth edition. London: Ward Lock.

National Reading Panel (2000) *Teaching Children to Read: An Evidence-Based Assessment of the Scientific Research Literature on Reading and its Implications for Reading Instruction.* Washington DC: NICHD. Available online at http://www.readingonline.org (accessed 2 August 2007).

Pressley, M. (1998) *Reading Instruction that Works: the Case for Balanced Teaching.* New York: Guilford.

Rayner, K. and Pollatsek, A. (1989) *The Psychology of Reading.* Englewood Cliffs, NJ: Prentice Hall.

Rose Review (2006) – *see* DfES (2006a)

Riley, J. (1996) 'The ability to label letters of the alphabet at school entry: a discussion of its value', *Journal of Research in Reading* 19 (2): 87–101.

Senechal, M. and LeFevre, J. (2002) 'Parental involvement in the development of children's reading skill: a five-year longitudinal study', *Child Development* 73 (3): 445–60.

Smith, F. (1971) *Understanding Reading: A Psycholinguistic Analysis of Reading and Learning to Read.* London: Hodder and Stoughton.

Stanovich, K. (1980) 'Towards an interactive-compensatory model of individual differences in the development of reading fluency', *Reading Research Quarterly* 16 (1): 32–71.

Stierer, B., Devereux, J., Gifford, S., Laycock, E. and Yerbury, J. (1993) *Profiling, Recording and Observing: A Resource Pack for the Early Years.* London: Routledge.

Taylor, B.M. and Pearson, P.D. (eds) (2002) *Effective Reading: Effective Schools, Accomplished Teachers.* Mahwah, NJ: Lawrence Erlbaum.

Wade, B. and Moore, (1996) 'Home activities: the advent of literacy', *European Early Childhood Education Research Journal* 5 (2): 63–76.

Whitehead, M.R. (1996) *The Development of Language and Literacy.* London: Hodder and Stoughton.

Children's literature referred to in the text

Aardema, V. (1981) *Bringing the Rain to Kapiti Plain.* London: Macmillan Children's Books.

Ahlberg, J. and Ahlberg, A. (1985) *Peepo!* Hamondsworth: Puffin.

Brown, R. (1981) *A Dark, Dark Tale.* London: Andersen Press.

Child, L. (2002) *I am not sleepy and I will not go to bed.* London: Orchard Books.

Donaldson, J. and Sceffler, A. (2005) *The Gruffalo's Child.* London: Macmillan Children's Books.

Linden, A.M. (1996) *One Smiling Grandma.* London: Mammoth.

Martin, B. (1995) *Brown Bear, Brown Bear, What Do You See?* Harmondsworth: Puffin.

Developing writing in the early years

Ann Browne

What is writing for?

Writing is an act of communication and can convey a variety of messages in many different ways. It can be used to establish contact with others, give information, persuade, entertain and exchange ideas. At times, writing may be used to conduct an internal dialogue or record information rather than to communicate with others. Writing things down can help to clarify and organise one's thoughts and make sense of experiences (Kress, 1997). This understanding of what writing is for should inform all our teaching of writing and about writing so that children recognise that it is a purposeful and significant activity.

Types of writing

Britton (1972) suggested that there are three main types of writing, each with a different function. These are expressive, transactional and poetic. Expressive writing is personal and most closely resembles speech. It is used to express the writer's thoughts, feelings and experiences in a relatively unstructured way and it is found in diaries, letters to friends and jottings. Transactional writing is used to 'get things done'. It is used to give instructions, persuade, advise, record, report and inform, and is generally impersonal. Poetic writing is valued for its artistic merit including the form, style and choice of vocabulary. It is carefully composed and crafted, since it is often used to entertain and interest others.

Young children's spontaneous, early writing is usually in the expressive mode. They often use writing to represent something that is significant to them. They may attempt to write their names, use writing to identify family members or label important possessions. They use writing to convey something about themselves and their experiences. Young children may tell adults that their writing 'is about my dog' and a little later, when they read back what they have written, demonstrate how they are using writing to communicate personal information such as 'I like playing with my dog'. Teachers of very young children capitalise on these personal written communications and children's understanding of the connection between speech and writing by encouraging children to use writing to tell them about their favourite toys, to describe their holidays and to write their news. This kind of writing exploits the relationship between speech and writing by showing that what is said can be written down and draws attention to the communicative purpose of writing, both of which are helpful to children who are just beginning to find out what writing is for and how it can be represented.

Young children are likely to be aware of transactional writing from the print they have seen in their homes and communities. They will have seen information conveyed through shop and street signs and print on packaging. They will also have observed adults reading instructions and making lists. Early years teachers are expected to introduce children to transactional writing through a writing programme which includes opportunities for children to learn how to write factual texts. The most obvious form of information texts that very young children see and write in nursery and school are labels and notices such as, 'The Book Area', or 'Three children can play in the sand'. From this, children can be gradually introduced to more complex, extended non-fiction writing, including recipes and information books and instructions.

The function of poetic or literary writing is to entertain through giving careful attention to the vocabulary, style and structure of the writing. Examples include stories, poems, plays, songs, rhymes and riddles. One of the starting points for developing poetic writing is through oral storytelling. This can be based on personal experience. When we talk we often share experiences with others in story form – 'Last Tuesday, just as I was going out, the telephone rang and ...' is the beginning of a story even though it is an account of a real event. Children are familiar with this way of using language from their own oral experiences. However, stories in books are not just anecdotes in story form or talk written down. They are usually third person, fictional narratives which have been composed and crafted with care in order to entertain others. They are carefully organised and come to a satisfying conclusion. Children's ability to tell good stories and use poetic language can be developed by sharing and discussing books with them, giving them opportunities to compose stories using puppets and small world equipment and developing their delight in language through singing and saying songs and rhymes.

What is involved in writing?

The act of writing involves three important elements – composition, transcription and review. All writing passes through these three stages at least once. Simple writing, such as a telephone message, is given some thought (composition), is written (transcription) and is quickly read through to make sure that it is clear (review). More significant writing, such as a letter to a newspaper, may go through each stage several times. As composition, transcription and review represent the process of writing that all writers use, it is important that children are given the time to explore each of these aspects.

Composition involves making decisions about the content of writing. There are two parts to this. First, generating ideas about what one wants to write and second, selecting the ideas that will be used. Composition is not just about writing it is also about thinking. It begins with understanding what is to be written, to whom and in what way. Teachers need to help children understand that writers consider what they write and can change and delete what is written.

Transcription is the process of converting what has been composed into marks on the page. It is dependent on composition since the way in which some aspects of transcription are used depends on the content of what is written and the audience and purpose of the writing. Transcription includes spelling, handwriting, punctuation, grammar and layout. It is a time-consuming part of writing and can be difficult for young writers. They need to learn a great deal about writing before they can transcribe accurately. They need to know how to form 26 upper and lower-case letters, how to combine these to create words and how to arrange writing on the page. Children want to and can write before they have control of the writing system and adults should encourage them to do so. As they become more aware of writing and receive guidance about writing, their transcription skills will develop. Focusing too much on transcription deflects attention from composition and may damage children's enthusiasm for writing.

Very little writing is perfect after a first draft because writing what one intends in the best possible way is difficult. Reviewing usually involves changing aspects of composition and transcription in order to improve what has been written. Introducing young children to this last part of the process of writing is often neglected in the early years. Teachers are often reluctant to ask children to re-read and alter their writing. They may think that because children have put a great deal of effort into composing and transcribing, asking them to alter what they have written could be tedious and deflating. This is true and so not every piece of writing needs to be revised. However, if children have spent time and taken care with a piece of writing there is good reason to review what has been produced. Encouraging children to re-read what they have written and discussing their writing indicates to them that what they have done is important and affords the child the opportunity to enjoy and take pride in what has been written.

The conditions for writing

All writing takes place in a context. It is undertaken for a reason, with an audience and outcome in mind. It is then composed and decisions are made about content, structure, style and vocabulary. It is transcribed and attention is given to spelling, punctuation and handwriting, and, finally, it is reviewed. Purpose, audience and outcome have an important effect on what is written and how it is written. Purpose describes the author's reason for undertaking a piece of writing. In the world outside nursery and school this will generally coincide with one of the many functions of writing, but in the classroom there may be a difference. This is because at school many writing activities are initiated by the teacher, and children write because they have been asked to rather than because they have an important personal reason for doing so. Whenever possible children need to engage in writing activities that have a purpose and they recognise as relevant. They need to be involved in writing that explores the different uses of writing.

Since writing is a communicative activity, what is written has both an author and an audience. Before beginning to write, authors need to know not only why they are writing but also who will read their writing. We write for ourselves, family members, friends and people who are unknown to us. The tenor of the relationship between authors and audiences can be friendly, hostile, intimate, correct, cautious or polite. Knowing about audience affects what is written, how it is presented, the time that is spent on it and the choice of writing implement. When writing to an unknown audience or formally to a known audience, writers may take a great deal of care to organise the content, present information clearly, ensure that the writing is legible and that words are used accurately and spelt correctly. Children need to experience as wide a range of audiences as possible in order to learn how to write in different ways and to suit their writing to the situation and the reader.

Outcome means what happens to writing when it is finished. It is linked to why the writing was undertaken and for whom it was intended. Writing can be read by others, replied to, kept as something worth re-reading at a later date or used as a starting point for a talk or a discussion. It can also be thrown away once it has served its purpose. Making this clear to children can help them to realise that writing does not always have to be undertaken with trepidation. The apparent permanence of writing can lead to anxieties that curtail risk-taking and experiment, and lead to the getting-it-right-first-time syndrome. Experimenting with writing on pieces of paper, rather than practising writing in exercise books, makes it easier to display, share what has been written with others or discard what is not wanted.

Early writing development

At one time it was common to see children being prepared for writing through pre-writing activities, such as tracing and copying handwriting patterns and words using chunky crayons and large pencils. These were intended to introduce children to the writing system, letters and directionality, and to develop the motor skills needed to control writing implements. Pre-writing was followed by set writing tasks. These usually began with children being asked to draw a picture. The content of the picture was then explained to the teacher who wrote down what was said and the children then copied or traced over the words (Beard, 1984). Practices such as these emphasised correct letter formation and spelling, and often neglected to widen children's understanding of the uses of writing. They reflected the belief that children have to be taught and then practise transcription skills before they can begin to write independently. They often curtail what children can or want to communicate as typically children produce a summary of their picture; for example, 'This is my dog'. If asked to talk about the picture; rather than write they could probably tell the listener a great deal about the dog's appearance and habits.

It is now accepted that even very young children know a great deal about writing and that they can and do produce unaided writing that demonstrates their understanding of the system and the function of writing (Clay, 1975; Ferreiro and Teberosky, 1983; Lancaster, 2003). Children learn through their experiences, experiments and observations. From the earliest stages, all children gain some experience of writing through seeing those around them producing and using writing. As children see others write and as they notice examples of writing in their environment they often begin to experiment with producing marks that are intended to represent writing. They try out the patterns of writing initially because it seems to be a satisfying activity (Dyson, 1983) and then later they begin to attribute meaning to their marks. These child-initiated experiments with writing are now recognised as an early stage of learning to write. As children produce more writing and notice writing more, their own writing shows an increasing resemblance to that produced by mature writers. Their early attempts at writing reveal how they learn to manipulate the principles of the writing system which are fundamental to becoming a writer (Clay, 1975).

The very earliest signs of writing development are seen when children begin to make marks on objects. They may do this even before they are able to hold and manipulate a writing implement. The satisfaction children demonstrate from leaving a mark on furniture or walls, and their embryonic awareness that such marks are enduring indications of their actions, may be their first lesson about writing (Whitehead, 1996). More intentional marks such as very early attempts at drawing help children to realise that objects or experiences can be represented by symbols (Kress, 1997). Writing uses a set of symbols to represent something other than itself. To use and read writing it is necessary to be aware that writing stands for something meaningful. Through their early experiments with making rudimentary marks on a variety of surfaces children may be learning about the permanence of writing and how symbols can be used to stand for things, people and events. Later, when they begin to talk about what their writing says, they are demonstrating their awareness that writing represents meaning.

The writing that young children produce, that might once have been dismissed as scribble, is now seen as an important first step in the development of literacy. The examples of writing that follow show how much young children know about writing. They reveal children's awareness of some of the organising principles of writing and show how independent practice, exposure to writing and discussions about

Figure 6.1   Aliza's writing

writing with adults enables children to refine their experiments and produce writing that gradually approximates to conventional models.

Children's earliest writing often contains shapes that are repeated. These may look like letters but can also take the form of joined-up scribble. Writing in this way shows a child's understanding of the linear and directional form of written language, and an appreciation that when writing, one uses a set of symbols. Aliza's writing in Figure 6.1 illustrates her understanding of these features of writing.

The 26 letters in the English alphabet can be combined to produce all the words contained in a dictionary. Fluent writers know that they can use this limited set of symbols in different ways to produce all the words and sentences that they want to write. Young children begin to discover this often using the letters of their names, which are the symbols that are most familiar to them. They use this limited set of letters to write sequences of words. Although the words they produce may not look like the words children say they have written, writing in this way demonstrates children's increasing awareness that the set of symbols used for writing is limited and regular. The following example, Figure 6.2, in which Louie is writing about himself and his friends, shows what this stage might look like.

Children need to discover what is and what is not acceptable in writing. The English language contains 26 letters that can be represented in many different ways. For example, 'a' may be written as 'A'. It may also vary in size and decorative features. However, not all

Figure 6.2   Louie's writing

Figure 6.3   Child's writing

characters that include curved and straight lines are acceptable as English language symbols. Although 'b', 'd', 'p', and 'q', which employ the same shapes but are orientated differently, are all acceptable as letters, 'a' does not become a letter shape if it is turned around. Other symbols such as numbers and small drawings are also not letters and are not found within words. In the writing in Figure 6.3 the child is exploring the English language. She is reversing letters, includes some numbers, which she called letters, in her writing as well as using conventional letter shapes. She is aware that writing consists of a range of signs but as yet is uncertain about 'what this range is' (Clay, 1975: 43).

Each of these manifestations of the principles of writing represents an important achievement in learning to write. When teachers are aware of the significance of these principles and recognise them in the writing that children produce, they can help children to understand other principles and progress towards conventional writing through their teaching. In order to do this, they will talk to children about their writing, provide demonstrations of writing and show children examples of writing for different purposes and different audiences.

During their time in the nursery and reception class children's writing might appear as:

- drawings
- random scribble
- scribble in lines
- letter-like shapes mixed with real letters and numbers
- groups of letters
- letters standing for words with recognisable connections
- sequences of complete words which are not spelt correctly.

All of these are normal. Willingness to write, intention to mean, and gradual changes which show progress towards conventional writing are evidence of successful learning in the early years.

Understanding that learning to write is a developmental process and that composition or the intention to mean emerges in advance of transcription has influenced what and how teachers teach children about writing. Practitioners now place less emphasis on children producing correctly transcribed writing through copying or using word books. Instead, the early writing curriculum includes many opportunities for young children to experiment with and see demonstrations of writing. Using the writing that children produce independently, adults work with children to extend their knowledge about writing and their ability to write. They respond to what children can do, discuss the content of what has been written and then give them guidance about transcription (Graves, 1983; Temple et al., 1988).

Writing experiences and activities

Nursery and reception classes incorporate many opportunities for writing development into their normal provision and daily routines.

Children learn letter names and sounds, and identify words through listening to and sharing stories, poems, rhymes and songs. Through their encounters with books and print in the classroom they begin to scrutinise letters and words in a meaningful context. Activities such as story sessions, literate role play and the provision of enticing reading and writing areas help children to see writing as a natural part of their daily lives. They enable children to appreciate the purposes of writing, to explore literacy and experiment with composition and transcription. When children incorporate writing into their play and write freely in the writing area they are discovering that they can contribute to and access the literate world, and their confidence as literacy users grows. Through their active involvement with reading and writing they are discovering that they can manipulate literacy for their own immediate purposes. Provision of this kind also gives children time and space to explore writing at their own pace and at a level that is appropriate to their existing abilities. When the emphasis is on experimentation and enjoyment, the possibility and experience of failure is reduced.

The curriculum for young children needs to be planned and sequenced so that it acknowledges children's existing abilities and extends these during the time they spend in nursery and reception classes. Teachers can present children with an appropriate and stimulating curriculum by providing models of literacy, devising activities which can be undertaken independently, teaching children about writing during discrete writing activities and planning varied ways for children to practise their developing skills.

Children need opportunities to explore the uses and the system of writing before and in addition to direct instruction about writing. Once children have been shown a model of writing, and maybe had the opportunity to practise with guidance from an adult, they are in a position to experiment further. Providing resources and reminding children that these are available encourages children to explore, gain practice and to extend their skills in their own ways and at their own pace. Opportunities to explore writing independently should be freely and frequently available to children since they enable children to 'attempt writing for various purposes' and 'explore and experiment with sounds, words and texts' (DfES, 2006: 22–23).

Writing across the curriculum

In order that children see writing as an integral part of their lives all activities can be resourced with writing materials. This provides opportunities for children to experiment with writing in many different situations. Paper and coloured pencils can be placed in the construction area so that children can record their plans for the models they intend to build. Pieces of card and felt-tip pens can be used to label models with the maker's name or other information. Large pieces of paper on an easel or smaller pieces on a clipboard can be used to record children's findings as they experiment with sand and water. Displays can be accompanied by paper and pens so that children can add their own thoughts, reply to questions or comment on the work that has been included. The results of matching, sorting and classifying activities can be noted. Sequences of notes and instruments can be written down so that the children's tunes can be played to the class during circle time. Pictures, cut out of catalogues, can be stuck into a blank book by children and an explanatory text added later when they are working in the writing area. Plastic, wooden and foam letters can be used for sorting and matching activities, so that children become familiar with the shapes of upper- and lower-case letters as well as learning their names and sounds. During outdoor play, children can be given buckets of water and large paintbrushes or chalk to write on the playground and the outside walls of the school. Plasticine, playdough, clay and individual trays containing small amounts of sand, damp cornflour or rice can be used to practise making letter shapes and patterns. When they paint and draw, children are learning about the representation of objects and experiences as well as developing increasing control of writing implements and using the shapes and strokes found in letters.

Writing books at home

Most children begin to learn to write before they enter nursery or reception classes. This can be capitalised upon by asking parents and carers to make a book with their child at home to bring to the nursery or reception class when the child starts. A common format for such books is to mount photographs of the child at different ages and engaging in favourite activities in a blank book. Together the child and the adult compose sentences that will tell the teacher and other children in the class about some of the child's interests, achievements, likes and dislikes. If carers are not able to participate in this activity, a member of the school staff can make a book for the child at school or during a home visit. Making a personal book that will be read many times by others, and by the child, provides many lessons about writing. Children learn about authorship, audience, the functions of writing, composition and transcription as well as the need to think about what one writes before writing. At a later stage, children can use their personal books for reference if they want to spell their names or words that are important to them.

The writing area

This is an important part of the provision for exploring writing in early years settings. It needs to be well equipped, with a wide a range of paper, card, prepared blank books and writing implements. Other resources such as folders, a stapler, hole punch, glue, Sellotape, paper clips and scissors give children additional ideas for the type of writing they do and how they present it. Reference materials such as displays of letters, writing styles and scripts in many languages, alphabet books, simple dictionaries, word lists and a noticeboard are also useful.

The children should be able to use the writing area independently and purposefully. They will be helped to do this if they are shown how to use the resources. The children can also be involved in organising the area. Working with an adult, they can compose notices and labels for the equipment. These could be transcribed by the teacher in a shared writing session or by the children themselves. Some of the writing that is produced in the writing area can be shared with the class, responded to and displayed.

Writing areas give children the chance to experiment with writing regularly and when they choose to do so. They can write for their own purposes, at their own pace and without needing adult attention. They can also explore the different uses and formats for writing as they use envelopes and blank books, write lists and letters and make cards. The writing area can provide opportunities for children to practise activities that have been introduced by the teacher. For example, if the children have been introduced to letter writing during shared writing or have been making greetings cards, they may spontaneously practise these in the writing area.

Reading and the reading area

Reading areas filled with carefully chosen books, including a selection of enlarged texts, non-fiction and books made by the teacher and the children, provide examples of writing being used for many purposes. Other reading resources also help to develop children's writing abilities. Tapes and story props give children additional opportunities to become familiar with the way that stories and non-fiction are written. Sets of props or puppets give children valuable practice at rehearsing plots and investing characters with personality traits. Sequencing activities using illustrations and words taken from a book or sets of photographs, and sentences recounting an activity the children have undertaken help to develop familiarity with story structure and narrative language. After the children have sequenced the cards they can use them as the framework for narrating a story or event to other children or an adult. Sequencing cards based on favourite books can also be made by the children. These experiences can add substance to the content of children's written stories.

Saying and learning nursery rhymes and encouraging children to join in the repeated refrains of stories is an excellent way for children to develop phonemic awareness (Goswami and Bryant, 1990). They provide an opportunity for adults and children to discuss rhymes and, if these are written on a chart, look at the letters and letter-strings that comprise the rhyme. Children who can identify onsets and rimes are taking their first steps in developing phonic knowl-edge, which helps them with their early attempts at spelling.

Sharing an enlarged text with the class or a group of children pro-vides another demonstration of the uses of writing, the enjoyment it can bring and the way it is constructed and arranged. Shared reading and story times offer the opportunity to introduce children to words and letters, to talk about content and illustrations. Not only does this help children to learn about writing, it also provides models of how to write.

Once children are ready to focus a little more on the writing, the teacher can introduce activities based on books which reinforce learning about letters, sounds and letter patterns, all of which help with spelling. The group can be asked to look out for a particular letter as the teacher reads. They may be looking for the first letter of someone's name or a letter that frequently appears in the text. They can be asked to look for lower- or upper-case versions. Enlarged texts can also be used to demonstrate punctuation marks, to reflect on how texts begin and end, to explore character and to recognise how books are often composed of a sequence of events. Because shared reading teaches children so much about reading and writing it can be tempting to overuse the teaching opportunities it presents. We need to be careful not to do this and to always remember that the main reason for sharing books is to enjoy a good read and that teaching should take second place to this.

Displays of print

Early years settings contain a considerable amount of writing. Cupboards, equipment and specific areas of the classroom are labelled. Lists, charts and children's writing are displayed. Displays of craft and art work are accompanied by explanations and titles. All these examples of print provide children with models for their own writing. Children can write captions and other contributions for displays. Questions and answers written in speech bubbles can help children to recognise the connection between speech and writing. Interactive displays, related to letters and sounds, support writing as well as reading. They help to reinforce the link between letter sounds and letter shapes, and teach children about letter formation. They can include chalks and a chalking board, whiteboards, plastic letters and other resources that encourage children to explore and make letter shapes.

Early years settings usually have a commercial alphabet frieze which can be used to show children how letters and some words are written. Even more valuable are alphabet friezes and books that are made by the class. They can be made relevant and interesting to children by concentrating on topics such as food, toys, countries or children's names. When children are involved in producing the environmental print in the classroom they become more aware of the writing that is displayed and are more likely to refer to it when they are writing alone.

Visits

Taking groups of children on visits provides them with models of literacy in the real world. Outings to local shops or a walk in the locality will reveal writing in use and demonstrate many of the functions and purposes of writing. Street signs, advertisements, shop names, newspapers and magazines in the paper shop, menus, order pads and bills in the takeaway, are just some of the types of writing which may be seen. An outing can be prepared for by making a list of things to take and a list of people who will be going. A shopping trip may require a written shopping list. After a visit children can try to incorporate the environmental print they have seen into their modelling, construction and imaginative play in the classroom. If appropriate, the teacher and children can write a letter together in a shared writing session to thank the shopkeepers they visited. Alternatively, the children can write their own thank you notes. Visits and follow-up activities stimulate discussion about language, its functions and its appearance and can raise children's awareness of writing.

Imaginative play areas

These are an important resource for all of sorts of learning in the early years classroom and need to be organised as carefully as any other planned learning activity. Adding literacy materials which encourage children to read and write provides opportunities for them to explore print in many forms. Books, magazines, brochures, telephone directories, calendars, diaries, maps, notices, forms, notepads, envelopes and a range of writing implements all have a place in the home, café, shop or garage. In dramatic play a few well-chosen props can be used by children to re-enact familiar stories and explore sequence and characterisation. For example, a crown and some cloaks might be sufficient for children to become Princess Smartypants (Cole, 1986) and her unfortunate suitors. Children's exploration benefits from adults who spend time modelling literate behaviour in play areas. They quickly imitate adult writing and reading behaviours and incorporate these into their play. To remain effective, the focus and the resources in role play areas need to be changed regularly. Involving the children in making changes draws their attention to what they can use and how.

Shared writing

In shared writing sessions the teacher records what the children compose. The teacher writes on a large flip chart or interactive whiteboard so that the children can see how words are written down, how they are arranged on the page and how they are spelt. They can also see how individual letters are formed. The adult can negotiate the children's suggestions and in doing so draw attention to how what is written has to be appropriate to the function and audience. As the children make their suggestions, the adult may need to make some revisions. This gives children a valuable message about the impossibility of producing perfect writing at a first attempt and shows them that it is important to review what has been written. A variety of text types, such as informative captions for displays, letters and stories, can be composed in this way.

Sometimes shared writing sessions are used to create stories modelled on known texts. This teaches children about story structure, plot and sequence. The characters or the objects in the story may be changed, but the language and the structures of the original text remain the same. For example, the model provided in *Where's Spot?* (Hill, 1980) could be used to write a book entitled 'Where's the Teacher?' Information texts, rhymes, poems and songs can also be used as models. When the writing is complete it can be made into a book for the class or copied out and displayed.

Guided writing

Guided writing gives the teacher the opportunity to work closely with a group of about five children. During the group session the teacher might demonstrate and discuss the writing that the children are about to do and then support the children as they write independently. The focus is on composition and the children are encouraged to think about what they are writing. Guided writing provides children with an opportunity to learn about the importance of thinking about what one wants to write before beginning to write and to review and improve writing once it has been produced. Young children's early writing is often spontaneous and impulsive; guided writing shows them that writing can be considered and crafted. Children can be introduced to different writing types through guided writing and they can begin to appreciate how writing differs according to its purpose and audience.

Direct teaching

Much of the direct teaching that takes place in the early years will occur when adults respond to and discuss children's writing. This may have been produced spontaneously or during one of the planned opportunities for writing. All the writing that children produce needs to be treated seriously. It merits comment that focuses on the content and the author's intention. Responses such as 'lovely writing' are insufficient as they do not do justice to the effort that the child has expended and do not give feedback that is helpful for the future. Using knowledge of the child's previous experience and understanding, adults can extend what the child knows and can do by acting in the following ways:

- Respond positively and with respect to what the child has done.
- Ask the child to read back or tell you what he or she has written.
- Talk about the content.
- Comment on any significant aspects of the transcription.
- Respond in writing with a comment, a question and a correct version.
- Write a reply if a child has written to you.
- Display the writing on the writing noticeboard.
- Use the writing if it is a notice or story, or has been produced for a play area or a display.

Writing for a range of audiences and purposes

Writing non-fiction usually takes place across the curriculum as part of learning about other things. It is rarely undertaken for its own sake. Its central function is to convey information clearly and accurately, and it often includes lists, headings and diagrams. Children's appreciation of the characteristics of non-fiction writing can be extended when adults share factual books with them and instigate discussions about the way the information is presented. Shared writing can also be used to demonstrate how information texts are organised. When children are asked to write factually, they will be helped if the teacher is clear about the purpose, audience and structure of the writing and makes this explicit. Placing writing resources alongside the many activities that are arranged in the class encourages children to use writing to record information.

Developing transcription

The *Primary Framework for Literacy and Mathematics* (DfES, 2006: 16–17) identifies the following as areas for attention before children are five years old:

- Word structure and spelling: use phonic knowledge to write simple regular words and make phonetically plausible attempts at more complex words.
- Presentation: use a pencil and hold it effectively to form recognisable letters, most of which are correctly formed.

As these concerns are returned to in Years 1 and 2 it is not expected that children's command of them will be complete at the end of the reception year. Some of the activities described in this chapter address these aspects of writing directly; for example, sorting and painting. In addition, children's competence in the transcription skills of writing does develop as they engage in writing and receive adult support.

Conclusion

During their time in nursery and reception classes, professionals help children to:

- understand the purposes of writing
- understand that what is said can be written down
- understand that speech sounds can be represented by letters

- become more familiar with writing implements and other resources for writing
- develop the skills needed to form letter shapes
- use writing in play and for their own purposes
- write their own names
- read or tell what they have written
- become familiar with different types of writing.

The above is achieved through providing children with opportunities to:

- browse, share and read books
- see writing as a natural accompaniment to a range of activities
- experiment with writing
- talk about writing with others.

The aim of practitioners who work in early years settings is to help children to become writers. This goes beyond merely teaching children to write. It involves developing children's confidence and understanding of writing as well as their skills. Practitioners who create a language-rich environment and provide activities and experiences that enable children to explore writing are helping children to establish the foundations for writing and become able and committed writers.

Suggestions for further reading

Godwin, D. and Perkins, M. (2002) *Teaching Language and Literacy in the Early Years.* Second edition. London: David Fulton.

Hall, N. and Robinson, A. (2003) *Exploring Writing and Play in the Early Years.* Second edition. London: David Fulton.

Whitehead, M. (2007) *Language and Literacy in the Early Years.* Third edition. London: Paul Chapman.

References

Beard, R. (1984) *Children's Writing in the Primary School.* Sevenoaks: Hodder and Stoughton.

Britton, J. (1972) *Language and Learning.* Harmondsworth: Penguin.

Clay, M. (1975) *What Did I Write?* London: Heinemann.

Cole, B. (1986) *Princess Smartypants.* London: Picture Lions.

DfES (Department for Education and Skills) (2006) *Primary Framework for Literacy and Mathematics.* London: DfES Publications.

Dyson, A.H. (1983) 'The role of oral language in early writing processes', *Research in the Teaching of English* 17 (1): 1–29.

Ferreiro, E. and Teberosky, A. (1983) *Literacy before Schooling*. Portsmouth, NH: Heinemann.

Hill, E. (1980) *Where's Spot?* Harmondsworth: Puffin.

Goswami, U. and Bryant, P. (1990) *Phonological Skills and Learning to Read*. Hove: Lawrence Erlbaum Associates.

Graves, R. (1983) *Teachers and Children at Work*. London: Heinemann.

Kress, G. (1997) *Before Writing*. London: Routledge.

Lancaster, L. (2003) 'Moving into literacy: how it all begins', in N. Hall, J. Larson and J. Marsh (eds) *Handbook of Early Childhood Literacy*. London: Sage. pp. 145–53.

Temple, C., Nathan, R., Burris, N. and Temple, F. (1988) *The Beginnings of Writing*. Second edition. London: Allyn and Bacon.

Whitehead, M. (1996) *The Development of Language and Literacy*. London: Hodder and Stoughton.

7

Multimodal literacies

Rosie Flewitt

This chapter introduces the terms *multimodality* and *multimodal literacies*. Drawing on social semiotic theories of communication and on early years research, it illustrates how children become literate in many ways, not just through language, but through learning to use combinations of different *modes*, such as gesture, gaze, movement, image, layout, music and sound effects. The chapter clarifies how children's uses of different modes are shaped by the social and cultural worlds in which they find themselves, and how learning to be literate in today's world involves acquiring a range of skills and practices in different media, such as personal computers, games consoles and mobile phones. These media require even very young children to use and interpret a varied repertoire of representational modes, and children's ability to negotiate new forms of literacy carries high stakes for social standing and life destinations. A major task, therefore, for practitioners is to reflect on their own practice so they can better support children's understanding and competence in diverse forms of visual, printed and digital literacies, in contexts that are meaningful to them.

What are multimodal literacies?

The word *multimodal* has begun to creep into curriculum and research documents to describe young children's learning, but what does it mean, particularly in the context of early literacies? Language has traditionally been the focus for the development of young children's literacy, but a multimodal approach broadens that view and regards learning as involving more than words. Multimodality takes into account the whole range of modes that young children encounter in a variety of texts (such as words, images and sounds in printed and electronic media and in face-to-face interaction) and the range and combinations of modes they use to make and express meaning (such as gesture, gaze, facial expression, movement, image, music, sound effects and language). The term *multimodal literacies* encompasses all the knowledge, skills and dispositions that children develop towards spoken, printed, visual and digital 'literacies'. These include, for example, listening to and using spoken language as they play, learning that printed language carries meanings, enjoying stories and rhymes, becoming familiar with literacies that are valued by their own communities, learning about symbols and numeric sign systems, and developing their skills and competences in new technologies.

The changing face of literacy

In today's world, young children encounter many different kinds of printed and electronic texts at home, in early years settings and in their everyday lives beyond schooling. Changes in the day-to-day uses of technology mean that learning to be literate involves not only learning to read and understand printed books, but also learning to read and understand screens, such as interactive television, video, personal computers, the internet, games consoles and mobile phones (Kress, 2003; Labbo and Reinking, 2003; Marsh et al., 2005). Traditionally, early literacy has involved learning to read the meanings conveyed by the combination of words and images in picture books, and to draw pictures to supplement early writing, but now even very young children are familiar with screen-based, digital texts, which present different challenges and demand high levels of visual literacy. Kress and van Leeuwen (1996) and Marsh and Millard (2000) discuss how words, images and sounds are juxtaposed in complicated ways in digital texts, and young children have to learn what to attend to, and in what order.

When children encounter storybooks in English and begin to read, they learn to follow a linear sequence, that is, to read each page from top to bottom, each line and word from left to right, and one page after another, reading a book from front to back. Books written in other scripts, such as Chinese, Arabic and Urdu, have different sequential patterns (for example, from back to front, reading vertically in columns from top to bottom), but they are still sequential. Illustrated non-fiction books often diverge from this sequence, offering bite-size nuggets of information with choices in the order of reading. When learning to read on-screen texts, children are confronted by more diverse spatial arrangements of meanings. Although words on a screen are still read from left to right, screens are rarely read top to bottom, with a neat ordering of one screen following another. Rather, the ability to 'read' a screen pivots on interpreting a medley of visual images, symbols and layout, and progressing from one screen to another through series of hyperlinks – often with several possible links from one screen, each of which takes the reader in a different direction.

The act of learning to write by holding a pen and forming letters and words is also a very different experience from learning to control a computer mouse, manipulating a cursor through the mouse, and identifying, finding and pressing the keys of a traditional keyboard to create letters and words on screens. Screen-based texts tend to have an array of font types, and young children who are learning non-cursive letter formation, such as 'ɑ', will be confronted with different cursive fonts, such as 'a' or 'ɑ', which to the unfamiliar eye look like different letters. Some advice is available for practitioners on using screen-based texts (e.g. Becta, 2004; DfES, 2007), but this is an area where practitioner guidance notes and training are lagging behind technological change.

A major task for young children in the twenty-first century is to develop their understanding and competence not just in traditional reading and writing, but in a range of printed, digital, oral and visual literacies. It follows therefore that a major task for practitioners and policy-makers is to respond creatively to young children's multimodal explorations of new and traditional forms of literacy.

Recent developments in early years literacy policy

The ability to negotiate new forms of literacy carries high stakes for social standing and life destinations, but in many countries, early literacy policy has tended to focus predominantly on spoken, written and printed language. Some countries have comparatively recently experienced a shift towards more prescriptive literacy policy, such as the move in the US towards more interventionist programs (United States Department of Education, 2001), and the emphasis on the teaching of phonics in England (DfES, 2006). These approaches, which view literacy primarily as an area of learning associated with reading and writing, may well help young children acquire some of the knowledge they need in order to produce and interpret written texts, but they fail to take into account the reality and the complexity of the multimodal and multimedia literacies that young children have to decipher as part of their daily lives (Plowman, 2006).

By contrast, other countries have adopted broader interpretations of literacy. For example, in Russia, oracy and literacy are taught together (Alexander, 2003), and in Reggio Emilia nursery schools in Italy, which do not follow a subject-based curriculum, literacy is not distinguished from other forms of expression. Here, children are encouraged to represent their thoughts and ideas in as many different ways as possible; for example, through dance, drawing, music, spoken and written language (Rinaldi, 1995). In the New Zealand early years curriculum (*Te Whāriki*), literacy is presented as one of the many facets of the broad area of 'communication', with an emphasis on how young children communicate their experiences through language, images, art, movement, etc.

These broader perspectives on literacy recognise the diverse ways in which young children express their understandings. The global challenge for equipping our youngest citizens for communication in the twenty-first century is to recognise and celebrate the many and varied digital, oral and visual literacies young children now encounter, the different combinations of modes (spoken and written language, images, symbols, sounds and so on) young children need to use to become 'literate' – and how practitioners can support the development of young children's multimodal literacies (UKLA/QCA, 2004).

Some key concepts

A multimodal perspective on literacy opens up new possibilities for considering what counts as literacy in young children's lives, and for bridging the gap between children's home and school literacy experiences. This section introduces some of the key concepts that underpin these new directions in our understandings of literacy.

Literacy as social practice

Traditional approaches to literacy have tended to focus on learning the skills of reading and writing, such as letter formation and phonological awareness. Underlying this approach has been an assumption that once these skills have been acquired, children will ultimately be able to use them in most situations where reading and writing are required. This model of literacy as the acquisition of a set of neutral, transferable skills has been termed 'an autonomous model' of literacy (Street, 1984; 1993). Street suggests that although the arguments for an 'autonomous model' may be coherent, the approach is fundamentally flawed as it ignores the fact that when we read and write, we do so in particular social contexts and for many and varied social purposes. Street (1984) proposed a new 'ideological model' of literacy as social practice began to emerge, which pays greater attention to how literacy practices take place in different social and cultural contexts and for different purposes. Viewing literacy as social practice acknowledges that children bring to school their varied, out-of-school experiences of different kinds of literacy, and that literacy is learnt most effectively when it is used in meaningful ways in real-life circumstances. This approach therefore opens the door to making connections between children's literacy learning in and out of school.

Literacies

Viewing literacy as social practice broadens the scope of what counts as literacy, and leads naturally to the plural term 'literacies', to capture how children's uses of literacy vary according to context and purpose. For example, writing a story in school is a very different kind of activity from writing a wish list for Father Christmas, and reading a storybook is very different to reading a computer screen. Young children encounter many and varied kinds of literacy practices as they grow up as members of families and communities, including listening, talking, reading, writing, viewing, visual and critical literacies. In today's world there are also digital literacies that have been introduced into everyday life by the widespread use of new technologies (see Chapter 10, this volume). These changes in the ways that young children experience literacy have implications for early years practice, demanding new ways of thinking about how to deliver the literacy curriculum.

Multimodal literacies

As mentioned in the introduction, the term 'multimodal literacies' refers to how meaning is expressed through different modes of representation, not just through words, but through combinations of different modes, such as words, images, sounds, movements, layout and so on. Makin and Jones Diaz (2004) discuss how different modes are sometimes used in different kinds of literacies and literacy practices. For example, spoken language and sound effects are often used in conversation, singing songs, telling and reading stories out loud, playing games and on digital media, such as television and computers. Written language is used in handwritten and printed texts, such as magazines, newspapers, food packaging and instructions. Visual images are used to create drawings, animation, three-dimensional models, on television, videos and computer games. Most forms of literacy combine modes: computers often use spoken and written language alongside images and sound effects; body movements and facial expressions usually accompany spoken language; layout always accompanies written texts. Children in the early years of education can be encouraged to develop critical literacy, that is, to reflect on the most effective way to convey a message – which modes and media to use, and why.

Case study 7.1 illustrates how a four-year-old boy in the first term of primary school used drawings and handwriting to complete a set task of writing about himself. It shows how when writing a story and drawing a picture to accompany it, some of the meanings are in the mode of words, some are in the mode of image, and other meanings are inferred by the way the words and pictures are laid out. It is the combination of the words, images and layout that convey meaning, literally and visually.

Case study 7.1   Using handwriting and drawing

Charlie is four years old, and is in reception year at an English primary school. As part of an activity relating to the Early Years Foundation Stage curriculum, the teacher has been talking with the whole class about themselves and their families. The class is then split into different activity groups, and Charlie finds himself at the writing table, where a teaching assistant (TA) helps a small group to write 'About Me'. Charlie completes the writing task, and finds time to draw a picture before moving on to the next activity. Charlie seems proud of the work he produces, which you can see below, and the TA congratulates him.

Figure 7.1   About me

(Continued)

(Continued)

Charlie's writing on the top left of the sheet reads:

my name is Charlie
I live in ...
I got a sid hur nem is tacats
and hery and 2 cats
I got owansg
and I nic ws2

He reads aloud to the TA:
My name is Charlie, I live in [name of town], I got a sister, her name is [sister's nickname] and [brother's name] and 2 cats. I got an orange and a nice ws2 [World Soccer 2, a table football game].

In his writing, Charlie has included many of the items mentioned during the class discussion, using simple linking words to list names and nouns. For the picture, positioned in the bottom right-hand side of the paper, Charlie has elaborated on the theme 'About Me' to show himself playing football with his new goal in the garden at home. In contrast to the writing, which contains a bare minimum of information (apart from the unsolicited detail of the 'orange' for a snack), the drawing reveals more personal details from his life at home: the close netting of the goal implies it is strong enough to stop a ball, his position in relation to the ball and goal suggests the high drama of a penalty shoot-out, and the huge smile on his face portrays his delighted anticipation. Conveying all these messages through words would have been very challenging, but by combining the modes of writing and drawing, Charlie is constructing a rich narrative about his home life within a school literacy activity.

Case study 7.1 illustrates how a young boy relates his own life experiences to a set classroom activity. He completes the writing task set by the teacher, using the tools available to him (pencils and paper) to compose a story in words. He then finds time to draw a picture, adding detail through images. The words give a sequence to his story, and the images highlight the intensity of his interest in one topic he has chosen to write about, and they also provide the reader with more descriptive and affective detail (for example, the close netting of the goal and his happiness). Through the combination of words and images, he constructs a rich and meaningful narrative that relates to the set task and to his home life.

Most young children's printed books combine the three modes of layout, images and words to convey the meanings of stories or non-fiction writing. They make use of spatial arrangements to convey meanings, sometimes allowing the reader to choose where to begin reading. When sharing the reading of books with another child or adult, readers also use the modes of speech, along with gaze, facial expression and body movements as they interpret the texts. Rather than just accompanying the words, or being 'unnecessary adornments', the use of other modes is often integral to the process of shared meaning-making, as shown in Case study 7.2, where a three-year-old boy is reading a non-fiction book at home.

> ## 🗁 Case study 7.2   Using multiple modes to share an illustrated non-fiction book
>
> *Jake is three years old. He and his mother are in the kitchen at home on a weekday afternoon, while Jake's older brother and sister are at school. Jake's mum is taking hot cakes from a baking tray at one end of the room, and Jake is sitting on a sofa at the other end, carefully studying an illustrated children's book on farm machinery – a favourite topic of his as he lives on a farm and his father is a farm worker. Because his mum is occupied with the hot cakes, she does not always respond immediately to Jake's questions (line 2), and he sometimes fills the gaps she leaves in her conversational turns (line 3). Although his mum is busy with the cakes, she prompts Jake to continue talking (line 4 and line 8), asks for clarification and encourages Jake to look more closely at the pictures in the book (line 14). She has high expectations of Jake's knowledge of specialist vocabulary, and sometimes relies on words for him to understand (line 8), and at other times she combines her use of words with actions to make her meanings clearer, and to bring the book illustrations closer to a reality that she knows Jake will understand (lines 16–17).*
>
> 1 Jake: *(gaze to book)* is dat a post one mum? *(studies picture)* dat not post one *(gaze to different picture on same spread, points)* digger *(moves finger towards picture, gaze always to book)* look digger dere
>
> *(Continued)*

(Continued)

2 Mum: *(no response, busy at other end of kitchen)*

3 Jake: *(looks through pages in book, gaze always to book)* I couldn't see digger on dis tactor an look is it *(turning page)* here? *(opens page)* yes *(opens book out, studies page)*

4 Mum: *(facing away from Jake, baking)* was that … is that a John Deere tractor?

5 Jake: yeh *(intake of breath as points to picture, gaze from book to Mum, pointing at picture)* I can see a grid here

6 Mum: *(baking)* it is yep

7 Jake: *(turning page, lilt/sing-song as speaks, gaze to book)* John De-er

8 Mum: *(baking)* an where's the um post banger?

9 Jake: *(glances at Mum, gaze to book, studies previous page)* it han't got post banger *(opening page, pointing to picture)* look *(pushing page open)*

10 Mum: *(glances to Jake while baking)* careful of the pages

11 Jake: see *(glances up, points to picture)* look it han't got post one on *(glances up at Mum, who walks towards him)*

12 Mum: it has hasn't it?

13 Jake: *(studies picture closely)*

14 Mum: what? it hasn't got a post you mean? it has I can see a post

15 Jake: *(studies picture closely)* can't *(?)*

16 Mum: *(comes over to Jake, points to picture in book)* this post *(points to other picture higher on page)* and that *(pointing)*, it drops down doesn't it? *(moves hand from top picture down to bottom, replicates dropping action with her arm, moves away)* like daddy's

17 Jake: *(gaze to pictures, studying them closely)* yeh tis like daddy's *(sighs, studies another picture on same page)*

Case study 7.2 shows how a mother and her three-year-old son share the reading of an illustrated non-fiction children's book in a relaxed and unhurried way, while the mother is busy baking in the kitchen. They share the book not just through talk, but through body movements for pointing and to act out what they mean, through exchanging gaze, through shared gaze attention focusing on the book and through shared knowledge and life experiences. In this instance, the mother draws on her familiarity with her son's knowledge to prompt him to look carefully for and to recognise the component parts of a tractor, and to relate the book to his life experiences.

In today's world, many young children also engage regularly in screen-based literacy practices, where the juxtaposition of images and words is more complex. In screen-based texts, words and images are usually combined with other modes, such as screen layout, sound and symbols, with the combinations of modes all contributing to meaning. Marsh et al. (2005) describe how parents and their young children share various communicative practices involving electronic and digital media (watching television together, playing with media texts, using mobile phones and engaging in online chat), and how these link in with parents' beliefs about literacy learning. For instance, one mother claimed her children had learned the alphabet by watching the television programme *Wheel of Fortune*. Under-fives also use media technologies independently: navigating computer screens, using 'favourites' on internet servers, printing out and colouring images from the web and using games consoles (Marsh et al., 2005). These new and emerging practices are continually reshaping how communication happens, and place new demands on early years practice in literacy.

Rethinking 'texts'

Traditionally, the word 'text' has been used to describe the written/ printed mode, and has sometimes been used to describe drawings and images, but changes in day-to-day uses of technology have led to a broader interpretation of 'text'. Jewitt (2006) describes how digital technology is reshaping the relationship between images and words, as screen-based, multimodal texts (which contain colour, image, layout, movement, words and sound) need to be read differently from monomodal or bimodal texts (which contain only one mode, such as written words, or two modes, such as written words and images). When using screen-based texts, young children have to read various meanings embedded in the different combinations of modes, and have to learn what they should attend to at any particular time. Reading any text involves paying attention to how the text is constructed, but screen-based texts are complex, and they rarely follow the conventional left-to-right, top-to-bottom, front-to-back sequence of traditional English books. Bearne (Bearne, 2003; Bearne and Wolstencroft, 2007) suggests that the prevalence of new kinds of multimodal texts in young children's lives is not only reshaping the practices of reading and writing, but is also creating new demands and new ways of thinking. Case study 7.3 illustrates a three-year-old girl's literacy practices using a computer game based on a popular children's television programme.

Case study 7.3   Using multiple modes to read and write a screen-based text

Cara is three years old, and one of her favourite computer games is 'In the Night Garden', an online game designed for young children that is based on a popular television programme. 'In the Night Garden' is an interpretation of a traditional nursery tale picture book, with a series of characters that resemble toys who live happily together in a woodland glade (filmed in a real wood). The characters are all of different sizes and shapes, each has its own unique song and dance and they use a language which is similar to that of the Teletubbies (see http://www.inthenightgarden. co.uk).

Cara confidently and competently uses the mouse to click on a symbol which has the words 'Play Game' and the images of some stars drawn on it. Clicking on this symbol takes her to a pop-up screen, showing the woodland setting with a familiar 'night garden' tune playing. Cara sighs happily in anticipation, and as she touches the mouse again, a flower-shaped cursor appears on the screen, followed by the images of characters from the television series. Cara's gaze moves along the characters as she moves the cursor over them. Each time she holds the cursor near a character, the narrator's voice says the character's name, accompanied by a few notes of each character's signature tune. After a few moments, Cara places the cursor over one of her favourites, Upsy Daisy – a happy, girl-like figure who loves to dance. Holding the cursor over Upsy Daisy makes the screen change, and leaves fall gently from the trees, first covering all the characters and then clearing to reveal Upsy Daisy in a setting associated with her character, next to her own special bed. Cara now creates a story about Upsy Daisy by moving the cursor over different objects on the screen, which makes the on-screen objects move and creates sounds. For example, moving the cursor over the bed makes it dash away, with Upsy Daisy chasing it. These animated actions are accompanied by automatically produced sounds, some of which resemble the intonation patterns and sounds of speech, but do not have discernible words, and some are more comic or reflect the emotional state of the character, forming an essential part of the narrative. If Cara's family had a webcam, she would be able to appear on screen alongside the characters, and to move her own image around on screen via the mouse.

When 'reading' and 'writing' these on-screen narratives, Cara uses a combination of modes, including whole body movements to position herself in relation to the screen; hand, arm and finger movements to manipulate the mouse; to point at and touch the screen.

> *She also sometimes talks to the on-screen characters, and moves her body to imitate the characters' activities. The narrative storylines are conveyed through combinations of the characters' actions, their (unintelligible) 'talk', comic sounds associated with certain actions, sounds that convey emotion, music that adds mood, a voice-over narrator and changes of colour and scene. Although only three years old, Cara appears to have mastered a fairly proficient level of performance of this relatively new form of literacy practice, and is able to use and interpret the combinations of symbols, sounds, language, images, animations and screen layout to create and enjoy her own stories from a varied, although limited, range of set options.*

In Case study 7.3 we see a three-year-old girl 'reading' and 'writing' narratives on a computer game that is based on a popular children's television programme. Through a series of on-screen links that are negotiated via the computer mouse, the game offers her the opportunity to select which characters to include in her narrative, and offers a fairly wide, if restricted, range of things that her selected characters can do. This computer-based medium combines several modes, including still and moving images, photographs, film, animated characters, sound effects, visual effects, music, talk-like sounds, layout, animation, etc. To interact successfully with the game, the child must be able to combine several modes: manipulate the computer mouse effectively, make choices about where to look on the screen and where to place the cursor. These activities require careful hand–eye coordination and stimulate her to talk to the characters, sometimes narrating what they are doing and imitating their movements. Using this medium, the three-year-old child shows sustained use of multiple modes while she is constructing multimodal stories.

Affordances and constraints

Different modes have different social and cultural histories of use and different 'affordances' and 'constraints'; that is, each mode has characteristics that make some things possible (affordances) and inhibit other things (constraints). In Case study 7.1 we saw how for Charlie, the mode of writing constrained the meanings he conveyed at that moment in his life, whilst the mode of drawing offered more potential for him to construct a detailed description. Case study 7.4 illustrates how a three-year-old girl responds to the affordances and constraints of speech.

> 📁 **Case study 7.4   Combining speech and body movement to convey meaning**
>
> *Zara, a three-year-old girl, was playing in the garden at home, with her mum and a researcher. On the whole, Zara spoke confidently, competently and clearly, but like many children (and adults!) she sometimes resorted to body movements to convey meanings when she could not find the right words to express what she meant, or when language alone 'constrained' the message that she wanted to convey. In the example below, Zara had said she would like to play with her 'bubble machine', and her mum had gone inside the house to fetch it. While they were waiting for her mum to return, the researcher asked Zara about the toy that was being fetched. Zara's response combined actions and words to overcome the need to use technical vocabulary and sequential expressions to explain how the machine worked. Her movements also conveyed her excitement and enjoyment of the machine in a way that even the bubbles themselves would struggle to do.*
>
> Researcher: *(to Zara)* what bubble machine?
> Zara: *(pirouettes on the spot, raises her arms in the air as though catching bubbles)* just a *(lowers her right arm, as though she were holding the machine, and raises her left arm up, opening her hand as she does so to indicate bubbles rising)* bubble machine *(lowers her left arm towards her right arm, with the fingers of her right hand makes a circle/hole)* you put in there *(lowers left arm and puts the index finger of her left hand into the hole she made with her right hand, indicating how to pour liquid into the machine)* and you push a button *(mimics pressing button with left hand)* and bubbles come out *(raises left arm high in the air and waves it rhythmically, imitating the movement of bubbles soaring up in the air)*

Case study 7.4 is an example of a young girl using the most practical resources available to her to convey the procedures of how a machine works. A purely verbal explanation would require particular vocabulary with connecting words to link her explanation of sequential processes. Instead, she uses body movements to act out the processes of bubble production, providing a clear, and far more vivid and entertaining account.

In contrast to speech, the mode of movement offers children a highly expressive way to convey action. The mode of speech is ordered by a logic of sequence – one word follows another word – with decisions about what will come first and last, what will be put in between, and whose turn it is to speak. This makes speech very useful for conveying information in a certain order. When using speech, a speaker can also create different effects by varying pitch, volume, emphasis and intonation. These are all 'affordances'. However, speech also has constraints – the fact that speech follows a sequence makes it difficult to talk about different things that are happening simultaneously, and adding movement helps to overcome these constraints.

Images also have certain characteristics that make it easier to express some aspects of meaning than writing, as we saw in Case study 7.1. In contrast to the sequential order of speech, images are ordered by a logic of space and different elements can appear simultaneously. Rather than deciding what should come first and next (as in writing), when thinking about images, decisions have to be taken about how to situate elements of an image in relation to each other (above, below, next to, overlapping, bordering, separated by space and so on). Decisions also have to be taken about colour (even if only black and white, there are still many shades of grey), and shape. The modes of dance and movement are also governed by the logic of space, but they are three-dimensional rather than two-dimensional, as are many on-screen images. Young children may sometimes be unsure of which words to use, or they may simply prefer to use combinations of different modes of expression to overcome the constraints of speech or writing, as shown in Case studies 7.1 and 7.4.

How can practitioners help young children to develop multimodal literacies?

In the examples above we have seen how literacy can take many forms, in different kinds of literacy practices, which vary with social and cultural influences, and which have begun to change significantly with everyday uses of new technologies. We have also seen how individual children experience literacy through their own personal histories, interests and ways of learning. Planning for literacy learning therefore means having clear goals *and* being constantly responsive to children's interests, preferences and child-initiated activities. If the ultimate goal is to foster young children's enthusiasm and independent learning, then it is essential for practitioners to provide varied opportunities for children to experience many different forms of literacy in contexts that are meaningful to them, and where there is a genuine reason to use and develop different literacies.

To give all children opportunities to develop multimodal literacies, practitioners should:

- organise the learning environment and planning of activities to ensure that 'the status of literacy is high and its value is reinforced by frequent occurrence' (Hall, 1987: 82). This means ensuring that the many different areas of the setting are rich in signs, symbols, notices, numbers, words, rhymes, pictures, music and songs that take into account children's different interests, understandings, cultures, writing scripts and different uses of literacy – including those that are spoken, handwritten, print-based and screen-based, and that reflect children's different home languages and scripts. (See also Chapter 4 in this volume)
- provide time and relaxed opportunities for children to have easy access to resources and to initiate activities that enable them to develop their understandings of diverse literacies, including print- and screen-based texts. These resources include games that use sounds and letters, poetry, fiction and non-fiction books, art materials and musical instruments, digital equipment, appropriate computer games, activities that draw on popular culture, and equipment that enables children to express their developing literacies through creative and imaginative play.
- show sensitivity to the many different modes that children use to express their understandings and be aware of how adults' non-verbal behaviour can encourage children to communicate their thoughts, ideas and feelings through a range of expressive modes, including when writing and speaking.
- have realistic expectations of children's developing uses of language and literacy, and respond to children sensitively, using rich language to help them develop vocabulary and linguistic structures whilst respecting that children learn in different ways and at different rates and may have preferences for other forms of communication, including their home languages, Braille, signing and silent modes of expression.
- provide opportunities for children to see adults engaged in a range of literacy practices in different media and for different purposes, for children to experiment with screen-based and print-based literacies, and to link language and literacy with physical movement through action in songs and rhymes, role play, art, dance and practical experiences, such as cookery and gardening.

- reflect on the role of the adult in supporting young children's multimodal literacy development, and share their reflections with colleagues. The role of the adult is far from straightforward: it involves providing resources, and setting them up in ways that are likely to stimulate interest and play. It also involves observing children closely, and getting to know more about their experiences of literacy out of the classroom, then building on all this knowledge to create further, authentic contexts for learning that respect the children's preferences for using diverse modes of expression.

Concluding thoughts

In this chapter, we have considered how the process of developing literacy is not just about acquiring the skills needed to speak and write a language. Literacy is always situated in particular social and cultural events, such as sharing a story at bedtime, making a shopping list, writing a letter, composing a story at school or reading and writing on-screen texts. So becoming literate means learning about how literacy is used in the varied social and cultural worlds that form part of young children's lives. Becoming literate is also a multimodal journey. Most illustrated storybooks, and young children's own stories, combine multiple modes. Traditional books tend to draw on the three modes of words, images and layout, and it is the combination of all these modes that create meaning. When sharing book reading, children and their carers also use other modes to supplement their reading, such as speech, body movement, facial expression and gaze. Nowadays, the prevalence of screen-based digital texts and interactive books has introduced new combinations of modes into everyday literacy practices, as they combine and exploit the affordances of several modes simultaneously (speech, sounds, music, movement, image, layout, etc.).

These new kinds of complex, multimodal texts are challenging current literacy policy and assessment practices. Changes to the ways that people encounter different literacies in their daily lives means that early years providers need to appreciate the complexity of children's textual worlds, to put traditional printed texts and new digital and interactive texts at the centre of literacy provision, to provide spaces for children to link their 'out-of-school' knowledge about literacy with 'schooled' versions of literacy, and thereby enable all young children to be secure in their ability to interpret and produce the kinds of multimodal texts that are central to life in the twenty-first century.

Suggestions for further reading

Gee, J.P. (2003) *What Video Games Have to Teach Us About Learning and Literacy.* New York: Palgrave MacMillan.

Kress, G. (2003) *Literacy in the New Media Age.* London: Routledge.

Kress, G. and van Leeuwen, T. (1996) *Reading Images: The Grammar of Visual Design.* London: Routledge.

Larson, J. and Marsh, J. (2005) *Making Literacy Real: Theories and Practices for Learning and Teaching.* London: Sage.

Marsh, J. and Millard, E. (2000) *Literacy and Popular Culture: Using Children's Culture in the Classroom.* London: Paul Chapman.

Marsh, J., Brooks, G., Hughes, J., Ritchie, L., Roberts, S. and Wright, K. (2005) *Digital Beginnings: Young Children's Use of Popular Culture, Media and New Technologies.* University of Sheffield: Literacy Research Centre. Available online at www.digital-beginnings.shef.ac.uk/DigitalBeginningsReport.pdf (accessed November 2006).

United Kingdom Literacy Association/Qualifications and Curriculum Authority (UKLA/QCA) (2004) *More Than Words: Multimodal Texts in the Classroom.* QCA: London.

Whitehead, M. (2004) *Language and Literacy in the Early Years.* Third edition. London: Sage.

Whitehead, M. (2002) *Developing Language and Literacy with Young Children.* Second edition. London: Paul Chapman.

References

Alexander, R. (2003) 'Oracy, literacy and pedagogy: international perspectives', in E. Bearne, H. Dombey and T. Grainger (eds) *Classroom Interactions in Literacy.* Maidenhead: Open University Press.

Bearne, E. (2003) 'Rethinking literacy: communication, representation and text', *Reading: Literacy and Language* 37 (3): 98–103.

Bearne, E. and Wolstencroft, H. (2007) *Visual Approaches to Teaching Writing: Multimodal Literacy 5–11.* London: Paul Chapman.

British Educational Communications and Technology Agency (Becta) (2004) *Using Web-based Resources in the Foundation Stage.* Coventry: Becta. Available online at http://www.becta.org.uk (accessed March 2007).

Department for Education and Skills (DfES) (2006) *Independent Review of the Teaching of Early Reading. Final Report, Jim Rose (The Rose Review).* London: DfES Publications.

Department for Education and Skills (DfES) (2007) *Statutory Framework for the Early Years Foundation Stage*. London: DfES Publications.

Hall, N. (1987) *The Emergence of Literacy*. London: Hodder and Stoughton.

Jewitt, C. (2006) *Technology, Literacy and Learning: A Multimodality Approach*. London: Routledge.

Kress, G. (2003) *Literacy in the New Media Age*. London: Routledge.

Kress, G. and van Leeuwen, T. (1996) *Reading Images: the Grammar of Visual Design*. London: Routledge.

Labbo, L.D. and Reinking, D. (2003) 'Computers and early literacy education', in N. Hall, J. Larson and J. Marsh (eds) *Handbook of Early Childhood Literacy*. London: Sage.

Makin, L. and Jones Diaz, C. (2004) *Literacies in Early Childhood: Challenging Views, Challenging Practice*. Sydney: MacLennan and Petty.

Marsh, J. and Millard, E. (2000) *Literacy and Popular Culture: Using Children's Culture in the Classroom*. London: Paul Chapman.

Marsh, J., Brooks, G., Hughes, J., Ritchie, L., Roberts, S. and Wright, K. (2005) *Digital Beginnings: Young Children's Use of Popular Culture, Media and New Technologies*. University of Sheffield: Literacy Research Centre. Available online at www.digitalbeginnings.shef.ac.uk/DigitalBeginningsReport.pdf (accessed November 2006).

Plowman, L. (2006) 'Entering e-Society: young children's development of e-literacies'. Available online at http://www.ioe.stir.ac.uk/research/projects/esociety/index.php (accessed November 2007).

Rinaldi, C. (1995) 'The emergent curriculum and social constructivism: an interview with Lella Gandini', in C. Edwards, L. Gandini and G. Forman (eds) *The Hundred Languages of Children: The Reggio Emilia Approach to Early Childhood Education*. Norwood, NJ: Ablex.

Street, B.V. (1984) *Literacy in Theory and Practice*. Cambridge: Cambridge University Press.

Street, B.V. (1993) (ed.) *Cross-Cultural Approaches to Literacy*. Cambridge: Cambridge University Press.

United Kingdom Literacy Association/Qualifications and Curriculum Authority (UKLA/QCA) (2004) *More Than Words: Multimodal Texts in the Classroom*. QCA: London.

United States Department of Education (2001) *No Child Left Behind*. Washington, DC: US Department of Education.

Looking with a different eye: creativity and literacy in the early years

Kate Pahl

Kate: It's like a person's house isn't it?

Pete: What colour's your house?

Child: Red.

Pete: Red is it?

Child: Chicken pox on! (see Figure 8.1 on page 151)

This chapter explores how young children's literacy activities can become more creative, particularly their drawings and early writing. The vignette above comes from a conversation with a group of four to five-year-olds, as they were sitting on the floor with large sheets of lining paper, drawing together. This data came from a research project involving an architect, an artist and a group of teachers, all working with children in a Foundation Stage classroom, for a project funded by Creative Partnerships on children's play. This part of the project involved the architect helping the children to design a play structure for their playground, utilising the children's previous play experience. The children were asked to draw their play activities at home, and this child was drawing his house (where he played) with chicken-pox spots. What this vignette illustrates is the importance of the 'unexpected outcome', that is, the bringing together of two different concepts – the red house and the chicken-pox spots.

What is creativity?

Creativity as a term has been variously interpreted, and carries a number of different meanings, often connected to artistic practice and literary ability. Banaji and Burn (2006) recently identified creativity as coming from a number of traditions, and suggested that as a term it has been understood in different ways. An image of the 'creative genius' in the attic, drawing on the muse, painting and writing individually, was identified with the Romantic movement of the eighteenth and nineteenth centuries and was traditionally why creativity was seen as special, unusual and about being gifted, or different. However, writers, artists and craftsmen saw this as an elitist definition, that excluded many people who created art collectively, in ordinary settings. In order to credit the often exciting and accidental creativities in daily life, another definition came to be recognised, that of 'everyday' creativity. An understanding of creativity developed, which asserted that ordinary, everyday acts could be seen as creative and transformative. Creativity could also be associated with 'craft' and the notion of 'fashioning', which implies the addition of skill as well as inspiration. Although some artists may not be able to describe where they get their ideas from, researchers are increasingly interested in understanding the transformations that make up creative acts. Carter (2004), in analysing everyday talk, described how small pieces of conversation can be understood as creative acts, as one idea is linked to another in unusual ways. The creative arts, both those that are seen as public art and the creative arts in everyday contexts include visual, aural, gestural, tactile and linguistic domains. A creative text can be a drawing, a model, or a piece of theatre, dance or painting as well as a linguistic representation. A multimodal analysis is useful to understand these different texts (Kress, 1997). Flewitt (Chapter 7, this volume) describes multimodality. Multimodality takes into account the whole range of 'modes' that young children encounter in a variety of texts (such as words, images and sounds in printed and electronic media and in face-to-face interaction) and the range and combinations of modes they use to make and express meaning (such as gesture, gaze, facial expression, movement, image, music, sound effects and language).

Multimodality can help extend an understanding of creativity. Creativity has been considered in connection with learning as being about stretching thinking as well as developing artistic and linguistic ability. Researchers working in the field of creativity have looked at how this happens, and have examined qualities like the 'unexpected outcome' in learning and teaching. Craft (2000; 2002) has considered ways in which teachers can foster this unexpected outcome. In relation to the above vignette, the creative aspect of the text can be understood as being about a mixing of different types of concepts, to produce something entirely new. Creativity can be enriched by the use of metaphor, and interesting juxtapositions, lifting things out of one domain of knowledge into another. For example, children can mix different concepts and come up with something that re-invents and transforms the concept. Creativity involves the use of different types of knowledge and thinking, bringing these together in an exciting collision of objects, ideas and images. Creativity can involve the sciences as well as the arts, and is interdisciplinary. Teachers can foster these unexpected collisions in many different ways. They can open up what Craft called 'possibility thinking' (2000; 2002). Asking questions is a good way of developing this thinking. The questions the architect, Pete, in the vignette above, asked of the child, followed the child into developing a new concept, that of the chicken pox house.

How can creativity be understood in early years settings?

The area of creative learning with young children has been described in a number of studies, including Jeffrey (2001) and Jeffrey and Craft (2004) as well as Craft (2000; 2002), as being a space where the following activities are important:

- relevance
- control of learning processes
- ownership of knowledge
- innovation. (Jeffrey and Craft, 2004)

Relevance is of particular importance to young children. As Jeffrey and Craft concur:

> The higher the relevance of teaching to children's lives, worlds, cultures and interests, the more likelihood there is that pupils will have control of their own learning processes. Relevance aids identification, motivation, excitement and enthusiasm. (Jeffrey and Craft, 2004: 47)

Teachers, they argue, can work with their pupils to create 'possibility knowledge' through imagination (Jeffrey and Craft, 2004). The idea of 'possibility thinking', was further explored in a study of teachers' practices in classrooms by Burnard et al. (2006) to describe the process by which teachers are given and also develop the space to profile learner agency, stand back and let go, and ask different kinds of questions.

Heath and Wolf (2004), in a study of visual learning in a community school in Kent, argue that children's involvement in the arts is cognitive work (2004: 5), in that it develops metaphor, and a steady sight when looking at things. When looking at the children's texts, such as the chicken pox house, ideas, objects and images formed a collage in which the metaphor became a critical part of the creative act. Metaphor becomes the space of possibility, and the children's ability to move across metaphoric domains is a sign of the complexity of the creative processes.

Work by Barrs (1988) and Safford and Barrs (2005) has emphasised the strong links between writing and drawing. Other forms of creative expression can also be linked to literacy learning. Safford and Barrs in their 2005 study, based on observation of a number of projects in London, were able to show how creative work such as dance could be explicitly linked to literacy outcomes. Children's speaking and listening goals were enhanced by a diverse range of creative activities. More recently creativity has been the subject of a study on 'Assessing learning in creative contexts', in which children's learning has been mapped as outcomes that teachers can use to present as evidence of creative learning (Ellis, 2007).

The focus of many of these studies has been on ways in which creative approaches open up different forms of learning. In a research project on the impact of a group of artists in Doncaster on very young children's learning in nursery settings, Nutbrown and Jones (2006) looked at ways in which creative practitioners stretched young children's learning through tactile experience of paint and dramatic play. They extended the ORIM framework (in which children are provided with Opportunities, Recognition, Interaction and Modelling in literacy learning) to create a grid that nursery practitioners can use to foster creativity in nursery settings. In the Nutbrown and Jones study, artists gave children opportunities to create different types of texts, recognise new creative interactions and model unusual ways of experiencing art activities, thus exploring the boundaries of their worlds through paint, texture and story.

Bringing creativity and literacy together

In this chapter, I outline some approaches to creativity and literacy. I draw on ideas from the New Literacy Studies, and argue that literacy is a set of *practices* (Street, 1984). Literacy takes place in a number of domains, including home, school and community (Barton and Hamilton, 1998). Children draw on these domains of literacy when they create texts. Texts can be drawings, writing or mixtures of the two, or can be realised in other modes such as moving-image media, sound and gesture. In some cases, the creative process of these texts is observable by teachers or parents, and these observable moments can be described as *literacy events* (Street, 2000). By understanding literacy practices as being bound up with everyday life, it is possible to make links with children's out-of-school literacy practices that they experience at home, and their literacy learning in school. This relates to Jeffrey and Craft's (2004) concept of relevance.

I also argue that literacy learning is multimodal (Flewitt, Chapter 7 in this volume) and that children come to read and write through visual means, often drawing their meanings before making marks, and then writing them (Barrs, 1988; Kress, 1997; Pahl, 1999). Literacy events and practices are observable, as are multimodal events and practices. It can then be understood that *multimodal texts can be connected to multimodal events and practices* (Lancaster, 2003). For example, teachers may set up a multimodal practice, that of map-making, and children will then be observed creating multimodal texts. This observable activity can be seen as a multimodal event. When looking at children's multimodal texts, I saw them as connected to a chain of events and practices that stretched outside of school and beyond (Rowsell and Pahl, 2007). By connecting up those chains, and identifying aspects of the text that came from home, and encouraging children to talk about those aspects, teachers could understand children's texts more clearly and expand the possibilities of what can be created from them. This can then lead to what Craft describes as possibility thinking, and create opportunities for unexpected outcomes (Craft, 2000; 2002).

I propose to describe, in this chapter, how children's texts can be seen as creative when they are 'thickened' by a combination of school and home domains that appear within their texts. The layering of many different experiences into one text can create unexpected and interesting outcomes (Jeffrey and Craft, 2004). In the example of May's map text (see page 152) teachers, artists and the architect, as well as her mother, all shaped the creation of one text. Likewise, when drawing spatial accounts of the playground, the children had a rich source of practices to draw upon. Creative texts can be seen as particularly rich in these layered domains. Children pour emotions, ideas and meanings into their drawn and written texts, and these are important sites for literacy learning. By recognising that children's experiences and practices can be inscribed within their texts, all kinds of options are available for teachers when a child makes a text. Questions can draw out the range of experiences within the text, and new thoughts and ideas emerge as a result.

Creative partnerships

The context for the work described in this chapter was a major funding initiative, involving partnerships between artists and schools, called Creative Partnerships (www.creative-partnerships.com). Based at the Arts Council, England, Creative Partnerships was set up in May 2002 to develop long-term partnerships between schools and cultural and creative organisations. The project ran as a pilot programme from 2002 to 2004, in 16 areas of England. Phases Two and Three followed, from 2005 to 2006. Between May 2002 and July 2005 Creative Partnerships ran 3,767 projects. The programme continued until 2008, with 36 areas around the United Kingdom involved. It aimed to foster:

- the creativity of young people, raising their aspirations and achievements
- the skills of teachers and their ability to work with creative practitioners
- schools' approaches to culture, creativity and partnership working
- the skills, capacity and sustainability of the creative industries.

Creative Partnerships has been positively evaluated. In 2006, Ofsted published a report on the Creative Partnerships initiative (Ofsted, 2006). The report concluded that:

> schools participating in the programme have stimulated pupils' creativity and have established the conditions in which pupils can further develop their creative skills. Most Creative Partnerships programmes surveyed were effective in developing the same attributes found in creative people, such as the ability to improvise, take risks, show resilience, and collaborate with others. (Ofsted, 2006: 2)

The Creative Partnerships initiative has enhanced opportunities for many schools to work with artists in unusual ways. By adopting a creative approach to the curriculum, teachers can extend children's learning, moving across curricula areas to develop literacy and language skills. Creative Partnerships came out of a number of policy documents and initiatives, all suggesting that creativity was an exciting tool for developing learning. In 1999, the National Advisory Committee on Creative and Cultural Education published *All Our Futures: Creativity, Culture and Education*, which argued that a national strategy for creative and cultural education was essential to unlock the potential of every young person (NACCCE, 1999). In 2000, the Qualifications and Curriculum Authority (QCA) commissioned a review of creativity in other countries, and developed a creativity framework, part of a three-year project designed to advise schools on how to develop pupils' creativity. This resulted in a website called 'Creativity: Find it, promote it'. This website contained resources and ideas for teachers (QCA, 2003). In 2001, the Department of Culture, Museums and Sport (DCMS) announced the setting up of the Creative Partnerships scheme. At the same time, the Office for Standards in Education (Ofsted) published the results of a small survey to identify good practice in creative pedagogy in schools (HMI/Ofsted, 2003). In May 2003, the Department for Education and Skills (DfES) outlined a new vision for primary education in a document called '*Excellence and Enjoyment: A Strategy for Primary Schools* (DfES, 2003). This new 'Primary Strategy' offered a more flexible approach to teaching, encouraging teachers to be creative and innovative in their approach to the curriculum. As teachers began to experiment with innovative and creative approaches to learning, and a more topic-based curriculum, the context for Creative Partnerships as an initiative, was very positive. This is the macro context for the study.

Looking with a different eye: the research study

The policy shift in England, towards creativity and greater flexibility in the classroom, can be seen reflected in micro terms in the research project I carried out between 2005 and 2007, to look at creativity and literacy in the Foundation classroom. Creative Partnerships funded a two-year research project, looking at the effect on children's learning of an intervention involving a group of artists, an architect and a group of Foundation teachers in an infants' school in Barnsley, Yorkshire (Pahl, 2007). The research aimed to look at ways in which the impact of the artists in the school enabled different types of literacy and language practices to take place. The research was carried out over two years, using an ethnographic perspective. I carried out interviews with teachers, artists, children and parents, together with a series of close observations of classroom practice all of which produced the data. I used an ethnographic perspective to explore what happened in the classroom when artists were present, and how teachers interpreted and developed creative practices. I focused on the creation of children's texts, on their drawings and literacy practices in the classroom.

The children drew and mapped the games they played in the playground in order to create plans for a new playground structure, which was then built. By working closely in partnership with the artists and the architect, the teachers were able to support children's text-making in ways that extended their literacy practices, bringing in, for example, experiences from home and the children's experience of out-of-school play. The children's multimodal texts drew on domains of school and home, and were created in a number of dimensions, including three-dimensional texts. The partnership between the artists, the architect and the teachers operated in a reciprocal and enabling way, moving the children on to new spaces, and taking forward ideas in unexpected ways. This facilitated creative approaches to literacy. For example, children drew maps that they then labelled and described, drew playground games, and told stories of the games they played. One of the outcomes was a day in which the whole Foundation team, the parents and the children, played for the whole day. The project involved looking at things differently, turning things upside down, and reconfiguring spaces and places. For example, the playground fence was used to display work, and everyday toys were used as painting implements. By looking at things differently, and reconfiguring uses, for example, stilts were used as painting utensils, material was used to create fantasy play spaces, the children's literacy learning was enriched. Teachers learned to listen to children and inhabit their cultural spaces. As one teacher commented of the project:

> It injected more creativity. Creative thinking, it's just like now we're doing a building project and we have incorporated Bob the Builder which is down onto their level and into their culture, so that's sort of helped us sort of relate more to what they are doing, and from that their creativity is more free. (Interview, teaching assistant, November 2005)

Creativity and multimodality

Creativity as an arts practice is intensely multimodal. A focus on multimodality enables children to open up their learning to include the visual, including objects and artefacts. Artefacts can be seen as key in opening up the 'figured worlds' that young children can then relate to in order to support creative approaches to literacy learning (Holland et al., 2001). Figured worlds are described by Holland et al. as imagined spaces of practice (2001:52–3). They are culturally shaped spaces where events and practices take place. Figured worlds hold narratives and narratives can evoke them. Figured worlds can also be transformed, or evoked, by artefacts. The figured world of home and its narratives can be evoked in classrooms through creating in the classroom a text derived from home. This text becomes an artefact that evokes a different figured world. For example, in a study of home and school meaning-making, a child who drew birds at home was able to transfer the bird enthusiasm and make model birds at school, transforming the classroom space into one where his meaning-making was recognised (Pahl and Rowsell, 2005). Many homes hold within them narratives, stories that young children are regularly exposed to, and often these stories relate to home artefacts. For example, a young child who loved 'Thomas the Tank' engine related this to a story about how his great-grandfather built the Indian Railways (Pahl and Rowsell, 2005). By drawing on home stories and encouraging the use of artefacts to support children's literacy learning, the relevance, in Jeffrey and Craft's words, of their learning is enhanced and the creative possibilities can be explored (Jeffrey and Craft, 2004).

A focus on multimodality in this project encouraged a link between drawing, painting and thoughts. The artist encouraged the parents and children to create paintings that reflected their feelings:

> I have been in groups when they have been doing painting about their feelings; you know, making different marks for the way that they felt. That's a little bit different. ... I was in when they did it and then were having their feelings through painting, so if their feelings were quite soft and gentle then they had a thick soft weavy [painting] and if they were doing about I think the dog ... they had some spiky bits because the dog were feeling quite active and things like that. And they all created really big patterns really, and we displayed them and put them in different groups of painting. (Interview, teaching assistant, November 2005)

By looking at ordinary objects in new ways, different types of practices associated with drawing, feeling and communication were developed, as this nursery nurse described:

I did work with [the artist] … and they did some printing with Lego and toys, and they were making the sounds of the cars and different marks so they were really having a good go at how they felt. (Interview, nursery nurse, November 2005)

Here, the teacher used the sound of the cars to create visual depictions of sound. The links between the marks and the sound were expressed through the printing. The artists encouraged the use of different materials to create meaning. For example, here, lengths of material were used to create opportunities for fantasy play:

On the final day it was this idea of these lengths of material, they then threaded them through the fence, at first it started off it was waves, we asked the children what are you doing what's happening here, and it was the sea and they were going through their waves and they were hanging their washing out and the same piece of materials changed as the different children got involved. (ibid.)

Play, creativity and map-making

From these activities developed an interest in creating a playground structure for the children that they would design themselves. An architect, Pete, an artist from an arts organisation, 'Heads Together', and several teachers and teaching assistants were all working together to find out and map what games the children played at playtime, and then to create a physical structure for the children to use as a play space in the playground. The idea for the project had its inception a few years previously, when the teachers at the school decided they wanted to find out more about children's play:

One of my big things was about children not having enough to do in the playground. (Interview, Foundation teacher, November 2005)

The artists worked with the teachers to develop activities to find out what kind of play space the children wanted. This would eventually be built as a playground structure. One of the aspects of the joint work that was created was to look at playtimes:

Where we went with the next thing, part of looking how they played was to try and make playtimes more creative. (Interview, artist, November 2005)

This resulted in the artists setting up days when the children and their parents played together. Following from this, the school and the Heads Together group hired a community architect, to work with them to realise the play structure:

> We worked with an architect, and he did a series of workshops to help design a new playground and he helped plan. ... We moved this work on and when they were having a new school built, we did a whole series of work around play and how they play, we did all sorts of stuff, drawing things. (Interview, artist, November 2005)

The architect came in and worked with the children. First, he went out into the playground and asked them to measure out how much space their games took up to play. He introduced them to the idea of making spatial maps of their play onto pieces of paper. At the same time, the teachers came up with their own activities to encourage spatial drawings, such as using squared paper to ask the children to draw maps and plans.

Mapping play

When I entered the classroom, on a February morning, the artist and the architect were both in the classroom, together with the two teachers and teaching assistants. I recorded the opening session in which the artist was setting up the activity. She sat a group of children around a long table, on which there was a large sheet of paper and some soft pastel crayons in their box. The aim was to create drawings that would become plans of the games the children liked to play. The artist began to explain the activity to the children. The children were given large sheets of paper in their wet-play area to colour in and draw the games they played:

> Artist: What we are going to do today is we have put some paper up in your wet-play area, a little bit like sitting inside this, OK, and you are going to be able to sit inside and write down and have a think about some of the things you could do in that space ...

The artist described the process of drawing spatially, the games the children liked to play at home and at school:

> Artist: We are going to have space to write lots of different games. What sort of pictures do you think would be interesting? If we make this really red, what kind of games do you think that would be good for?
>
> Child: Red!
>
> Artist: The Barbie, red. What other colours would be good for Barbie?
>
> Child: Purple and pink!

Figure 8.1   Chicken Pox house

The artist took on the role of teacher to enable the children to understand what she wanted them to do. As she talked, the children began to draw. Her aim was to encourage the children to use colour to describe the games they played at home, and to draw these out on the paper. Meanwhile, in what was described as the children's wet-play area, another group of children was drawing games they played at home, with the architect as their guide. The architect and I watched as the children drew, often sitting alongside them, as they were drawing, and playing in between the drawing activity. Some of the drawing was concrete, some abstract. The resulting text was a multi-authored complex text, in which swirls and squirls co-existed alongside more conventional drawings. Figure 8.1 shows the drawings by the children, and one of the children accompanied their drawing with this interchange:

Kate: It's like a person's house isn't it?

Pete: What colour's your house?

Child: Red.

Pete: Red is it?

Child: Chicken pox on!

Figure 8.2   May's plan

About mid-morning, I was told that one of the children, May, had brought into school a plan of her house. The teacher mentioned that they had done an exercise involving squared paper the day before, following from the work by the architect on drawing maps of the playground. Both the artist and the architect reported to me that they were pleased the teachers had developed their own activity following the spatial work they had initiated. I sat down with May, who started to tell me about her plan (Figure 8.2).

As May talked me through her plan, I taped the interaction:

Kate: Is this your house?

May: Yes, that's the grass, that's a fireplace, that's a card and that's a card.

Kate: That's your brother's cards?

May: That's a beer bottle. That's a box on top of the fireplace, that's a fire brush so we don't get burned, and this is a chair.

Kate: What's this here? *(pointing to a calendar)*

May: Saturday 9 February

Kate: What's this bit there?

May: That's turns the telly off and change it over.

Kate: Turns the telly off?

May: Change it over, this is the aerial, that's a juice bottle, that's the telly.

Kate: What's this here?

May: That's two cupboards.

Kate: Where is all this?

May: Its daddy's um [room]. Its for the weathers, and ...

Kate: I see, I understand now, that's your calendar.

May: Yeah.

Kate: What's this?

May: A brush, it's for weathers.

Kate: That was a pot. And that's your brother's cards.

May: This is me brother's and this is me sister's. And they – its about the weather.

Kate: Does it tell you the weather? That's good. What's this bit? (*I pointed to the right-hand section of the drawing*)

May: A table.

Kate: What's this say down here?

May: That's skips.

Kate: That's skips, packets of skips.

May: And this is ... I don't recognise this. (*looks at drawing*)

Kate: What's this here?

May: Smarties.

Kate: That's skips. ...What's this up there?

        (*The architect appears and talks to May about the picture*)

        [...]

Kate: What gave you the idea?

May: My mum was drawing the plans.

Kate: Why was she doing a plan?

May: I don't know. She was doing a plan because she wanted the house to be nice.

Kate: Yeah.

May: We are getting our kitchen made.

Kate: Is she doing an extension?

May: (*louder*) We haven't got no builders. Our builders have gone to
         a different (*unclear*).

Kate: Oh no!

May: So me dad's got to do it all by hisself!

Kate: That's terrible, May!

(February, 2006)

May's description of her home plan is very detailed. Her account begins with a description of the fireplace and what is on it (cards and box). She alludes to the social practice of having a fire with her reference to the fire brush (so we don't get burned). Much of her description involves a practice and an enactment of a practice; for example, turning over the television channel (the television is in the left-hand corner of the image). Her interest in the crisps (Skips) and Smarties is evident in the prominence she gives them in the drawing – the Skips are carefully labeled with writing on the bottom right-hand corner and the Smarties are very large round circles in the same area. May presents this detailed spatial account of family life in the context of a crisis – no builders. Her mother drawing the plans was May's conception of where she got the idea. Her plan is a detailed account of family life, from her dad's beer bottle, to the cards sent to her brother and her own beloved packets of Skips.

If we apply the lens of multimodal events and practices (Lancaster, 2003) to May's text, the complexity of the text is apparent. I mapped out the different events and practices that could be connected to the text. In this analysis (Table 8.1), I have divided the chart into multimodal practices, events and texts. Over a period of time, I had collected data about the project. The artist had previously initiated a project where the children drew things from above, below and behind. The architect had also asked the children to peg out the space their games took up in the playground. At the same time, the teachers used squared paper with the children to create maps. May's text can be traced back to six different kinds of practice, events and texts, including the mother drawing the plan, the teacher's drawing at school using squared paper, the idea from the artist of drawing above, below, behind and to the side, the mapping of games in the playground, the drawing of games, and the drawing of the plan at home. May's text is a combination of different factors. It instantiates what happens when an artist, an architect and teachers work closely

Table 8.1   May's Text

	1	2	3	4	5	6
Multimodal practices	Mother drawing the plan	Plan drawing at school using squared paper, teacher initiated	Artist inspired practice: drawing from above, below, behind and to the side	Architect asks children to map out games on playground	Architect asks children to map out games from home	May draws her plan at home
Multimodal events	The mother's drawing as observed by May	The drawings the children did observed by the teachers	Artist described a day when the children did this 'and things just exploded'	Day when games were mapped out observed by architect	Day observed by me, when children drew games	Unobserved event when May drew her plan
Texts	Mother's plan at home	Children's drawings on squared paper	Children's texts of objects from different angles	Pegged games on large paper	Large scale drawings on paper	May's plan collected by me

Figure 8.3   May's playground game, 'Tig'.

together. It is evidence of close-partnership work. It also is a text from home.

In my analysis of May's drawing, I consider that her creativity is connected strongly to the everyday, but bringing in different domains. What is rich and unusual about the text are the number of literacy practices and events recorded in it. From the practice of watching the calendar, to recording birthdays, writing cards, looking at the weather and considering sweet wrappings and crisp packets, May's literacy practices are reflected in the many examples of writing within the text. These literacy practices stemmed from everyday domains of practice, but creatively mixed with the idea of drawing a plan and representing it at school in the context of a focus on map-making. Creativity here involves the transformation of May's home knowledge, daily experience, into something new and different – a plan, drawn from memory, in the context of map-making at school.

Drawing children's play

On another occasion, I watched the architect, Pete, and the artist encourage the children to draw what games they play in the play-ground. After a long discussion with the children about their favourite games, May announced that hers was called Tig. She then went to the drawing table, and drew an image of the game (Figure 8.3).

Kate: Tell me what the picture is?

May: She's it. (*Drawing is of girls with linked hands and in two separate spaces*)

Kate: They are very far away aren't they! Who are those people?

May: That's the guy.

Kate: What are they doing?

May: They are holding hands.

Kate: Is that the game?

May: They are holding hands because they are there and she's there, ... (*unclear*) and that's why they are holding hands.

Kate: Are they running?

May: No standing.
(*May has drawn speech bubbles, I ask about them*)

May: One is saying 'neh, neh' and one is saying 'ye' and one is saying [person's name].

Kate: What's that one doing?

May: She is a girl and she's 'Tig'.

May's description of the playground is enacted through her vivid account of the children's taunts, and her use of the speech bubbles (depicted in the drawing) to describe the hostile world of the playground, complete with the taunt, 'neh, neh, neh, neh, neh!' Here, the literacy practices, that of drawing a speech bubble and writing the taunts in the bubble, are embedded within a wider multimodal text. The creative aspect of the text comes from the way it spans domains of practice, from the world of the playground to the world of cartoons and speech bubbles, enacted in the talk. In this text, as in May's other text, the literacy event (written text, depicting speech) sits embedded within a wider mesh of communicative practices, and the meanings cross three domains, from home to school, to playground.

Crossings and creativity

Creativity in this chapter has been about facilitating crossings, so that literacy practices and events, embedded in everyday domains of practice, can re-surface in children's texts in interesting and unexpected ways, from home to school and back again. Teachers have stood back and allowed the spaces of possibility, letting the children lead the way, and enabling the children's thinking to flow (Burnard et al., 2006). The close connection in the nursery setting between children's drawing and writing provides an ideal site to explore crossings between home and school in children's play. Burnard et al. (2006) developed a notion of 'possibility thinking' to describe what teachers and children can do. They suggest that creative teaching involves the following types of activities of the teachers:

- posing questions
- play
- allowing time and space
- standing back.

It also involves the children:

- taking risks
- being imaginative
- innovation
- self-determination.

Children can be encouraged to take the lead, and then ask questions of the text. Burnard et al. suggest that teachers can ask different types of questions in order to develop different types of answers (2006: 244). Teachers can then extend the boundaries of what can be developed from them, making connections across domains and from home to school and back again as part of that process of exploration. May's map text and the chicken-pox house as well as the 'Tig' text can be seen as creative because they generate new questions.

One aspect of the work the teachers did in the Foundation classroom was the holistic nature of their planning. Teachers took on what the artists offered them in terms of the curriculum to explore the world around them and bring home experiences into the classroom. They made their topic the ideas that the artists brought in. In an interview with the artist involved in the project, she described how the project work permeated the activities in the Foundation classroom:

> They took it on across the whole nursery so when I would go in, everything would be related to the activity. (Interview, artist, November 2006).

The coherence with which the teachers worked with the artists and the architect to develop work focused on maps, space and spatiality was reflected in the quality of the children's text-making.

☐ Summary

Here, I offer a few points for reflection that can help strengthen a creative approach to literacy learning in the Foundation classroom. Teachers can:

- recognise the link between children's narratives from home, and their drawings in the classroom
- create opportunities for children to move home experience to drawing, to narrating and then to early writing
- develop ideas for writing and drawing which link to everyday rituals and practices
- extend the text as a space for possibility thinking, where the child and the teacher could both ask of a text – Where is this from, and where is it going?
- encourage talk about a drawing, and then develop literacy activities from that text, as a 'way in' to early writing.

I argue that it is in these connections with everyday worlds that young children's text-making is most harnessed to their agency. This creates relevance and ownership of knowledge for children (Jeffrey and Craft, 2004). When many worlds are represented in one text, we need to celebrate that achievement, and take account of that process when considering creative practices in schools. Children's literacy practices can be stretched across the domains of home and school, and acknowledged in new ways in the Foundation classroom, taking everyday knowledge, and transforming this knowledge into something new in creative and unexpected ways.

Suggestions for further reading 📖

Craft, A. (2002) *Creativity and Early Years Education*. London: Continuum.

Heath, S.B. and Wolf, S. (2004) *Visual Learning in the Community School*. London: Creative Partnerships.

Jeffrey, B. (ed.) (2006) *Creative Learning Practices: European Experiences*. London: Tufnell Press.

Safford, K. and Barrs, M. (2005) *Creativity and Literacy – Many Routes to Meaning: Children's Language and Literacy Learning in Creative Arts Projects*. London: CLPE.

Acknowledgements

I would like to thank the Heads Together group and Wilthorpe Infants School, Barnsley, for their generosity in sharing their work with me.

A shorter version of this chapter in a slightly different form can be found as Pahl, K. (2007) 'Creativity in events and practices: a lens for understanding children's multimodal texts', *Literacy* 41 (2): 86–92.

References

Banaji, S. and Burn, A., with Buckingham, D. (2006) *Rhetorics of Creativity: A Review of the Literature*. London: Creative Partnerships. Available online at http://www.creative-partnerships.com/content/gdocs/rhetorics.pdf (accessed December 2007).

Barrs, M. (1988) 'Drawing a story: transitions between drawing and writing', in M. Lightfoot and N. Martin (eds) *The Word for Teaching is Learning*. London: Heinemann. pp. 51–69.

Barton, D. and Hamilton, M. (1998) *Local Literacies: Reading and Writing in One Community*. London: Routledge.

Burnard, P., Craft, A., Cremin, T., Duffy, B., Hanson, R., Keene, R., Haynes, L. and Burns, D. (2006) 'Documenting possibility thinking: a journey of collaborative inquiry', *International Journal of Early Years Education*, 14 (3): 243–62.

Carter, R. (2004) *Language and Creativity: The Art of Common Talk*. London: Routledge.

Craft, A. (2000) *Creativity Across the Primary Curriculum: Framing and Developing Practice*. London: Routledge.

Craft, A. (2002) *Creativity and Early Years Education*. London: Continuum.

DfES (Department for Education and Skills) (2003) *Excellence and Enjoyment: A Strategy for Primary Schools*. London: DfES Publications.

Ellis, S. with Lawrence, B. (2007) 'Assessing learning in creative contexts'. Talk given at the UKLA conference, Swansea, July 2007. Available online at www.clpe.co.uk/pdf_assessing_learning_in_creative_contexts.pdf (accessed 15 April 2008).

Heath, S.B. and Wolf, S. (2004) *Visual Learning in the Community School*. London: Creative Partnerships.

HMI/Ofsted (2003) *Expecting the Unexpected: Developing Creativity in Primary and Secondary Schools*. HMI 1612: Ofsted. Available online at www.ofsted.gov.uk/assets/3377.pdf (accessed March 2008)

Holland, D., Lachicotte, W., Skinner, D. and Cain, C. (2001) *Identity and Agency in Cultural Worlds*. Harvard: Harvard University Press.

Jeffrey, B. (2001) 'Primary pupils' perspectives and creative learning', *Encyclopaedia* 9 (Spring): 133–52.

Jeffrey, B. and Craft, A. (2006) *Creative Learning Practices: European Experiences*. London: Tufnell Press.

Lancaster, L. (2003) 'Beginning at the beginning: how a young child constructs time multimodally', in C. Jewitt and G. Kress (eds) *Multimodal Literacy*. New York: Peter Lang. pp. 107–22.

Kress, G. (1997) *Before Writing: Rethinking the Paths to Literacy*. London: Routledge.

National Advisory Committee on Creative and Cultural Education (NACCCE) (1999) *All Our Futures: Creativity, Culture and Education*. London: DfEE.

Nutbrown, C. and Jones, H. (2006) *Daring Discoveries: Arts Based Learning in the Early Years*. Doncaster: Darts and Creative Partnerships.

Ofsted (2006) *Creative Partnerships: Initiative and Impact*. HMI 2517. Crown copyright: Ofsted. Available online at http://www.ofsted.gov.uk/assets/Internet_Content/Shared_Content/Files/creativeprtnrshps.pdf (accessed December 2007).

Pahl, K. (1999) *Transformations: Children's Meaning Making in a Nursery*. Stoke-on-Trent: Trentham Books.

Pahl, K. (2007) 'Looking with a different eye: report on a Creative Partnerships research study', http://www.creative-partnerships.com/content/researchAnd EvaluationProjects/181129/?version=1 (accessed December 2007).

Pahl, K. and Rowsell, J. (2005) *Literacy and Education: The New Literacy Studies in the Classroom*. London: Paul Chapman.

Qualifications and Curriculum Authority (2003) *Creativity, Find it, Promote it!* London: QCA. http://www.qca.org.uk/qca_9915.aspx accessed. July 2008.

Rowsell, J. and Pahl, K. (2007) 'Sedimented identities in texts: instances of practice', *Reading Research Quarterly* 42 (3): 388–401.

Safford, K. and Barrs, M. (2005) *Creativity and Literacy – Many Routes to Meaning: Children's Language and Literacy Learning in Creative Arts Projects*. London: CLPE.

Street, B.V. (1984) *Literacy in Theory and Practice*. Cambridge: Cambridge University Press.

Street, B.V (2000) 'Literacy events and literacy practices: theory and practice in the New Literacy Studies', in M. Martin-Jones and K. Jones (eds) *Multilingual Literacies: Reading and Writing Different Worlds*. Amsterdam/Philadelphia: John Benjamins Publishing Company. pp. 17–29.

Play, drama and literacy in the early years

Julie Dunn

📁 **Case study 9.1   The Magic Carpet Tour Office**

Several early years teachers are planning for the forthcoming term. Their task is to generate a series of experiences that will stimulate the children's interest in their own city. They want the class to appreciate its key geographical features, forms of transport, and places of interest. The children themselves have had no say in the development of this topic, but the teachers are nevertheless keen to incorporate their ideas as the work progresses and want to ensure that the learning takes place in an environment encouraging of playfulness. The teachers decide therefore that a socio-dramatic play space should be a key component of the plan, and are agreed that this play space should also offer the learners opportunities to develop their literacy skills by engaging with a range of context-appropriate text types.

One member of the planning team suggests that a possible way to introduce the children to the topic might be to shift their perspective, encouraging them to explore the city from above, adopting a bird's eye view as they look down on the zoo, the lake, the river, the central business district and indeed their own school. This suggestion prompts one of the team to recall that the children had been most excited last term by the story of Aladdin and wonders if the most effective vehicle for this aerial tour might be a magic carpet! Instantly a series of exciting ideas is generated and a loose structure for learning begins to emerge. The children will be the owners of a magic carpet tour company and the play space will be a text-rich Magic Carpet Tour Office.

Ideas for teacher-structured activities that relate to this initial idea are also suggested, with a range of drama strategies and conventions including teacher-in-role being keenly discussed. The teachers agree that these will be used to scaffold the children's participation in this new context, introduce appropriate vocabulary and language registers, model situated literacy practices, ensure that all participants have a shared understanding of the roles and situations possible within this dramatic world, and perhaps most importantly of all, provide the ongoing input and tension that will serve to keep the children playing. They understand that it is only by maintaining interest in the notion of a Magic Carpet Tour Office that contextualised and purposeful interactions with the literacy materials contained within the office will continue.[1]

The above case study is reflective of the key philosophies underpinning this chapter. Most important of these is the view that adult-structured drama and child-structured dramatic play can work together in a highly effective manner to generate rich literacy opportunities for children in the early years. It also reflects the notion that the active involvement of the teacher is critical to the successful application of these two related, but distinct, pedagogical approaches, not only at this initial planning stage, but also later as modelling, scaffolding and other forms of support are needed to initiate the dramatic action or sustain it. Finally, and perhaps most significantly, it reflects the notion that in order to be effective in developing literacy, dramatic play contexts must engage and excite as many of the children as possible for as long as possible, with dramatic tension being a key part of this process. An understanding of what is meant by the term 'dramatic tension' and the strategies teachers can use both within and beyond the play space is therefore critical.

Within this chapter, case studies of teacher planning, including the one above, will be used to explore how teachers might take advantage of the powerful relationship between dramatic play and drama to generate literacy outcomes for their students. This three-way relationship has been only partially explored within the literature, as researcher-interest has steadily and increasingly focused on the interface between just two of these dimensions – play and literacy. As far back as the 1980s, researchers, such as Hall (1987), were exploring

---

1   This Case study relates to a planning meeting conducted between the author and a team of teachers at Kaohsiung City Kindergarten, Kaohsiung City, Taiwan.

the possibilities of transforming play spaces into print-rich environments, where children were provided with contextualised opportunities to engage in literacy learning. Since then, these possibilities have been the subject of a great deal of research, with Roskos and Christie (2001) conducting a critical analysis of 20 of the most important of these projects generated between 1992 and 2000 in order to achieve an overall sense of what all this activity has revealed. They suggest that together these studies provide strong evidence that play can serve literacy by:

- providing settings that promote literacy activity, skills and strategies
- serving as a language experience that can build connections between oral and written modes of expression
- providing opportunities to teach and learn literacy. (Raskas and Christie, 2001: 83–4)

However, they also caution that one of the weaknesses of these claims is that little research has been focussed on the microlevel of play in terms of who is engaging in the activity and how individual play preferences and motivations impact upon the literacy outcomes achieved. Clearly teachers need to be aware of this risk, exploring ways to extend play involvement.

One way of supporting a broader range of learners, and of keeping them interested in the literacy materials offered within a play space, is to take advantage of the motivating and uniting force of drama education strategies. How teachers might do this and what they need to understand about this three-way relationship is the focus of this chapter.

Child-structured dramatic play

Although not always seen in this light, dramatic play sits within the broader field of drama, being the most improvisational and spontaneous of all the dramatic forms. Here the participant, either individually or in a group, freely manipulates the elements of drama, such as role, place, time, symbol and tension, to create a dramatic world that temporarily allows them to become 'other' or be 'elsewhere'. Within this world, the child can become a superhero, a parent, a vet, a dog, or all of these. The player is completely free and unrestricted, being able to shift role at whim. Similarly, time and place can also be transformed, with the player choosing to experience an ancient land inhabited by dinosaurs or a shoe shop filled with customers. Sticks become horses and cardboard boxes become cars. In each case, the dramatic world has become a vehicle for the child to explore alternatives beyond the actual worlds they inhabit in their everyday lives and according to Booth these experiences are significant because they give the child the opportunity to 'leave the narrow confines of their own worlds giving them entry into new forms of existence' (1994: 22).

In the playground, the home, the garden, at the beach and in the classroom, children create these dramatic worlds, structuring their own experiences and making spontaneous decisions about content and direction. For some children, this structuring comes easily and they are able to generate for themselves and their play partners, rich and exciting play experiences. Creaser (1989) has adapted Fein's (1987) use of the term 'master player' to describe these children as 'master dramatists' in recognition of their intuitive ability to manipulate the elements of drama in fluid, flexible and effective ways. For other children however, these structuring skills are not so strong and support is needed if their play episodes are going to be engaging and exciting. In the playground or at the beach, this support may come from other children, but in the classroom context, support can also come from the teacher through careful planning, scaffolding and participation in play.

The dramatic play of children is often viewed by adults as being an unstructured activity, with this viewpoint being most famously reinforced by Piaget (1962: 87) who suggested that it is 'without rules or limitations'. However, Vygotsky (1976: 542) was one of the first to challenge this ruleless view of play arguing that there can be no imaginative or pretend play without rules, saying that 'to imagine that a child can behave in an imaginary situation without rules, i.e. as he behaves in a real situation, is simply impossible'. More recently, writers from a range of fields (Guss, 2005a; Lobman, 2003; Lofdahl, 2005; Sawyer, 1997) have suggested that not only does play have rules, but that it is in fact a form of improvisation and as such has its own inherent structure. Rules, whilst not written down or even explicitly understood by the players, must be followed and the spontaneous text, co-created by the participants as the action itself unfolds, is not random, but rather is the result of some very careful structuring and manipulation by the players themselves. Later in this chapter, the notion of the 'playwright function' in play will be discussed (see pages 176–177), but for now, it should be understood that the players, even those who are very young, are engaged moment by moment in the task of structuring their play to ensure that it offers them an enjoyable experience.

However, while structured, a key characteristic of dramatic play is that it has no specific, external goal for the player. The child is not playing in order to develop their literacy skills, enhance their ability to socialise or extend their vocabulary. These may of course be the parents' or teachers' goals, but for the player, it is in fact the freedom of play that drives them (Bolton, 1985; Kelly-Byrne, 1984). In summary:

- Play's principal features are spontaneity and enactment.
- The experience is not easily repeatable.
- The mode of the action is an intense 'living through'.
- It can survive changeable degrees of individual cooperation.
- It is usually conducted in small groups but may be a solo activity.
- There are rules, but these are generally imposed by the players themselves.
- A high level of cooperation between the players is required as control of the action rests with the children themselves.

Dramatic play preferences

Within the overarching category of dramatic play, three main types of play are generally recognised: solitary, parallel and socio-dramatic play. For some theorists (from Parten in 1971 [1933] to Broadhead in 2006), solitary play is viewed as being less complex, requiring less from the player in terms of cooperation than the highly collaborative socio-dramatic play, with the result being that solitary play is viewed by many educators as being developmentally inferior. However, an increasing understanding is emerging that each of these forms of play has its own benefits and that adults need to offer children opportunities to engage across this range.

When offered such a choice, some children, in some circumstances, will choose to create a dramatic world alone. Here the action may be either partially or completely internalised, with roles being projected onto toys or other objects. The action will most often also be miniaturised, with blocks or dolls being key props, but, whilst not always involving an embodied role, the action is still essentially dramatic and often quite intense for the player. When internalised in this way, it may be difficult for the observer to fully grasp what is taking place in the play situation, for often the language remains unspoken or is fragmented. However, in spite of its seemingly incoherent external presentation, the dramatic world being spontaneously created by the child playing alone may in fact be extremely rich.

At other times, the child's preference may be to engage in parallel play. Here two or more children create personal dramatic worlds in close proximity to each other, being able to overhear each other and share ideas or storylines. These contexts may be similar or quite distinct, and there may be some overlapping or momentary merging of situations or roles, but essentially the players have chosen to play out their ideas individually, maintaining their distinct dramatic worlds.

Within the education environment where play partners abound, socio-dramatic play is another option and the one that has been most thoroughly researched in terms of its value to literacy development. Here, two or more children co-create a play episode within a shared dramatic context. These episodes may be of extended duration or may last for just a few minutes, depending on the experience of the players, the level of understanding they share about the dramatic context and roles inherent within it, and the play situation itself – where and when it is occurring, and the level of control over time and space that is exerted by the adult. Cooperation between players is also of key importance, but as noted above, child-structured dramatic play is capable of surviving even fairly low levels of collaboration, especially when a master dramatist is present. The topics/situations played out by children will also have an impact on the duration of a play episode, with the level of shared understanding of this context being of key significance. Children's popular culture texts such as films and television shows generally influence play choices, but programmes such as the news will also have an effect. Adults often underestimate the impact on children of big stories such as global catastrophes or local troubles (Weddell, 2003), but young children regularly explore these events within their play texts, with the episodes generated sometimes being distasteful to the adults who might observe them. In these cases, adults often intervene to 'sanitise' the play that emerges (Sutton-Smith, 1985), either by asking the children to stop, or by trying to divert the play towards other more 'acceptable' topics.

Socio-dramatic play in early years settings

In early years learning situations, the most common socio-dramatic play space provided for children is the home corner. Here, they are given the time and resources to explore a context that is generally familiar to most children, with cooking activities, parenting tasks and pet management being some of the main family situations played out. Increasingly, teachers are taking advantage of the literacy opportunities inherent within such a setting and flooding the play area with recipe books, shopping lists, food labels, telephone contact lists and magazines, along with the tools they might need to interact with these materials or indeed to create their own texts, including computers. However, the roles inherent within any individual child's home and indeed the amount of print material found within them will not be universally common, as many children live in non-traditional family units, while the situations that children experience in their homes will also differ widely. These differences may be minor and collaboration between children will still be possible, but they may also be quite complex and these complex differences in life experience may make it difficult for children to create a shared dramatic world with their peers, or indeed engage in meaningful ways with the literacy materials.

Other play contexts generally made available to children include shops, hairdressing salons, post offices, and hospitals, with each of these spaces offering different possibilities, including opportunities to use context-specific vocabulary, and to explore roles and situations beyond those made possible by the domestic nature of the home corner. Here teachers can offer opportunities for young children to write and post letters, count out change, write names in appointment books or 'read' patient charts, depending upon the play space and the tasks generally required within such a place.

Hall and Robinson (2003) provide us with a well-documented example of such a space in the form of their now well-known garage play space. Here the children began their set of experiences by visiting a local garage before formally seeking written permission to create a garage of their own, filling out application forms, drawing up plans, defending a threat to its development in the form of a letter of complaint, planning a grand opening, applying for jobs and eventually simply dealing with the day-to-day operation of such a workplace. Throughout all of these processes the children were reading, writing and speaking – using new vocabulary to convey meaning to others and doing this in a purposeful and contextualised manner.

In the learning context described in case study 9.1, the Magic Carpet Tour Office play space has the potential to achieve similar outcomes. Through the various stages of designing the magic carpet, planning its itinerary, and preparing to launch their new tour business, children may decide to create brochures, design advertising, map journeys, take bookings over the phone and in person, record these on a booking sheet, create and issue tickets, and of course go on journeys themselves, reporting their adventures to others through written and spoken recounts, letters, emails and even digital photo stories.

However, in spite of these exciting possibilities, teachers cannot control children's play and a space created to give children opportunities such as those described above may not attract all children. In addition, some children may not fully understand the possibilities inherent within a context as fanciful as a Magic Carpet Tour Office, and as a result may choose not to engage with peers in such a space. What they lack may be a shared understanding of the roles, activities, language and indeed print-related practices that would generally be experienced there, with this lack of knowledge not only preventing them from playing, but also from engaging in the literacy learning on offer.

Using drama to support literacy through play

As we have seen from Hall and Robinson's garage example above, an excursion can be one way of providing this access for all learners, but an alternative or indeed additional approach is to make use of the strategies of adult-structured drama. Here the teachers may use drama to introduce the children to the dramatic context (for example, by meeting their classroom teacher who has adopted the role of the owner of the Magic Carpet Tour Office), support the children to take on roles themselves (for example, by using enrolment strategies to help them become the manufacturers of the flying carpet itself), plan places the carpet may fly to (by meeting key people in the city via the strategy of hot seat), and create images of key city locations (by making freeze frames).

Significantly, the teacher-in-role work will also provide valuable modelling of context-specific literacy practices. For example, when in role, the teacher may have checked off the passengers' names as they stepped aboard the carpet, or chatted on the telephone taking a booking and recording it on a booking sheet. The teacher may also have modelled the practices of a passenger, signing a credit card slip and filling out details on a booking form. Oral language will also have been modelled by the teacher during the drama component of the experience, with appropriate vocabulary and a range of language registers being used (Grainger and Pickard, 2004) so that once the children shift into child-structured play later in the experience, they will be able to experiment with this language, while also playing around with status and tone, using language styles appropriate to the roles they have chosen, such as customer, tour guide, or even Aladdin himself.

Tensions may also be introduced, with the teacher writing to the students as one of Aladdin's friends to suggest that he needs his magic carpet back, or as a customer forwarding by email a complaint that during her journey the carpet went off course, travelling to places not on the itinerary. These interventions all need to be responded to, with the tension created by such written texts generating the kind of excitement and energy that Hall and Robinson's (2003) letter of complaint generated in their garage experience. Without this tension, interest in the garage space may have waned early on, and with this loss of interest, the many opportunities for meaningful text creation that were documented as part of that project may also have been lost.

These various forms of teacher intervention serve then both to prepare children for play and to support them as they engage in child-structured play experiences, with the drama strategies opening up new pathways for the children to pursue in their play and a clearer idea of how they might engage with the array of text types included in the space, such as maps, charts, brochures, telephone books, timetables, photographs, booking sheets and even internet sites. Children will draw on their experiences within the adult-structured drama to support them in the development of written and spoken texts, with this also supporting their emerging understanding of the relationship between genre and purpose. Given sufficient modelling, even the most inexperienced child will be capable of participating in a play episode related to this context, while drama strategies can also be used to stretch those children whose understanding is already strong. Of course, modelling of this kind can also occur when teachers adopt a co-player role in a play space, but these adult-structured drama strategies offer a more efficient way of demonstrating these practices for the whole group, while also generating opportunities for shared reflection and discussion after the activities.

Finally, as the Magic Carpet Tour Office example above suggests, drama opens up possibilities for children to engage in play contexts that are far beyond those that could ever be experienced as part of children's normal lives and because of their fanciful nature don't exist as excursion possibilities. For example, a Giantologist Headquarters (O'Toole and Dunn, 2002), established especially to support the work of a visiting giant specialist who is endeavouring to find out what is making a local giant throw tantrums, offers quite different possibilities compared with a more realistic office environment, while a kitchen established to mix up and create dreams for a missing Dream-Maker (Dunn and Stinson, 2002) is sure to engage some children who would not normally be interested in playing within a more traditional 'home' space. New language possibilities are also opened up as children create recipes with ingredients quite different from those generally found in meals, while recording on a town map reports of the latest incidents of giant trouble differs markedly from other forms of report writing.

In these examples, three common occupational play spaces (travel agency, office and kitchen) have been enriched through the addition of a dramatic frame, with adult-structured drama strategies being used to tap into the imagination of the young child to motivate their involvement and keep them playing, while at the same time offering opportunities to generate and respond to a more diverse range of text types.

What is important to note here, however, is that teachers should avoid using these or any other strategies to dominate the learning environment, for within the context of early years education, adult-structured drama, like play, should be both spontaneous and improvisational. It should not look like or be derivative of those forms that are mainly performative or text-based, but rather, should simply be a more structured and goal-oriented version of what children do naturally, with the key difference being the structuring provided by the teacher. A number of different names has been given to the various forms of adult-structured drama used in early years settings, with process drama (O'Neill, 1995), 'living through drama' (Bolton, 1992) and story drama (Booth, 1994) being just three of these. Similar in terms of approach, each one of these approaches should be highly playful and provide opportunities for the participants to make decisions about the action from within it. Process drama, for example, is an approach which according to O'Neill 'proceeds without a script, its outcome is unpredictable, it lacks a separate audience, and the experience is impossible to replicate exactly' (1995: xiii). She goes on to add to these characteristics by suggesting that process drama generates a dramatic 'elsewhere' – a dramatic world (1995: 12).

These of course sound like the characteristics of play, and that is as it should be, but with the key differentiation point being the purposes and goals of the teacher. Explicit links to the curriculum and specific learning outcomes will have been planned for, with the development of specific or more general literacy goals being part of this.

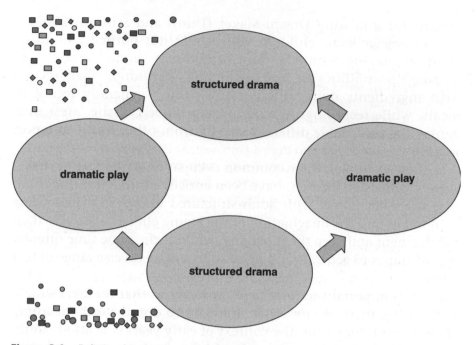

Figure 9.1   Relationship between child-structured dramatic play and adult-structured drama

Planning and the role of tension

As we have seen above, adult-structured drama with the whole class or a segment of the class group can create new contexts for children to explore through play. However, an alternative planning approach is for adults to observe the natural play of small groups of children and build on this as the basis for later drama experiences. Indeed, the diagram in Figure 9.1 suggests that children can be given the opportunity to move back and forth between these two approaches, starting anywhere.

In the Magic Carpet Tour Office example, the teachers chose to commence the work with the structured drama as the children had no common experience of this context and therefore were in need of the modelling that these teacher-led experiences provide. Later the children will shift into socio-dramatic play mode via the Magic Carpet Tour Office or perhaps to solitary play by creating miniature playscapes of key city locations, such as the zoo. Eventually, in order to sustain interest or to introduce new tensions or developments, structured drama may be needed again and these strategies will be used before the focus returns once more to child-structured play.

At other times, however, these same teachers may have chosen to work in the opposite direction. Let us look at a different example.

Case study 9.2   The lighthouse playground

During storytime, the teacher of a group of four-year-olds had shared with them the first book in the 'Lighthouse Keeper' series by Ronda and David Armitage entitled 'The Lighthouse Keeper's Lunch'. The children were fascinated by the setting of the story and the idea of the lighthouse keeper's lunch being sent across the sea in a basket hanging from a high wire. At outside playtime the children asked their teacher if they could create a similar device and soon they were atop the climbing frame sending a basket of goodies back and forth across the playground to their peers on the classroom veranda. Before long lighthouses were being made during block time and boats were constructed and sailed to islands. A torch appeared the next day and in a darkened part of the classroom a lighthouse was created to keep these boats safe.

Later that week, more books in the series were read and new ideas for play were generated. Eventually however, the play began to peter out but the teacher felt that even more learning could be generated from this context and so she looked for a way to rejuvenate it. Using drama strategies, she introduced a new character, the lighthouse keeper's nephew, an inexperienced lad who would be left in charge of the lighthouse while his uncle went away. Needing the children's help to light the light and keep the lighthouse functioning, the children participated in drama strategies specifically designed to train the young man for his new role. This help included making lists of jobs, naming parts of the lighthouse, and writing reminder lists. But the nephew falters and one night the light is not lit. The next morning mysterious boxes wash ashore and the nephew (teacher-in-role) brings these to the children seeking their advice about what might be inside and where they may have come from. Of different sizes and shapes, two of the boxes have words written on them such as 'Handle with care!' and 'Danger!', while another is labelled with a mysterious address. Great interest is generated and lots of group reading of these messages takes place.

These brief dramatic encounters stimulate the children's imaginations and once again the child-structured play takes off. Later the nephew will return with more troubles, but for now the play, originally generated by the children, has been given a new lease of life through the use of adult-structured drama.[2]

---

2   For a full account of this experience see J. O'Toole and J. Dunn (2002) *Pretending to Learn: Helping Children Learn Through Drama*. Frenchs Forest, NSW: Pearson Education.

In the case study above, it was the children's enjoyment of a picture book that initiated the entire experience, with the situation and roles from the book being the stimulus for the play that followed. However, it was the adult-structured drama that provided the necessary momentum and interest to get the children playing again, achieving this by introducing a new set of roles and tensions for the children to explore, whilst importantly reintroducing literacy-related aspects to the experience in the form of labels and addresses.

Tension is the driving force of all drama (O'Toole, 1992), and without it even play can become repetitive or mundane causing participants to lose interest, just as a boring film or television show causes us to switch off. To avoid this sense of repetition, something always needs to be happening, something has to be 'up'. Players therefore need to be supported in generating a 'What's up?' factor each time they play, and while the master dramatists, as previously discussed in this chapter, are quite capable of generating these on their own, other children need support to understand and apply this aspect of play.

In the lighthouse context, interest waned because the novelty of using the rope and basket could not sustain the children's interest and some form of tension was needed. This could have been introduced by a child, but in this case it was the teacher, using adult-structured drama conventions to support her, who intervened. The need to train and support the young, inexperienced lighthouse keeper replacement was the first intervention, while the mysterious physical arrival of the three boxes was the second, with this latter one creating a wide array of print-related activity. Children immediately began to make their own boxes, placing messages inside and then labeling and addressing them to others.

Haseman and O'Toole (1987) suggest that there are five main forms of dramatic tension: task, relationship, mystery, surprise and metaxis (the tension between the real and the fictional world), and while other drama theorists may contest this list (Bundy, 2004), an understanding of how these tensions can be used to support and extend play is highly useful. For example, by asking the children to engage in the process of training a young replacement lighthouse keeper, the teacher was generating tension of the task, while the introduction of the boxes brought both tension of surprise and mystery to the play episode. In both cases an understanding of the impact of tension coupled with an ability to apply dramatic strategies was used to enrich and develop child-structured play.

However, for the teacher interested in developing tension in children's play, other options that do not necessarily involve the use of adult-structured drama strategies are available. The teacher may, for example, use group or circle time to review play experiences, asking the children to provide a summary of what happened as they played. During these times the teacher might ask the children to identify any 'What's up?' factors that might have been present in their play, thus providing ideas for other children to adopt and explore later. Alternatively, ideas about possible 'What's up?' factors might also be discussed prior to play, with the children supporting each other in the brainstorming of possible ideas. Of course, the children may not make use of any of these ideas, but the process itself will have served to remind the children that in play something needs to be happening. Such learner scaffolding should begin the process of developing what Guss (2005b) calls dramatic intelligence by generating an explicit understanding of dramatic form.

As we have seen above, the teacher may also enter the children's play as co-player making offerings in role that may or may not be picked up by the children as their texts develop. Such intervention in play has been hotly debated within the play literature, with a romantic notion of play as the child's domain dominating for some time. Within this view, direct adult intervention is viewed negatively. However, as Best points out, 'to fail to intervene is to fail to educate' (1992: 75), and, as such, early years teachers are now more inclined to get involved in play.

The purpose of the intervention is critical, however, for as Rogers and Evans point out, play benefits most from those styles of intervention that 'extend and rejuvenate rather than constrain and frustrate' (2007: 163), with those that constrain and frustrate often being generated in order to control the players or sanitise the content of the play (Sutton-Smith, 1985). However, for those who prefer extension and rejuvenation, there are some important decisions to be made when intervening in order to ensure that the offerings have a positive impact on the play and, in turn, the literacy opportunities available.

Planning to intervene

Before a teacher opts to intervene in a particular fictional context, either as a co-player or by making use of drama strategies, a role must be chosen and this role must not only be relevant to the specific dramatic world the children have created, it must also have a status level (high, medium or low) that meets the needs of both this context and the individual children playing. Adults must also time their entry, observing the action closely prior to joining the children in order to ensure that their contribution is still needed. Play texts move rapidly and if the children have already re-generated the play for themselves intervention may not be needed. Finally, and most importantly, the teacher must decide how they want to influence the text, making a decision about the kind of offering they will make once they enter the play frame. Do they, for example, want to support the current direction of the text, change it radically, or simply offer support for a textual direction offered by one of the children but not taken up by the group? In terms of literacy, the teacher must also decide how their intervention will influence the way the children interact with the print materials in the space.

These can be complex decisions, and yet this is an under-theorised aspect of the play literature, with little support being offered to teachers in terms of understanding 'how' they might best engage in play so that their offerings make a positive contribution to all aspects of the experience. One useful framework for thinking about these interventions is that of the 'playwright function'. The term 'playwright function' was first devised by O'Neill (1995) to suggest that within all improvised texts, including play, the participants are engaged in a text creation process that, while spontaneous and oral, still requires the services of a playwright. She reminds us that improvised texts are not prior documents, but an 'animating current' to which the participants submit and, in submitting to this current, each person involved assumes at least part of the playwright function, doing this from *within* the event (1995: 24). Building upon O'Neill's initial application of this term, four playwright functions have been identified and described (Dunn, 2003) with each of these having a different impact upon the collaboratively generated play or improvised drama episode. These functions include the narrative, intervening, reinforcing and reviewing playwright functions which should not be thought of as being in any way fixed or pre-determined, or understood as being a way of labelling an individual person. Rather, control of these functions should be understood as being fluid, shifting rapidly from one player to the next in a spontaneous attempt at structuring the action.

The narrative playwright function is used to continue the planned or current line of action, creating dialogue and action that falls into line with the existing direction of the text, while the intervening playwright function provides textual innovations that are aimed at either subtly or radically changing its direction. The reinforcing playwright function is used to support and extend these interventions, ensuring that useful tensions become incorporated into the emerging text. Finally, the reviewing function serves to call the group together in order to review what has happened thus far. Without these reviewing moments, coherence can be lost, but this function is the one used least within young children's play.

Knowledge of these functions, coupled with an understanding of status and tension, is therefore particularly useful for teachers. In case study 9.1 for example, a teacher entering the Magic Carpet Tour Office taking on a high status role such as a demanding customer who wants to complain about the trip she has just been on, will clearly have a different impact on the children's play responses compared with another who enters the office in a low status role as a lost visitor who has just dropped in, map in hand, to seek directions. The first teacher, by adopting an intervening playwright function will change the direction of the action completely as the children struggle to meet the needs of this high status customer. The second teacher however, by opting to use a reviewing function and low status role, may be able to engage with just one child at this time, perhaps targeting someone whose involvement is low or whose participation in the literacy-related aspects of the space is minimal.

A third alternative may be for the teacher to enter the booking office in a mid-status role seeking a journey to some unexpected place, such as under the sea, providing the children with the option of reinforcing this offering by agreeing to take them there, or maintaining a narrative function by explaining that the carpet cannot 'fly' under the sea. Either way, the children are in control, with the teacher simply providing a stimulus that opens the door for new textual opportunities, allowing herself to be 'tossed around' by the play rather than driving it to a pre-determined destination.

If the teacher is going to be an effective participant, decisions about the use of the playwright function need to be carefully made and constant use of high status roles combined with adoption of the intervening playwright function might not provide the best outcomes for the players or their literacy development. By adopting a range of status positions and playwright functions, teachers are able to model for children options that may lead not only to the enhancement of individual texts, but possibly also to the development of individual player skills to the point where the teacher no longer needs to take on such a role.

Solitary play and literacy development

As we have seen in the two case studies above, published and on-screen texts can play a key role in stimulating the initial play experience. Within the drama education literature these materials are known as pre-texts, with the people, places and situations explored within them offering plenty of opportunities for transformation into play. Picture books are particularly useful, as the visual images offer children a real sense of place, supporting their imaginations and providing important scaffolding for the creation of shared dramatic worlds, while other texts such as non-fiction books, street directories, charts, telephone books and websites can support the children's action in the play.

Case study 9.3 provides an example of these processes at work, with a picture book stimulating the initial interest of the children, while a range of other text types are used later in the experience to support the children's ongoing learning and engagement, resulting eventually in the spontaneous development of written texts by the children themselves.

Case study 9.3   Trouble beneath the sea

Matilda returns from holidays with a beautiful conch shell she has found at the beach. The children in her reception class enjoy holding the shell up to their ears and listening for the sounds of the sea. Their teacher, Thomas, recalls one of his favourite stories about shells and introduces the children to the picture book There's a Sea in my Bedroom *by Margaret Wild (1989). The story explores what happens when a similar shell magically pours sea water from its opening, flooding a child's bedroom and turning his bed into an island complete with seagulls and a rocky shoreline. The children love this text and develop a rich interest in shells and the creatures that live in them. Thomas decides to build on this interest, sharing with them further stories about shells including those relating to hermit crabs and uses these stories to build the children's scientific knowledge about shell creatures. The children are soon pretending to be hermit crabs themselves, using cardboard boxes as their shells, but the play opportunities inherent within this context are limited and Thomas needs a way to develop them. He decides to extend this play by suggesting that the children create miniaturised undersea playscapes using unstructured collage materials. Great enjoyment is generated during their development, but many of the children still seem to be struggling to engage dramatically in these undersea landscapes. Tension is lacking and Thomas decides that this could be generated through adult-structured drama.*

Discussing with the children why the sea may have poured out of the shell in the picture book and then gaining the children's agreement to pretend that the reason was that there was trouble under the sea and help was needed, Thomas enters the classroom in role as the boy from the picture book. He shares with the children the terrible news that some wicked crabs have been collecting all the shells they can find and hoarding them in an underwater cave, meaning that other sea creatures who depend upon them for their homes are now at risk from predators as they outgrow their old shells and have none to move into. The children question the boy, using the hot-seat strategy, gathering information about this undersea situation and how he might have heard this news. The boy reveals that the message came out of the shell with the water and goes on to explain that many of the larger creatures like dolphins, whales and even swordfish have all tried to intercede, but so far have not been successful.

Immediately upon hearing this news many of the children return to their undersea playscapes keen now to explore through solitary play these new developments. Other children respond by adopting some of these roles themselves and engaging in socio-dramatic play, using the playground as their undersea world complete with a cave. Texts in the form of letters to King Neptune, rescue plans and even 'Wanted' posters are soon generated, with reference materials in the form of non-fiction texts and websites being called upon as part of the now energised learning experience.[3]

Once again, this case study highlights the possibilities that are made available to teachers when play and drama are brought together as partners in literacy education. Here the arrival of the shell stimulated a series of experiences scaffolded by the teacher to provide useful learning and engagement with written texts, but not fully exploiting the dramatic and literate possibilities of the situation. It is only when the teacher intervenes by introducing tension (in this case tension of relationships) using the key drama strategy of hot-seating, that the learning really accelerates with the children not only generating more dramatically rich play episodes within their playscapes, but also engaging with a range of texts as both readers and writers.

---

3   The drama experience described here was created in conjunction with Andrea Burton, Griffith University.

Conclusion

The interface between drama, play and literacy has been explored within this chapter, with the role of the teacher being highlighted as being particularly critical in the achievement of literacy outcomes for young children. These outcomes, such as the three important ones outlined by Roskos and Christie (2001) at the outset of this chapter, cannot be achieved through play if there are individuals who have become disengaged and are no longer interested in participating within the developed context. This aspect poses one of the biggest challenges to the argument that play can be an effective literacy tool, for learning can occur only when there is play, and when children 'opt out' of play because it is boring, does not meet their needs or has become repetitious, the value of this approach is clearly limited to those children who have engaged.

Drama strategies were therefore suggested as offering support for play, while an understanding of dramatic tension and its role in generating engagement was outlined.

Tension was described as the driving force of all dramatic activity, with the 'What's up?' factor being highlighted as requiring the explicit attention of both the teacher and the learners. Use of the intervening playwright function was identified as being one way for the teacher to introduce tension into either child-structured play or adult-structured drama, with an understanding of status also being highlighted as an important consideration for teachers who wish to enter the dramatic frame.

Picture books were discussed as having a role to play in children's understanding of the 'What's up?' factor, as well as in the support they offer children in terms of motivation and contextualisation. By building on children's interest in these texts, teachers can provide children with opportunities to explore beyond the author's ideas using the images and narrative of the text as a springboard. Armed with this understanding, early years teachers can extend and support the literate potential of play, generating opportunities for young children to engage with a range of text types in a meaningful and contextualised manner. Reading, writing, viewing and speaking all become part of the fun of play and drama, but it is not magic ...

Suggestions for further reading 📖

Booth, D. and Neelands, J. (eds) (1998) *Writing in Role: Classroom Projects Connecting Writing and Drama.* Hamilton, Ontario: Caliburn Enterprises.

Dyson, A.H. (2003) *The Brothers and Sisters Learn to Write: Popular Literacies in Childhood and School Cultures.* New York: Teachers College Press.

Wood, E. and Attfield, J. (2005) *Play, Learning and the Early Childhood Curriculum* Second edition. London: Paul Chapman.

Wright, S. (ed.) (2002) *The Arts, Young Children and Learning.* Boston: Allyn and Bacon.

Wright, S. (ed.) (2003) *Children, Meaning Making and the Arts.* Sydney: Pearson Education.

References

Armitage, D. and Armitage, R. (1994) *The Lighthouse Keeper's Lunch.* London: Scholastic.

Best, D. (1992) *The Rationality of Feeling – Understanding the Arts in Education.* London: Falmer Press.

Bolton, G. (1985) *Towards a Theory of Drama in Education.* London: Longman.

Bolton, G. (1992) *New Perspectives on Classroom Drama.* Hemel Hempstead: Simon and Schuster.

Booth, D. (1994) *Story Drama: Reading, Writing and Roleplaying across the Curriculum.* Markham, Ontario: Pembroke Publishers.

Broadhead, P. (2006) 'Developing an understanding of young children's learning through play: the place of observation, interaction and reflection', *British Educational Research Journal* 32 (2): 191–207.

Bundy, P. (2004) 'Dramatic tension: towards an understanding of intimacy', *Youth Theatre Journal* 18: 17–29.

Creaser, B. (1989) 'An examination of the four-year-old master dramatist', *International Journal of Early Childhood Education* 21: 55–68.

Dunn, J. (2003) 'Enhancing dramatic activities in the early childhood years', in S. Wright (ed.) *The Arts, Young Children and Learning.* Boston: Allyn and Bacon. pp. 211–29.

Dunn, J. and Stinson, M. (2002) *The Dream-Maker.* Brisbane: Queensland Studies Authority.

Fein, G. (1987) 'Pretend play in childhood: an integrative review', *Child Development* 52: 1095–118.

Grainger, T. and Pickard, A. (2004) *Drama: Reading, Writing and Speaking Our Way Forward.* Royston: United Kingdom Literacy Association.

Guss, F. (2005a) 'Reconceptualizing play: aesthetic self-definitions', *Contemporary Issues in Early Childhood* 6 (3): 233–43.

Guss, F. (2005b) 'Dramatic playing beyond the theory of multiple intelligences', *Research in Drama Education* 10 (1): 43–54.

Hall, N. (1987) *The Emergence of Play.* London: Hodder and Stoughton.

Hall, N. and Robinson, A. (2003) *Exploring Writing and Play in the Early Years* Second edition. London: David Fulton.

Haseman, B. and O'Toole, J. (1987) *Dramawise.* Melbourne: Heinemann.

Kelly-Byrne, D. (1984) 'Dramatic play, childhood drama and the classroom', *Australian Journal of Reading* 7 (2): 89–97.

Lobman, C. (2003) 'What should we create today? Improvisational teaching in play-based classrooms', *Early Years* 23 (2): 132–42.

Lofdahl, A. (2005) '"The funeral": a study of children's shared meaning-making and its developmental significance', *Early Years* 25 (1): 5–16.

O'Neill, C. (1995) *Drama Worlds: A Framework for Process Drama.* Portsmouth, England: Heinemann.

O'Toole, J. (1992) *The Process of Drama: Negotiating Art and Meaning.* London: Routledge.

O'Toole, J. and Dunn, J. (2002). *Pretending to Learn: Helping Children learn through Drama.* Frenchs Forest, NSW: Pearson Education.

Parten, M.B. (1971 [1933]) 'Social play among preschool children', in R. Herron and B. Sutton-Smith (eds) *Child's Play.* New York: John Wiley and Sons. pp. 83–95.

Piaget, J. (1962) *Play, Dreams and Imitation in Childhood.* New York: Norton.

Rogers, S. and Evans, J. (2007) 'Rethinking role play in the reception class', *Educational Research* 49 (2): 153–67.

Roskos, K. and Christie, J. (2001) 'Examining the play–literacy interface: a critical review and future directions', *Journal of Early Childhood Literacy* 1 (1): 59–89.

Sawyer, K. (1997) *Pretend Play as Improvisation: Conversation in the Preschool Classroom.* New York: Lawrence Erlbaum Associates.

Sutton-Smith, B. (1985) *The Denial of Play.* Paper presented at the 'Hot Housing of Children' symposium (Philadelphia, PA, 25–26 October). ERIC Document ED 275 397.

Vygotsky, L.S. (1976 [1933]) 'Play and its role in the mental development of the child', in J.S. Bruner, A. Jolly and K. Sylva (eds) *Play: Its Role in Development and Evolution.* Middlesex: Penguin. pp. 537–54.

Weddell, C. (2003) 'The child as audience', in S. Wright (ed.) *Children, Meaning Making and the Arts.* Frenchs Forest, NSW: Pearson Education. pp. 135–59.

Wild, M. (1989) *There's a Sea in My Bedroom.* Sydney: Puffin.

10

ICT and literacy

Tim Waller

Introduction

This chapter critically reviews recent international literature and research concerning early literacy and ICT. Over the past few years significant developments in digital technology have changed the nature of print-based literacy and led to the recognition of multiple literacies. Emerging literacy practices are being fostered though the use of small handheld devices, moving communication from the page to the screen and requiring a redefinition of the literacy curriculum. There is also a growing appreciation of the impact of digital technology on childhood, children's lives and children's communicative practices. The impact of ICT on a range of communicative literacy practices in children's lives at home and in early years settings and schools is considered in this chapter. However, many children still do not have access to modern technology, and the chapter also acknowledges the range of digital divides and the implications for children who are excluded from modern communicative practices. The chapter also discusses possibilities for developing and documenting children's narratives through digital technology and what teachers can learn from children's literacy play experiences with new digital technology.

Recent international literature and research concerning early literacy and ICT

As soon as they are born, many children across the world are immersed in a way of life where digital technology is used for a range of complex social and literacy practices. These practices, which are constantly changing, include using a range of handheld devices such as mobile phones, multimedia players (iPods) and games consoles, playing interactive games on digital and satellite television, and accessing the internet to communicate images and text, hold telephone conversations and play games with participants across the world. Currently, social network websites (shared databases of photographs which facilitate group discussion) and blogging (contributing to online web diaries) are very popular, but as the technology develops new and different communicative possibilities and practices will evolve. For many people, therefore, paper-based literacy is no longer the preferred mode of communication and the dominance of writing through the medium of the book has been replaced by the dominance of the image through the medium of the screen (Kress, 2003). Jewitt and Kress (2003) have argued that there has been a perceptible shift from the traditional logic of the page to the much more visual logic of the screen and, that as a result, writing has become subordinated to image. For Snyder (2003) these developments represent a new 'communication order'.

Larson and Marsh (2005) contend that recent changes in literacy practices precipitated by developments in technology have been so profound that they have challenged our understanding of the very nature of literacy itself. Consequently, as Marsh (2004), for example, has argued, the plural form 'literacies' has become widely adopted to acknowledge the range of literacy and communicative practices developed through computers, television and mobile phones. Currently, learning to be literate involves developing an understanding of and familiarity with electronic literacies; this is a necessary accomplishment for both children and adults (Waller, 2006a). Larson and Marsh (2005) outline a number of phrases now in common use which demonstrate the way in which lettered representation is being transformed and shaped by digitised technologies. They discuss how phrases such as 'digital literacy' (Glister, 1997), 'new literacies' (Lankshear and Knobel, 2003), 'media literacy' (Buckingham, 2003) and 'moving image literacy' (Burn and Leach, 2004), 'all have currency and appear to address similar issues, namely the ability to decode, encode and make meaning using a range of modes of communication including print, still and moving image, sound and gesture, all mediated by new technologies' (Larson and Marsh, 2005: 69).

An enduring dilemma is that changes in technology are always ahead of the published research and literature and that detailed knowledge of new literacy practices that have evolved through digital technology is rather limited, especially with young children. Further, most studies of emergent literacy still focus on print-based literacy which can lead to an (over-) emphasis on the formal skills of reading and writing print (Waller, 2006a). For example, Lankshear and Knobel (2003) conducted an extensive review of international research concerning new technology and early childhood literacy. They found a very limited number of articles concerning new technology and literacy, and almost none concerning early literacy. In addition, Lankshear and Knobel established that the overwhelming emphasis was on how technology was used to support traditional alphabetic and print-based literacy and that, in general, literacy was treated in a non-dynamic manner. Also, there is little research on new technology and literacies out of school. Marsh (2005) argues that the emergent digital literacies of young children should be more widely acknowledged. These include the narratives influenced and developed by film, television, computer games and on mobile phones.

There is also a need to comprehend the accelerating technological change in our daily educational and working lives, and how this impacts on teaching and learning in the classroom. Luke (1999) challenges us to examine the way in which young children are navigating the worlds of technologically mediated childhoods. Waller too has argued that:

> as we move from 'e-learning' (electronic learning) to 'm-learning' (mobile learning), using small multi-function devices and out of the computer suite and into the classroom (not before time), one important question is how these initiatives combine so that the potential of ICT is fully utilised to support young children's emerging literacy. (2006a: 38)

As Luke and Luke (2001) point out, many teachers continue to feel unsure about rapid technological change and feel concerned that they are not able to provide a curriculum appropriate for a digital generation.

A large scale *Digital Rhetorics* project (Lankshear et al., 1997; Lankshear and Snyder, 2000) investigated the relationship between digital technology and literacy education in Australia over two years and developed a 'three-dimensional' theoretical approach to literacy and technology. The study argues that in the context of increasing and changing demands for literacy and technology learning worldwide, education must enable students to become proficient in the 'operational', 'cultural' and 'critical' dimensions of literacy and technology (originally developed by Green, 1988). The 'operational' dimension of literacy education, as it involves new technologies, focuses on how to operate the language system (making sense of print) as well as on how to operate the technology system. Understanding and being able to draw upon the 'cultural' dimension of literacy involves awareness of style, audiences and purposes, and the realisation that the ability to operate language and technology systems is always in the service of participating in 'authentic' forms of social practice and meaning. The 'critical' dimension means that teachers and students need to be able to assess and critically evaluate software and other technology resources (Lankshear and Snyder, 2000). The critical dimension is highly significant, as Snyder points out:

> the ability not only to use such resources and to participate effectively and creatively in their associated cultures, but also to critique them, to read and use them against the grain, to appropriate and even re-design them. (Synder, 2003: 270)

Despite a number of concerns about the limitations of published research focussing on digital technologies and literacy practices, two factors are evident from recent studies. Firstly, it is clear that many young children develop significant competence with technology at home well before they attend an early years setting or school (Marsh et al., 2005). Secondly, children's participation in the use of digital technology helps to transform the literacy. Gregory et al. (2004) demonstrate the capacity of young children across cultures to draw from home, community and school contexts to make sense of literacy. They develop a model of 'syncretic literacy' to acknowledge what children take culturally and linguistically from their families, and how they gain access to existing funds of knowledge in their communities as well as how they transform existing literacy practices to create new forms. Here, important recognition is given to the possibility that children are not passive recipients of existing literacy practices but active agents in developing new practices through their participation and shared use of digital technology in multiple communities. As Kenner (2003) has argued, children do not remain in separate worlds but acquire membership of different groups simultaneously – they live in simultaneous worlds.

For Gregory et al. (2004) simultaneous membership means that children syncretise the literacies, narrative styles, discourse, communicative practices and social activities, etc. appropriate to each group and go on to transform languages and cultures they use to create new forms relevant to the purpose needed. For example, Helavarra Robertson (2004) showed how a six-year-old Pahari and English speaking boy of Pakistani heritage in England used the participation structures and learning approaches of both his English and Quranic (Arabic) schools in learning how to read and speak Urdu in his fourth language Urdu class. As Lankshear and Snyder (2000) acknowledge, being literate involves the capability to actively create, shape and *transform* social practices and meanings. The model of syncretic literacy advocated by Gregory et al. (2004) can help us to understand how recent technological developments have led to significant changes in the ways in which we communicate and impact upon literacy as a social practice (Knobel and Lankshear, 2007). In particular, the significance of this model of syncretic literacy is that it gives recognition to the role of children in the transformation of literacy practices.

The impact of digital technology on childhood, children's lives and children's communicative practices

Firstly, it must be acknowledged that many children still do not have access to modern technology, both within the UK and across the world. As Waller (2007a) argues, there is not one, but multiple digital divides caused and reinforced by global capital's control of new technologies. There are clear divisions based on class, race, gender, age and geography. For example, in a current world population of six billion, less than one billion people have regular access to computers. In wealthy countries there are 563 computers per 1000 people but in less wealthy countries only 25 per 1000 people (Social Watch, 2006). Castells has argued that 'exclusion from these networks is one of the most damaging forms of exclusion in our economy and in our society' (2001: 3). In the UK there is evidence of a class-, race- and gender-based access and use of ICT, both at home and at school. National Statistics (2006) show that an estimated 13.9 million households (57 per cent) in Great Britain could access the internet from home between January and April 2006. According to Owen (2003), minority ethnic people living in deprived areas have less access to home computers than their white neighbours. However, minority ethnic families with a PC were more likely to use it for work and education. Only 36 per cent of children in single-parent households had internet access – with almost double that number able to surf the net in two-parent homes (the Office for National Statistics, 2002).

As children from affluent socio-economic backgrounds usually have greater access to new technologies it becomes vital that schools equip children, at all levels, with the appropriate experiences and competences in the use of digital technologies (Waller, 2006a). A further important point, as Marsh (2007) and Facer et al. (2003) note, is that patterns of technology *use* are different from patterns of *access*. Some children have access to a range of digital technology at home but either choose not to use it, or it is used solely by the adults in the house. There is therefore a strong argument that the role of the teacher changes as a result of the introduction of new technologies into the classroom. This new role includes providing opportunities and contexts to exploit the potential of children's experience of electronic literacies in the wider community. Teachers need to know their children's capabilities and interests, to understand how to organise their classroom and to structure the teaching of their children so that ICT resources become an integral part of the learning (Waller, 2006a).

Further, although there are concerns about children who are excluded from modern communicative practices, there is a growing recognition of the impact of ICT on many children's lives. For example, the United States (Gee, 2003; Labbo and Reinking, 2003), Australia (Knobel and Lankshear, 2007; Lankshear and Knobel, 2003; Lankshear and Snyder, 2000; Luke and Luke, 2001; Yelland, 2006) and the United Kingdom (Facer et al., 2003; Marsh, 2005, 2007; Marsh et al. 2005) put forward the view that electronic media has a significant influence on childhood and suggested that children's early literacy and play experiences are shaped increasingly by electronic media.

Marsh (2007) contends that young children are just as engaged in current digital communicative and social practices as the older members of their families and communities. She compares the findings of the *Digital Beginnings* survey in England (Marsh et al., 2005) with the *Zero to Six: Electronic Media in the Lives of Infants, Toddlers and Preschoolers* report from the US (Rideout et al., 2003). Much of the data gathered in the two studies demonstrates a correlation between the digital experiences of young children in England and the US. The data indicated that children in the studies had access to a wide range of media and technologies and were generally 'immersed in media-rich homes' (Marsh, 2007). Findings from the study in England (Marsh et al. 2005) identified 126 minutes as the mean time for children to be engaged in screen activity (including watching television, watching videos/DVDs, using computers, playing console games and playing handheld games, such as *Gameboy*). Also, parents reported that their children were independent users of computers and that the children participated in a wide range of activities on computers, including sending emails, using internet chatrooms (both with adults as scribes), playing internet games, writing stories and making cards (Marsh, 2007).

Digital Beginnings (Marsh et al., 2005) reported almost universal family ownership of at least one mobile phone. It appears that children often prefer text to talking and that teenagers are particularly dependent on their mobile phone as a tool for social interaction (Timms, 2006). However, while independent use of mobile phones by young children in the *Digital Beginnings* study was reported by parents as minimal (1 per cent), Marsh (2007) gives examples to show that mobile phone use was firmly part of some families' communication practices with their young children. Marsh suggests that:

> a clear theme to emerge from the data was that children were saturated in the discourses and iconography of media narratives. These permeated children's everyday experiences, they were woven into the fabric of their daily lives. (2007: 13)

As Carrington (2005) has shown, children are learning to engage in culturally valued textual practices.

The potential of computer games to support learning has been a contentious issue in the media in the UK, but has been recently recognised within the literature (Yelland, 2002; Knobel, 2006). Verenikina, et al. (2003) argue that for many children computer games are a significant part of their daily experiences and that early years practitioners need to understand how the games impact on the children's lives. A study by Livingstone and Bovill (1999) showed that for children aged 6–17 playing computer games is a favourite leisure activity outside school. Carrington (2005: 19) argues that 'computer games are the prime popular culture multimodal text for children young and old. Mastery with, and knowledge of, these texts are highly valued commodities in peer cultures'. A number of other recent studies also emphasise the significance of this activity for children and the range of different and complex competences involved. For example, the TEEM Project (McFarlane et al., 2002) found that whilst the majority of children surveyed played games at home, usually in their bedrooms, they were more likely to play with one or more friends. Approximately 25 per cent stated that they played for over two hours at a time and half those surveyed reported that they played games on the internet. Facer et al. (2003) highlight the social aspects of playing computer games and Whitebread (2006) discusses the contribution that computer games can make to children's thinking. Also, Bolstad (2004) has developed a useful table for assessing the contribution of computer games to children's play.

As Carrington asserts, 'deeply entrenched in popular culture, computer games are increasingly complex interactional texts which have much to tell us about the literate practices and identities of the children entering our classrooms' (2005: 18). Carrington argues that there are many implications for literacy in this engagement:

> Many of these texts have quite distinctive features – non-linear narrative structure, quite distinctive spatial layouts, ongoing and cumulative challenge levels, multiple and interactive cueing systems. As a result quite different approaches to text and reading are encouraged and rewarded. Different literate habitus are developed via these readings. (Carrington, 2005: 18)

Prensky (2001) has argued that the use of computer games produces a specific games literacy that involves changes in skills and educational processes from more traditional forms of ICT. Further, he maintains that computer games afford specific attributes which can lead to increased motivation for learners and that this aspect has been ignored by educators (Prensky, 2003). Gee (2003) also argues for the recognition of the unique educational environment of computer gaming. Further, Gee (2005) emphasises the theme of empowerment through gaming. He discusses 13 effective learning principles evident in 'good' video games in relation to 'empowered learners', 'problem solving' and 'understanding'. He suggests that these principles are inherent in the design of computer games, and that they could promote critical thinking and be usefully embedded within educational programmes. Thomas (2005) investigated the practices of a virtual community of children participating in an online role-playing game space based on the Tolkien world of Middle Earth. Thomas draws on Wenger (1998) to argue that the participants of this particular virtual community are learning through their participation in the discursive and social practices of the community.

The digital and communicative practices in which many young children have become embedded, as shown in the studies above, clearly involve and afford a number of literacy and social competences. Lankshear and Knobel (2004b) use the phrase 'digitally at home' to describe a generation comfortable with and competent in the use of new technologies. They have identified four roles which they suggest characterise the practices people engage in as they learn to produce, distribute and exchange texts in a new media age:

1   A 'designer of texts': the concept of design (as opposed to author) is important in the production of multimodal texts – recognises the range of resources drawn upon in creation of digital texts.
2   A 'text mediator or broker': mediates texts between author and reader – for example, people who manage discussion boards.
3   A 'text bricoleur': emphasing the inventiveness involved in drawing on whatever is at hand to create texts.
4   A 'text jammer': describes the process of changing or adapting texts in order to subvert messages given – Larson and Marsh describe this as online critical literacy (2005: 72).
    (Lankshear and Knobel, 2004b; as discussed in Larson and Marsh, 2005: 71)

For Lankshear and Knobel (2004a and b) the development of these roles represents a challenge to conventional literacy practices in the classroom. As digital literacies become established outside the classroom and more and more children become 'digitally at home' it is also important that teachers learn about the effect of their influence on children's learning. Yelland (1999; 2006), for example, has raised the significant issue of the need to consider the nature of the impact of digital technology on childhood and take account of the child's perspective of electronic media. Yelland (1999) points out that developments in technology have moved with extreme speed over the past few years and argues that there is a need to consider new definitions of what it means to play with both physical objects and digital ones. She contends that traditional activities can now be complemented with different experiences that have been made possible with the new information and communications technologies. For Yelland, these technologies, and the activities that children may engage in with them, have the potential to extend learning in new and exciting ways. Yelland (1999) considers the impact of the new information technologies on play and *as* play. She suggests that ICT has the potential not only to enhance learning, but also to promote engagement with ideas in new and dynamic ways as in the example of the availability of digital toys which enable the child to engage in fantasy contexts, as well as to create interactions which have personal significance.

Luke (1999; 2000) and Yelland (1999; 2006), therefore, present an argument that the use of digital play opportunities can strengthen everyday literacy teaching and learning in early childhood classrooms. However, as Dombey (1998; 1999), Roskos and Hanbali (2000) and Roskos and Christie (2007) point out, there is a concern amongst early childhood educators that the important role of play in the process of learning to read and write might be misunderstood, if not overlooked altogether. They argue that the current reality of early literacy practice is that it involves intensely instructive activities that are seen as best led by adults who impart essential literacy knowledge and skills that children must learn.

Waller (2006a) maintains that long-established play and literacy activities in early years classrooms can now be complemented with different experiences that have been made possible with the new digital technologies. These technologies, and the activities that children may engage in with them, have the potential to extend learning in new and exciting ways and strengthen everyday literacy teaching and learning in early childhood classrooms. In this context, learning is not only fun but children actively construct their own meaning and make sense of the world in their own ways. It is a direct contrast to much of the current literacy practice, where the learner is often passive and the teacher acts as the conductor of content and actions. If the potential of ICT is not exploited in this way it seems that there is a possibility of a mismatch between the learning process of children and teaching methods (Yelland, 1999). Knobel and Lankshear (2003) also draw our attention to a possible mismatch between children's early digital experiences at home and in their community and those provided by the school. They argue that for many children activities offered in school appear unexceptional by comparison, and this can lead to disaffection and disengagement.

There is therefore a number of implications for early years teachers: firstly, maintaining an appropriate literacy curriculum that includes suitable opportunities for play, and, secondly, including activities that allow children to draw on their experiences of digital technology in their play (Waller, 2006a). In terms of the school curriculum and digital literacies, there are two possible developments: schools can support and promote the digital literacies emerging from communicative and social practices out of school; or digital literacies can develop independently in the community irrespective of any school involvement. Kerin has argued that, 'the new digital world is a place that educators must begin to engage with and explore more thoroughly and seriously so that they are fully able to appreciate its educational potential' (2005: 176).

This dichotomy is also apparent at policy level, within the literacy curriculum in England. Larson and Marsh (2005) discuss Burnett et al.'s

(2004) contrasting conceptions of the curriculum and pedagogical change within the UK in relation to new media education: the 'blue-sky' thinking of the government's e-learning strategy (with a vision of schools and learning transformed by technology), as opposed to the Primary National Strategy enrichment view (where technology is added to support existing practice – for example, Smart Boards are used to replace blackboards).

There are now numerous publications illustrating how technology can be used to enrich the traditional literacy curriculum, but relatively few concerning transformation. A number of examples of transformative literacy practice is now discussed.

Van Scoter and Boss (2002) describe an early years setting in Oregon where teachers often send home digital photos of children's activities and out-of-school visits. Working with children to put captions on these photos offers an opportunity to develop children's written language skills as children use their own words to describe what the photos show. This strategy is considered a particularly useful one to support children's oral language development in their native language. Shepherd (2002) reports on a project in Scotland involving the creation of software to support the transition from home to nursery, particularly for children whose first language is not English. A digital camera was used to take photographs of children following nursery routines. Clicker software was used to present these, together with spoken commentary in English and other relevant languages. Bolstad (2004) discusses a number of examples of ICT used to support early literacy in both English and Maori in New Zealand. Several early childhood centres have used ICT to produce multimedia learning stories co-authored between children, educators and, sometimes, parents (for example, Lee et al., 2002; Wilson et al., 2003). Also, Ferguson and Mellow (2004) describe a resource, available online and as a CD-ROM, which they developed to support young children's development of Maori.

Nixon and Comber (2005) provide a very interesting account of film-making in two South Australian primary classrooms. Here, children and teachers were engaged in the co-construction of movies that involved scripting and producing narrative films. As Nixon and Comber argue, the film scripts not only arose from children's daily lives, but were also inserted back into them. Crucially, there was also an authentic purpose for the film-making closely related to the children's lives. As Nixon and Comber point out, 'The films were deliberately positioned in the public arena where they can be experienced and responded to by a range of audiences' (2005: 229). Also, the teachers assisted the children in engaging in the full range of cultural practices associated with film-making, such as world premieres, film-screenings, film clubs and libraries of children's films, and entry into film festivals, and so on. In addition, Marsh (2006) gives an overview of a project in which aspects of moving image education were introduced into the curriculum of a nursery (with children aged three and four years). Marsh argues that this evidence indicates that very young children are able to develop digital, animated films if they are given appropriate resources and support.

Merchant (2005a) discusses how early years practitioners should respond to the emergence of the new (on-screen) writing. He argues that new writing tools, including portable handheld devices such as palmtops, 'change the physical actions necessary for text production' (2005a: 185). Interestingly, Merchant provides a table updating Clay's (1975) 'Principles of Writing' to include on-screen writing, making a very useful comparison of writing on screen and on paper. Merchant (2005b) also reported an on-screen writing project in England where children collaborated with researchers who wrote in role as web journalists. Merchant showed how children's awareness of the different characteristics of digital texts shaped their on-screen writing, and he argued that most of the children involved in the project were well able to draw on experiences of electronic literacy gained outside the classroom to inform their online publications.

Larson and Marsh (2005) provide a case study of a primary class in which traditional models of literacy practice have been extended. Here, they argue that the literacy curriculum is developed from the skills and competences children bring to school, including the regular use of mobile phones and email. Examples of innovative practice include regular documentation and publication of children's literacy through an electronic whiteboard, which is also used for whole class composition and review. In addition, children are organised in pairs and ICT is used to facilitate peer review, critical reflection and response to peer comments.

The above examples demonstrate that many children are already participating in a range of digital literacies outside school and that new technology has significant potential to support young learners in educational settings. The next section explores how digital literacies can be fostered and facilitated in early childhood settings.

Documenting children's narratives through digital technology

An example of transformative practice with digital technology is discussed briefly below in relation to an outdoor learning project (see

Waller, 2006b; 2007b). The project is ongoing and involves children aged three to seven in two different settings: a nursery school in England (Setting 1) and a primary school in Wales (Setting 2). The children are given regular access to extensive wild outdoor environments (such as woodland, riversides, mountains and beaches) and are afforded the opportunity to explore and play in the environment with minimal adult direction and intervention. The design of the project draws on the framework for listening to young children – the multi-method 'Mosaic approach' described by Clark and Moss (2001; 2005). The method uses both the traditional tools of observing children at play and a variety of 'participatory tools' with children. These include taking photographs, creating books, tours of the outdoor area and map-making. 'The Mosaic approach enables children to create a living picture of their lives' (Clark and Moss, 2005: 13). Also, part of the Mosaic approach is to involve adults in gathering information in addition to perspectives from the children.

The outdoor learning project adapted the Mosaic approach into a two-stage model. Stage one involves children and adults in using tools to gather and document perspectives. Firstly, data collection starts with children using digital photographs and film to record their perspectives, which then become a starting point for discussion with an adult. The discussion is then recorded as a 'learning story' (Carr, 2001). Learning stories are structured narrative documentation based on critical incidents of children's learning, including the child's own comments (Carr, 2001: 96). The child and a practitioner discuss a child's drawing, painting or photograph (that is a representation of the child's interest, play or activity). The discussion is then recorded by the practitioner and published alongside the image. In stage two the information gathered is reviewed and reflected on for action (Clark and Moss, 2005). Publication and presentation of the learning stories are enhanced through display on a whiteboard which extends opportunities for individual and group review. Also, digital images and learning stories are regularly taken home by children to share with their families. The learning story is then used to inform planning and act as a record of learning by the practitioners (Waller, 2006b; 2007b).

In the outdoor settings, once familiar with the outdoor environment, all children were given opportunities to record image-based data, revealing an interesting range of both 'social spaces' and 'individual landmarks' (Clark and Moss, 2001; 2005). As the visits increased children re-visited and named familiar places, evolving a range of shared narratives around the spaces. These shared narratives included 'The Octopus Tree', 'Eeyore's Den', the woods, 'The Top of the World', 'The Giant's Bed' (of leaves), 'The Goblin's House' and 'Dragonfly Land' (Setting 1) and 'Morgan's Mountain', 'The Crocodile Tree', 'The Giant's Den', 'The Trampoline Tree' and 'The Troll Bridge' (Setting 2).

One example of the development of a shared narrative is given below to illustrate the role and process of transformative technology. The following extract is taken from field notes over a number of visits to a riverside woodland:

> As a group of children and adults walked along the path, in through the riverside woodland on first visit, they came to a fallen tree which had blocked the path. The first adult walked around the tree and started a discussion with other adults as to how the tree had fallen. The children stopped to play on the tree. They found that the lower branches were ideal to bounce on whilst holding onto a higher branch. Rosalynn named this 'The Trampoline Tree'. Thereafter, the children stopped regularly to bounce on the tree and, as their confidence grew, climb higher up the tree. In some visits a number of children spent most of their time on these activities. All the children identified the tree on their maps of the riverside woodland.

This narrative was developed back at school through the publication of pedagogical documentation over the following week. The initial review of the images of 'The Trampoline Tree' on the whiteboard, by children and a practitioner, involved discussion about bouncing on the branches which led to some children discussing the possibility of the experience being like riding on a horse. Subsequently, a number of children drew pictures of themselves on the tree 'riding a horse', several of these were published as a learning story and the children incorporated this into their play regularly in future visits. It is interesting to note that adult discourse was around the cause of the tree falling and being burnt (a lightning strike) and the dangerous nature of the branches sticking out at head height. Children's discourse, however, was around climbing high up the tree, hanging on, sliding and jumping down. They saw the play potential (Hakkarainen, 2006); adults were more concerned about safety.

As Waller (2006b) discusses, the publication of pedagogical documentation enabled all those involved in the project (children and adults) to suggest developments and alternatives in the shared narratives. A crucial factor in the construction of these narratives is the reification of shared knowledge. Cowie and Carr (2004) draw on Wenger (1998) who describes this process of documentation as an example of 'reification' – informal practice that has been concretised or reified (making public, making concrete). Not only are children's ideas reified and legitimated through the co-construction of meaning but, as Cowie and Carr (2004) point out, in a learning community in which they fully participate children behave and act in competent ways. The role of the digital technology, controlled and used by the children, would appear to be significant in the reification of shared knowledge.

The purpose of documenting children's experiences in this manner was to make children's views, research and pedagogical practice visible and subject to discussion and reflection by practitioners, parents, children and other interested parties. This method is consistent with the principles of the well-known Reggio Emilia approach to pedagogical documentation where learning processes are documented in various ways so that they can be shared, discussed, reflected upon and interpreted (Dahlberg et al., 1999). As Hoyuelos suggests, this documentation represents an extraordinary tool for dialogue, exchange and sharing (2004). Also, Rinaldi and Moss argue that it is 'a unique source of information – precious for teachers, children, the family and anyone who wants to get closer to the strategies in children's ways of thinking' (2004: 3).

This model demonstrates, firstly, that young children's views about their environment and experiences within that environment are crucial insights and, secondly, that children can be involved in reporting, discussing and documenting these insights through digital technology. The project found, like Clark, 2004 and Burke, 2005, that the process of using participatory tools increased our understanding of the children's lives.

Conclusion

This chapter has presented a critical overview of recent international literature and research concerning early literacy and ICT. It has discussed the significance of developments in digital technology and emerging literacy practices over the past few years that have led to the recognition of multiple literacies and required a reconsideration of the traditional notions of literacy (Larson and Marsh, 2005). Whilst the chapter acknowledges the range of digital divides and the implications for children who are excluded from modern of communicative practices, the impact of ICT on a range of communicative literacy practices in children's lives at home and in early years settings and schools is considered.

The challenge is for early years practitioners to do more with digital technology than use it to enrich or bolt on to traditional literacy practices (Knobel and Lankshear, 2007; Marsh, 2007). As Siraj-Blatchford and Siraj-Blatchford (2006) point out, young children entering early years settings and schools today will be adults in 15 years' time and, given the rapid nature of technological change, by that time literacies and cultural practices will be very different from those of today. As a result Thomas (2005) argues that professional development in digital and cyberliteracies for teachers is essential. Here, the principles developed by Larson and Marsh (2005), discussed earlier in the chapter, are important for practitioners wishing to develop a transformative curriculum. Useful lessons can also be learned from Gregory et al. (2004) and studies adapting a model of syncretic literacy. They point out that, 'many teachers realised that building on children's home literacy experiences was much more difficult than they had originally believed and they could not simply assume that children shared their own literacy lives' (Gregory et al. 2004: 3). Feiler argues, 'where there is flexible, negotiated collaboration between school staff and families, it is possible for home-based practice to influence the school literacy curriculum' (2005: 146). An example is given by Pahl and Roswell who assert that teachers must:

> redefine the way we see and interact with texts and build bridges between the student's home and school in every way. As far as possible, teachers should:
>
> - find out about the literacy practices of their children
> - share them in a community of practice with the class
> - build on these practices in classroom settings. (Pahl and Roswell, 2005: 70)

If practitioners are to develop a *transformative* pedagogy (Larson and Marsh, 2005) then they will need to build on children's digital and online experiences, and involve the children as experts. This process will be enhanced by a consideration of all three dimensions of literacy and technology – operational, understanding and critical (Lankshear and Snyder, 2000). A particularly significant aspect concerns issues around the commercial context of much of the digital technology promoted in homes and schools. Bigum (2000) and Buckingham (2005), for example, argue for critical engagement on the part of both children and teachers in their use of online activities. As Buckingham stated, 'the internet is now an essentially unregulated and commercial medium, a medium for selling; and while this does not mean that it can no longer be of value, it does mean that it can no longer be seen as a neutral conduit for information' (2005: 7).

It is therefore vital that both teachers and children engage in 'critical' reflection and thinking about the impact of technology as they participate in the construction of new literacies (Vasquez, 2004). Also, children and practitioners need to be enabled to be involved in more collaborative processes of hardware and software design (Cooke and Woollard, 2006).

Recent literature and research in the field of literacy education has a firm message about practice in schools. If practitioners are to build on many young children's experiences of digital literacies (and empower those who do not have these experiences), and involve children as experts in aspects of a new literacy curriculum, then a transforming pedagogy is necessary (Knobel and Lankshear, 2007; Larson and Marsh, 2005). However, there is also a clear need for much further critical reflection, discussion and articulation of possible models of classroom practice, particularly in relation to early childhood (Lee and O'Rourke, 2006; Merchant, 2005b). Whilst much attention at policy level is given to the technology, it is children, teachers and parents who hold the key to supporting and promoting the digital literacies emerging from contemporary communicative and social practices.

Suggestions for further reading 📖

Hayes, M. and Whitebread, D. (eds) (2006) *ICT in the Early Years of Education*. Milton Keynes: Open University Press.

Marsh, J. (ed.) (2005) *Popular Culture, New Media and Digital Technology in Early Childhood*. London: RoutledgeFalmer.

References

Bigum, C. (2000) 'Managing new relationships: design sensibilities, the new information and communication technologies and schools'. Paper given to the APAPDC Online Conference. Available online at http://www.beecoswebengine.org/servlet/Web?s=157573&p=Con2000_wk4_cbigum (accessed 22 August 2007).

Bolstad, R. (2004) *The Role and Potential of ICT in Early Childhood Education*. New Zealand: Ministry of Education.

Buckingham, D. (2003) *Media Education: Literacy, Learning and Contemporary Culture*. Oxford: Polity Press.

Buckingham, D. (2005) *Schooling and the Digital Generation: Popular Culture, New Media and the Future of Education*. London: Institute of Education.

Burke, C. (2005) 'Play in focus: children researching their own spaces and places for play', *Children, Youth and Environments* 15 (1): 27–53. Available online at http://www.colorado.edu/journals/cye (accessed 7 July 2005).

Burn, A. and Leach, J. (2004) 'ICTs and moving image literacy in English', in R. Andrews (ed.) *The Impact of ICTs on English 5–16*. London: RoutledgeFalmer.

Burnett, C., Dickinson, P., Malden, H., Merchant, G. and Myers, J. (2004) 'Digital connections: purposeful uses of email in the primary school'. Paper presented at the United Kingdom Literacy Association (UKLA) Annual Conference, Manchester.

Carr, M. (2001) *Assessment in Early Childhood Settings*. London: Paul Chapman.

Carrington, V. (2005) 'New textual landscapes, information and early literacy', in J. Marsh (ed.) *Popular Culture, New Media and Digital Literacy in Early Childhood*. London: RoutledgeFalmer. pp. 13–27.

Castells, M. (2001) *The Internet Galaxy: Reflections on the Internet, Business, and Society*. Oxford: Oxford University Press.

Clark, A. (2004) 'The Mosaic approach and research with young children', in V. Lewis, M. Kellet, C. Robinson, S. Fraser and S. Ding (eds) *The Reality of Research with Young Children*. London: Sage with the Open University. pp. 142–61.

Clark, A. and Moss, P. (2001) *Listening to Young Children: The Mosaic Approach*. London: National Children's Bureau.

Clark, A. and Moss, P. (2005) *Spaces to Play: More Listening to Young Children Using the Mosaic Approach*. London: National Children's Bureau.

Clay, M. (1975) *What Did I Write?* London: Heinemann.

Cooke, J. and Woollard, J. (2006) 'Visual literacy and painting with technology: observations in the early years classroom', in M. Hayes and D. Whitebread (eds) *ICT in the Early Years*. Maidenhead: Open University Press. pp. 107–203.

Cowie, B. and Carr, M. (2004) 'The consequences of socio-cultural assessment', in A. Anning, J. Cullen and M. Fleer (eds) *Early Childhood Education*. London: Sage.

Dahlberg, G., Moss, P. and Pence, A. (1999) *Beyond Quality in Early Childhood Education and Care: Postmodern Perspectives*. London and New York: RoutledgeFalmer.

Dombey, H. (1998) 'A totalitarian approach to literacy education?', *Forum* 20 (2): 36–41.

Dombey, H. (1999) 'Picking a path through the phonics minefield', *Education 3–13* 27 (1): 12–21.

Facer, K., Furlong, J., Furlong, R. and Sutherland, R. (2003) *Screen Play: Children and Computing in the Home*. London: RoutledgeFalmer.

Feiler, A. (2005) 'Linking home and school literacy in an inner city reception class', *Journal of Early Childhood Literacy* 5: 131–49.

Ferguson, S. and Mellow, P. (2004) 'Whakahihiko te Hinengaro: lessons from a preschool te reo e-learning resource', *Computers in New Zealand Schools* 16 (2): 41–4.

Gee, J.P. (2003) *What Video Games have to Teach us About Learning and Literacy*. New York: Palgrave/Macmillan.

Gee, J.P. (2005) 'Learning by design: good video games as learning machines', *E-Learning* 2 (1): 5–16.

Glister, P. (1997) *Digital Literacy*. New York: John Wiley and Sons.

Green, B. (1988) 'Subject-specific literacy and school learning: a focus on writing, *Australian Journal of Education* 32 (2): 156–79.

Gregory, E., Long, S. and Volk, D. (eds) (2004) *Many Pathways to Literacy*. Abingdon: RoutledgeFalmer.

Hakkarainen, P. (2006) 'Learning and development in play', in J. Einarsdottir and J. Wagner (eds) *Nordic Childhoods and Early Education*. Connecticut: Information Age Publishing. pp. 183–222.

Helavarra Robertson, L. (2004) 'Multilingual flexibility and literacy in an Urdu community school', in E. Gregory, S. Long and D.Volk (eds) *Many Pathways to Literacy*. Abingdon: RoutledgeFalmer. pp. 171–81.

Hoyuelos, A. (2004) 'A pedagogy of transgression', *Children in Europe* (March) 6: 6–7.

Jewitt, C. and Kress, G. (2003) *Multimodal Literacy*. New York: Peter Lang.

Kenner, C. (2003) 'Embodied knowledges: young children's engagement with the act of writing', in G. Kress and C. Jewitt (eds) *Explorations of Learning in a Multimodal Environment*. New York: Peter Lang.

Kerin, R. (2005) 'The review essay', *Journal of Early Childhood Literacy* 5 (2): 175–84.

Knobel, M. (2006) 'Technokids, Koala Trouble and *Pokémon*: literacy, new technologies and popular culture in children's everyday lives', in J. Marsh and E. Millard (eds) *Popular Literacies, Childhood and Schooling*. London: Routledge Falmer. pp. 11–28.

Knobel, M. and Lankshear, C. (2003) 'The out-of-school literacy practices of children', in N. Hall, J. Larson and J. Marsh (eds) *Handbook of Early Childhood Literacy*. London: Sage. pp. 51–65.

Knobel, M. and Lankshear, C. (eds) (2007) *New Literacies Sampler*. New York: Peter Lang.

Kress, G. (2003) *Literacy in the New Media Age*. London: Routledge.

Labbo, L. and Reinking, D. (2003) 'Computers and early literacy instruction', in N. Hall, J. Larson and J. Marsh (eds) *Handbook of Early Childhood Literacy*. London: Sage. pp. 338–54.

Lankshear, C., Bigum, C., Durrant, C., Green, B., Honan, E., Morgan, W., Murray, J., Snyder, I. and Wild, M. (1997) *Digital Rhetorics: Literacies and Technologies in Education – Current Practices and Future Directions*. Canberra: Department of Employment, Education,Training and Youth Affairs.

Lankshear, C. and Knobel, M. (2003) 'New technologies in early childhood literacy research: a review of research', *Journal of Early Childhood Literacy* 3 (1): 59–82.

Lankshear, C. and Knobel, M. (2004a) 'Planning pedagogy for i-mode: some principles for pedagogical decision making'. Paper presented at the Annual Meeting of the American Education Research Association, San Diego, CA, April.

Lankshear, C. and Knobel, M. (2004b) 'Planning pedagogy for i-mode: from flogging to blogging via wi-fi', published jointly in, *English in Australia*, 139 (February) and *Literacy in the Middle Years*, 12 (1): 78–102.

Lankshear, C. and Snyder, I. with Green, B. (2000) *Teachers and Technoliteracy: Managing Literacy, Technology and Learning in Schools*. St Leonards, Sydney: Allen and Unwin.

Larson, J. and Marsh, J. (2005) *Making Literacy Real*. London: Sage.

Lee, W., Hatherly, A. and Ramsey, K. (2002) 'Using ICT to document children's learning', *Early Childhood Folio* 6: 10–16.

Lee, L. and O'Rourke, M. (2006) 'Information and communication technologies: transforming views of literacies in early childhood education', *Early Years* 26 (1): 49–62.

Livingstone, S. and Bovill, M. (1999) *Young People, New Media: Report of the Research Project: Children, Young People and the Changing Media Environment*. London: London School of Economics and Political Science.

Luke, C. (1999) 'What next? Toddler netizens, playstation thumb, techno-literacies', *Contemporary Issues in Early Childhood* 1 (1): 95–100.

Luke, C. (2000) 'Cyberschooling and technological change: multiliteracies for new times', in B. Cope and M. Kalantzis (eds) *Multiliteracies: Literacy Learning and the Design of Social Futures*. South Yarra: Macmillan. pp. 59–71.

Luke, A. and Luke, C. (2001) 'Adolescence lost/childhood regained: on early intervention and the emergence of the techno-subject', *Journal of Early Childhood Literacy* 1 (1): 91–120.

Marsh, J. (2004) 'The techno-literacy practices of young children', *Journal of Early Childhood Research* 2 (1): 51–66.

Marsh, J. (2005) 'Ritual, performance and identity construction: young children's engagement with popular and media texts', in J. Marsh (ed.) (2005) *Popular Culture, New Media and Digital Technology in Early Childhood*. London: RoutledgeFalmer. pp. 28–50.

Marsh, J. (2006) 'Digital animation in the early years: ICT and media education', in M. Hayes and D. Whitebread (eds) *ICT in the Early Years of Education*. Milton Keynes: Open University Press. pp. 122–34.

Marsh, J. (2007) 'Digital beginnings: conceptualisations of childhood'. Paper presented at the WUN Virtual Seminar, 13 February. Available online at www.wun.ac.uk/download.php?file=2488_Childrenpaper13Feb.pdf&mimetype=application/pdf (Accessed 11 August 2007).

Marsh, J., Brooks, G., Hughes, J., Ritchie, L. and Roberts, S. (2005) *Digital Beginnings: Young Children's Use of Popular Culture, Media and New Teachnologies*. Sheffield: University of Sheffied. Available online at http://www.digitalbeginnings.shef.ac.uk (accessed 15 March 2006).

McFarlane, A., Sparrowhawk, A. and Heald, Y. (2002) *Report on the Educational Use of Games*. Cambridge: TEEM.

Merchant, G. (2005a) 'Barbie meets Bob the Builder at the workstation: learning to write on screen', in J. Marsh (ed.) *Popular Culture, New Media and Digital Literacy in Early Childhood*. Abingdon: RoutledgeFalmer. pp. 183–200.

Merchant, G. (2005b) 'Digikids: cool dudes and the new writing', *E-Learning* 2 (1): 50–60.

National Statistics (2006) 'Internet access – households and individuals'. Available online at http://www.statistics.gov.uk/StatBase/Product.asp?vlnk=5672 (accessed 4 December 2006).

Nixon, H. and Comber, B. (2005) 'Behind the scenes: making movies in early years classrooms', in J. Marsh (ed.) *Popular Culture, New Media and Digital Literacy in Early Childhood*. Abingdon: RoutledgeFalmer. pp. 219–36.

Office for National Statistics (ONS) (2002) *UK 2002 Yearbook*. Available online at www.statistics.gov.uk/statbase/Product.asp?vlnk=5703&More=N - 21k (accessed 4 December 2006).

Owen, D. (2003) 'Digital divide hits black families', BBC News Online. Available online at http://news.bbc.co.uk/1/hi/education/3193512.stm (accessed 14 June 2004).

Pahl, K. and Roswell, J. (2005) *Literacy and Education: Understanding the New Literacy Studies in the classroom*. London: Paul Chapman.

Prensky, M. (2001) *Digital Game-based Learning*. New York: McGraw-Hill.

Prensky, M. (2003) 'Beyond the exam'. Presentation at NESTA Futurelab Conference, Bristol, 19 November. Available online at http://www.nestafuturelab. org/events/past/be_pres/m_prensky/mp01.htm

Rideout, V.J., Vandewater, E.A. and Wartella, E.A. (2003) *Zero to Six: Electronic Media in the Lives of Infants, Toddlers and Preschoolers*. Washington: Kaiser Foundation.

Rinaldi, C. and Moss, P. (2004) 'What is Reggio?' *Children in Europe* 6 : 2–3 (March).

Roskos, K. and Christie, J.F. (2007) *Play and Literacy in Early Childhood*. New York: RoutledgeFalmer.

Roskos, K. and Hanbali, O.M. (2000) 'Creating connections, building constructions: language, literacy, and play in early childhood'. An invited commentary, *Reading Online*. Available online at www.readingonline.org (accessed 1 August 2000).

Shepherd, K. (2002) 'A multi-lingual introduction to the nursery'. Available online at www.ltscotland.org.uk/ictineducation/innovationawards (accessed 13 January 2004).

Siraj-Blatchford, I. and Siraj-Blatchford, J. (2006) 'Towards a future for early years: ICT curriculum', in M. Hayes and D. Whitebread (eds) *ICT in the Early Years of Education*. Milton Keynes: Open University Press. pp. 152–61.

Snyder, I. (2003) 'A new communication order: researching literacy practices in the network society', in S. Goodman, T. Lillis, J. Maybin and N. Mercer (eds) *Language, Literacy and Education: A Reader*. Stoke-on-Trent: Trentham Press/ Open University Press.

Social Watch (2006) *Information, Science and Technology. Digital Gap, People Gap*. Available online at http://www.socialwatch.org/en/informeImpreso/pdfs/ informationsciencetech2006_eng.pdf (accessed 4 December 2006).

Thomas, A. (2005) 'Children online: learning in a virtual community of practice', *E-learning* 2 (1): 27–38.

Timms, D. (2006) 'UK teens are worst misusers of mobile phones', *Guardian Online*, Monday February 13. Available online at http://education.guardian. co.uk/schools/story/0,,1708992,00.html (accessed 13 March 2006).

Van Scoter, J. and Boss, S. (2002) *Learners, Language, and Technology: Making Connections that Support Literacy*. Portland, Oregon: Northwest Regional Educational Laboratory. Also available online at www.netc.org/earlyconnections/ pub/index.html (accessed 1 August 2004).

Vasquez, V. (2004) *Negotiating Critical Literacies with Young Children*. Mahwah, NJ: Lawrence Erlbaum.

Verenikina, I., Harris, P. and Lysaght, P. (2003) 'Child's play: computer games, theories of play and children's development'. Paper presented at the Young Children and Learning Technologies conference, UWS Parramatta, July.

Waller, T. (2006a) 'Early literacy and ICT', in M. Hayes and D. Whitebread (eds) *ICT in the Early Years of Education*. Milton Keynes: Open University Press.

Waller, T. (2006b) 'Be careful – don't come too close to my Octopus Tree': recording and evaluating young children's perspectives of outdoor learning', *Children Youth and Environments* 16 (2): 75–104.

Waller, T. (2007a) 'ICT and social justice: educational technology, global capital and digital divides', *Journal for Critical Education Policy Studies* 5 (1) ISSN 1740–2743.

Waller, T. (2007b) '"The Trampoline Tree and the Swamp Monster with 18 Heads": outdoor play in the Foundation Stage and Foundation Phase', *Education 3–13* 35 (4): 395–409.

Wenger, E. (1998) *Communities of Practice: Learning, Meaning and Identity.* Cambridge: Cambridge University Press.

Whitebread, D. (2006) 'Creativity, problem-solving and playful uses of technology: games and simulations in the early years' in M. Hayes and D. Whitebread (eds) *ICT in the Early Years of Education.* Milton Keynes: Open University Press. pp. 85–105.

Wilson, P., Clarke, M., Maley-Shaw, C. and Kelly, M. (2003) 'Smile, you're on digital camera! Collaboration between communities, children, and computers', *Early Education* 33: 39–46.

Yelland, N.J. (1999) 'Technology as play', *Early Childhood Education Journal* 26 (4): 217–25.

Yelland, N. (2002) 'Playing with ideas and games in early mathematics', *Contemporary Issues in Early Childhood: Technology Special Issue* 3 (2): 197–215.

Yelland, N. (2006) *Shift to the Future: Rethinking Learning with New Technologies in Education.* New York: RoutledgeFalmer.

11

Media literacy in the early years

Jackie Marsh

This chapter focuses on 'media literacy', a term which now has widespread currency as a result of the Office of Communication's (Ofcom) remit to develop media literacy amongst the general population[1]. Ofcom define media literacy as 'the ability to access, understand and create communications in a variety of contexts' (Ofcom, 2004). Many people, myself included, would argue that it is confusing to align the word 'literacy', a term relating to lettered representation, with other nouns, as this means that the use of 'literacy' simply becomes a way of signalling competence in a particular area (Kress, 2003). Rather than separating 'literacy' from 'media literacy', in this way, we need to review the traditional language and literacy curriculum altogether in order to recognise the way in which communication is changing in the twenty-first century and include media texts as a focus of study alongside other texts. Nevertheless, having stressed this as an underlying principle, there is some value in looking at media texts in some depth and examining how children's analytic and productive skills in relation to media can be developed. In the first part of this chapter, I will explore in particular how early years teachers can develop children's understanding of film texts, given the key role these texts play in children's lives. In the final part of the chapter, I move on to outline how key concepts used in media studies with older children can inform young children's engagement with media in early years settings.

---

1   See http://www.ofcom.org.uk/media/news/2004/11/nr_20041102

Media texts in the home

Engagement with a wide range of media and technologies can facilitate the development of media literacy. As research in relation to print-based emergent literacy suggests, simply by engaging in daily practices in which print plays a part, children learn much about its role, nature and purpose (Hall, Larson and Marsh, 2003). It is inevitable that the same processes should occur in relation to media literacy. Indeed, in a review of research in the field, Buckingham (2004) suggests that, 'Children develop media literacy even in the absence of explicit attempts to encourage and promote it' (2004: 2). There is growing evidence to suggest that young children are engaged in a wide range of media literacy practices at home from birth (see Chapter 10, this volume, for a review of the literature in this area). In the *Digital Beginnings* survey (Marsh, Brooks, Hughes et al., 2005), a study of the media literacy practices of children aged 0–6 in 1,852 families in England, young children were reported as engaging in a variety of activities, detailed in Table 11.1.

Moving image media were central to children's practices. Children enjoyed a range of television programmes and films and liked to replay them through the use of a DVD player. Parents reported that their children gained a wide range of skills, knowledge and understanding from their engagement with film and television, which included knowledge and understanding about the world, songs, rhymes, new vocabulary, colour, shape, letter and number recognition, and social and personal skills.

However, children are not just users of moving image media; increasingly they produce it, as the popularity of internet sites such as YouTube, which enables users of the site to upload films they have made, demonstrate. Some parents reported that children in the *Digital Beginnings* study could use the video camera feature on mobile phones and could also use digital video cameras. There are certainly products now marketed at young film-makers in the home, with plastic-cased video cameras retailing for less than £100. This 'D-I-Y media culture' (Sharp, 2006) is becoming prevalent across society, to the extent that it is now possible for Sky TV viewers to send in their home-made videos for broadcast on the satellite television channel 'Sky News', and for satellite/cable viewers to receive a channel entitled 'Bedroom TV', which broadcasts karaoke-style videos made by members of the general public and uploaded to the channel's website, featuring themselves, family and friends miming along to popular songs.

Such engagement with moving image media in the home is not universal, of course, as there are issues of access to hardware and

Table 11.1   Young children's use of media and new technologies in the home

Using TVs and DVDs	Using computers	Using games consoles	Using mobile phones	Other technologies
• Watching television • Watching films • Using the remote control to change channels • Rewinding and forwarding DVD/video players • Playing games on interactive TV using the red button	• Playing computer games • Using art packages • Using word-processing packages • Using desktop publishing packages • Surfing the internet • Playing games on the internet • Printing off pages (for example, pictures to colour in) • Using chat room and MSN (with adult as scribe)	• Playing a range of console games, for example, *Rugrats, Sonic the Hedgehog* • Using PlayStation® 2 EyeToy, which projects children's images on the screen	• Playing with toy or discarded mobile phones to conduct 'pretend' conversations • Using real mobile phones to speak to relatives (with adult support) • Pretending to send text messages • Sending text messages with adults acting as scribes • Using the camera feature of mobile phones	• Using dance mats • Using karaoke machines • Using handheld computers to play games • Using electronic laptops • Using electronic keyboards • Reading electronic books • Playing with robot pets • Listening to radios and CD players • Using digital cameras – both still and video • Playing with electronic toys (for example, PDAs, microwave, bar scanners)

software, as well as issues relating to the way in which family dynamics might contribute to use of computers in the home (Valentine, Marsh and Pattie, 2005). Nevertheless, many young children enter early years settings and schools with a broad and rich experience of media and are ready to have their skills, knowledge and understanding developed further in this area through schooling. However, opportunities to do this are not always proffered, as a review of research in the area might suggest.

Media literacy in early years settings and schools

In a review of research which has focussed on the analysis and production of the moving image, Burn and Leach (2004) identified only
twelve studies in the UK which were relevant to their review and, of
these, four involved children of primary-school age. None involved
children in the Foundation Stage (three- to five-years-old). This lack
of attention in the early years to a range of contemporary communicative practices is of concern, as it is clear that in this post-Fordist
society, young people will be leaving school and emerging into the
labour force needing a range of skills and knowledge which will
equip them sufficiently well for employment in technologically
driven, globalised societies (Luke and Luke, 2001). The concern to
develop media literacy is not confined to employment needs;
technology-mediated literacy forms a large part of children's and
young people's out-of-school social practices (Lankshear and Knobel,
2005). These developments require an education system which
acknowledges the centrality of media literacy practices from birth in
order to build on and develop these in appropriate, incremental
ways, instead of viewing such practices as suitable for development
only at a later stage of schooling, once children are competent with
alphabetic print.

There have been a few studies conducted which have explored
the production of films in schools. Reid et al. (2002) evaluated the
work of 50 schools which introduced digital filming and editing
into the curriculum and found that introducing work on moving
image media supported the development of a range of transferable
skills, including 'problem-solving, negotiation, thinking, reason-
ing and risk-taking' (Reid et al., 2002: 3). In addition, they determined that the opportunities afforded by animation work were
strong because of the way in which children could combine voice,
gesture, music, image and language. It may be the case that the difficulties in developing sustained analyses of media production in
schools lie in the area of assessment and evaluation (Goodwyn,
2004). There has been little documented work on the assessment
of production skills, and most acknowledge the complexities and
challenges faced by this aspect of media education (Buckingham
et al., 1995).

There have been a few projects that have been successful in
developing teachers' competence in using film in the curriculum. An

action-research project carried out by the Primary National Strategy and the United Kingdom Literacy Association (PNS/UKLA, 2004) developed teacher-research networks in three local authorities in England in which the use of film in the literacy curriculum was explored. More recently, the British Film Institute's (BFI) Lead Practitioner Scheme For Moving Image Media Literacy, also known as 'Reframing Literacy.' took place from 2005 to 2007 (BFI, 2008). The BFI worked with over 60 local authorities in England in order to develop expertise in moving image media teaching and learning (see Marsh and Bearne, 2008, for an evaluation of this project). Teachers across England developed innovative projects in which they engaged children in the production and analysis of film. In this chapter, I outline the practice of one early years teacher involved in the project in order to indicate how moving image media can be embedded in the early years curriculum.

Using film in the early years curriculum

Lynn Scott is an advanced skills teacher for Foundation Stage, Literacy and ICT. She works at Childwall Valley Primary School in Liverpool where she manages the Foundation Stage unit and Key Stage 1, and coordinates Literacy and ICT across the primary age range. Childwall Valley Primary School opened as a Fresh Start school in 2003. Fresh Start refers to a scheme in which schools deemed to be failing under the Ofsted inspection scheme are closed and then reopened on the same site, normally with new management. The school serves an area of considerable socio-economic deprivation.

The work featured in this chapter took place in the Foundation Stage, with three- and four-year-old children. Lynn undertook a programme of study based on the moving image text *Baboon on the Moon*, which is one of a series of films the British Film Institute (BFI) includes in an educational pack for schools, *Story Shorts* (BFI, 2002). The children watched the film and then retold the story orally and in writing. The children moved on to develop soundtracks for the film and created animated films of their own. Throughout this work, they reflected critically on the process and their work.

At the time of the study, Lynn's planning related to the 'communication, language and literacy' strand of the Early Years Foundation Stage (DfES, 2007). The following early learning goals are embedded in this strand. By the end of the Foundation Stage, children should be able to:

- listen with enjoyment and respond to stories, songs and other music, rhymes and poems and make up their own stories and poems
- retell narratives in the correct sequence, drawing on the language patterns of stories
- show an understanding of the elements of stories, such as main character, sequence of events, and openings. (DfES, 2007)

Lynn was able to ensure that the children she worked with not only met these targets but moved beyond them to develop a range of skills, knowledge and understanding appropriate for a new media age. She interpreted the goals in a way that enabled her to focus on a moving image story, *Baboon on the Moon*. The film is a short animation, without dialogue, that features a baboon living alone on the moon. The baboon maintains the machine that makes the moon shine. At the end of the film, the baboon is portrayed looking longingly towards earth, crying, accompanied by a melancholic soundtrack. The children watched the film a number of times and analysed it using the 'three Cs and three Ss' model advocated by the BFI. This involves examining colour (how colour is used in the film), characters, camera (how camera shots/angles are used), and story, setting and sound (how sound/silence/layered soundtracks/dialogue work). Detailed guidance on using this framework can be found in the BFI materials listed at the end of this chapter and in *Reframing Literacy* (BFI, 2008).

Children in Lynn's class undertook a range of activities in relation to the film *Baboon on the Moon*. After viewing it several times, they then wrote or orally retold the story, demonstrating their understanding of the elements of the story (see an example in Figure 11.1).

Lynn felt that the children's writing had improved through the analysis of the film. By viewing it together and developing children's language, scaffolding their ability to retell the story, the children were more confident and competent in their written work.

The children who had retold the story orally onto the computer added a soundtrack to their stories by importing a sound file to their tracks. The children then worked on recreating a soundtrack for the original film, using the Apple software *Garageband*, which involved them discussing the relationship between mood and music in film. Once the work on the analysis of and response to the story was complete, the children moved on to create their own stories, drawing on

Figure 11.1   Retelling the *Baboon on the Moon* story in writing

Text: In creepy dark spais the planits wher scery. There a Baboon lived in a creepy cotig The Baboon was lonly Beecos he missed his mum and DaD But he had to stay on the moon Beecos he had to make the moon shine.

the themes raised in the film. This included the creation of moving image stories in the form of short animated films.

An example of this can be seen in Figure 11.2. This portrays a selection of still shots from a clay animation produced by the children, which tells the story of *Little Beaver and his Friends*. As can be seen from the stills, the key events consist of Little Beaver and his friends falling out of a boat, watched keenly by a few ducks who swim idly by. In the final scene, Little Beaver manages to climb back into the

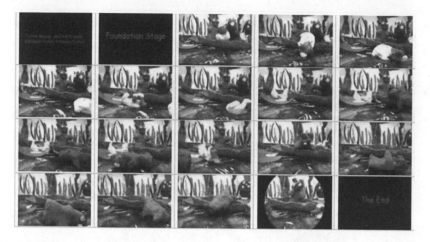

Figure 11.2   *Little Beaver and his Friends*

boat. Apart from the titles which open and close the film, this animation was produced independently by children in Lynn's class. They developed the set, produced a storyboard and manipulated the figures as they created the animation frame by frame. At approximately 23 seconds in length, this film required a large number of still frames and took the children a few weeks to complete.

Animations can also be completed using plastic figures, such as Playmobil figures, which are easier for young children to manipulate than plasticine. The only equipment required for such work is a webcam, laptop/PC and simple film-editing software. (For a more detailed analysis of young children's production of animations, see Marsh, 2006).

In this sequence of work, Lynn enabled children to demonstrate attainment of the early learning goals outlined previously. However, she also moved beyond them to ensure that these three- and four-year-old children developed skills, knowledge and understanding of multimodal texts appropriate for a digital age. Figure 11.3 outlines some of these, although this is not intended to be an exhaustive list.

As Parker and Pearce (2002) suggest, offering children the potential to engage with narrative across modes allows them to:

> switch from regimes of reception associated with visual practice – aspects such as framing, composition, shot, sequence, colour, shade, tone, etc. – to those acquired through the decoding of text – for example, paragraphing, style, intonation, voice, grammar. (Parker and Pearce, 2002: 4)

The relationship between film and traditional literacy can be a very positive one. Research indicates that work on moving image media

- Knowledge that stories can be told in a range of media and that aspects of narrative are the same across different media; for example, plot, setting, character.
- Ability to identify how sound is used in moving image texts to create mood.
- Understanding of the use and effects of camera angles; for example, close-up, long shot.
- Understanding of the way in which mood and atmosphere is created in moving image texts through the use of colour and imagery.
- Ability to use a range of hardware to create oral and moving image texts; for example, microphone, computer, camera.
- Ability to use a range of software to create oral and moving image texts; for example, imovie, Garageband.
- Understanding of the process of creating stop-motion animation.
- Understanding of the affordances of different modes and media.
- Understanding of the processes involved in transduction (movement of semiotic material across modes).

Figure 11.3 Skills, knowledge and understanding developed in the work on the film *Baboon on the Moon*

can raise attainment in aspects of writing, including composition and effect, text structure and organisation and sentence structure and punctuation (Marsh and Bearne, 2008; PNS/UKLA, 2004). Work on moving image texts can also enhance inferential reading skills (Oldham, 1999), understanding of narrative (Parker, 1999) and raise motivation for reading (Marsh et al., 2005), in addition to impacting positively on speaking and listening skills (Marsh et al., 2005). In the BFI Lead Practitioner scheme, teachers in Birmingham analysed examples of children's writing before and after units of work that were undertaken on film. Table 11.2 outlines the impact on children's writing.

Whilst this kind of evidence is important in convincing those who might think otherwise that work on media does not mean traditional literacy skills are neglected, we need to guard against film being used simply to enhance writing; films should be a focus for analysis in their own right. Thus far, the chapter has focused primarily on film as the unit of analysis. There are many other media texts that can and should be the focus of study. What approaches can be taken to these? In the next section, I will look briefly at a framework for the analysis of other media in early years settings.

Media literacy in the early years

At GCSE level, the subject of media studies provides a systematic framework for the analysis of media (Buckingham, 2003), but at

Table 11.2   Impact on children's writing when using film

Composition and effect	
Before	*After*
• Vocabulary limited • Narrative writing limited in terms of ideas and complexity • Writing brief and lacking in detail • Authorial voice missing	• More sophisticated vocabulary • More able to describe characters' motives and feelings • Development of narrative viewpoint • More understanding of the importance of settings • Effective use of description • Stories came alive
Text structure and organisation	
Before	*After*
• Limited use of different text types • Writing usually in chronological order • Ideas written in isolation • Ideas muddled	• Writing at greater length • Greater independence in the writing process • Improved structure including use of paragraphs • Greater cohesion and coherency • Improved presentation
Sentence structure and organisation	
Before	*After*
• Simple sentence construction • Limited sentence openers • Basic punctuation used	• More complex sentences • Variety of connectives used • Improved use of punctuation – both accuracy and variety • Ideas linked more cohesively • Effective word choice established

other key stages, such work is undertaken only when teachers have particular interests in media. There is a need to develop a curriculum framework for media at all key stages. As Learmonth and Sayer state:

> Amongst the most important characteristics of effective teaching and learning in media education are [...] a clear conceptual framework shared by all colleagues involved in teaching media education. (Learmonth and Sayer, 1996: 10)

A set of key concepts underpin media studies at Key Stage 4. These include a focus on:

- Media language – how meanings are produced by media, the conventions and codes that are used to make meaning.
- Genre – what type of media text a specific text is.
- Representation – how does a particular text represent its subject matter?
- Institution – who produced the text and why?
- Audience – what are the audiences for a particular text and what meanings might they make of it?

Obviously, what can be expected of three- and four-year-old children using these concepts will be very different from what pupils undertaking a GCSE in media studies will explore. However, there is a number of ways in which we can begin to develop young children's understanding of the media, using these categories as a framework. In the next section, I will look at each of these categories in turn and explore how they can be addressed in the early years.

Media language

The practice undertaken by Lynn at the Childwall Valley Primary School outlined previously is an excellent example of a teacher engaged in enabling children in the early years of schooling to look at aspects of media language, in this case, film language. However, the same principles can be applied to other media. For example, children can explore codes and conventions used in newspapers, or comics and magazines. Work on the language of comics can involve children in a consideration of features such as cartoon drawings, speech bubbles, special effects and onomatopoeia. In one nursery which contained a majority of bilingual children, work on comics excited the children and stimulated much conversation about books they had at home or programmes they had seen on television. The children discussed whether the comics used photographs of real things and people, or drawings. They then went on to produce their own comics, some of them following conventions such as placing a sequence of drawings in boxes.

In another Year 2 class of six- and seven-year olds, children drew on the conventions and codes of radio broadcasts when making podcasts of interviews. In Monteney Primary School in Sheffield, Peter Winter, the IT teacher, enabled children from different classes to create blogs (online weblogs). One of these blogs was linked to a topic a class was undertaking on Egypt. Children developed an 'Egyptian News' blog, on which they reported key events and stories relating to Egyptian history. Inevitably, one of the main stories related to the discovery of the Tutankhamun tomb. In one of the blog posts, a child can be heard interviewing another child who was posing as Howard Carter, the archaeologist who discovered the tomb. At the end of the podcast, the interviewer draws from his knowledge of news genre as he signs off from the interview, saying: 'That was the Egyptian News. All you watching at home, it'll be back soon'. This indicates the extent to which this child was aware of the conventions of news reporting, although a little confused with regard to the modality. He would be helped by further work in which children identified the ways in which news reports on radio and screen were started and completed, comparing and contrasting the words and phrases used.

Work on media language is most effective when analysis and production are linked. It is through the process of design that children have to make judgements about the elements needed in a particular production and they draw normally on their well-established knowledge of media texts in order to do this, as the podcast example demonstrates. However, levels of knowledge and expertise should not be assumed and children benefit from the input of informed adults who extend their understanding in ways which offer both reassurance and challenge.

Genre

Work on genre requires children to reflect on genres of media texts and how those genres can be identified and categorised. This involves an analysis of the common features across a particular genre. Children's skills in identifying genres can be sophisticated at an early age because of their extensive engagement with media texts in the home. Various activities can be used to develop children's understanding of genre. In a Year 1 class in a school in the north of England, children were presented with a series of short clips from the television genre of game shows. They were asked to identify a common set of characteristics that typified the genre and they came up with the following list:

- The programmes always feature a game with rules.
- There is always a presenter who manages the game.
- There are contestants.
- Different sounds feature in the game (such as a buzzer).
- Music is used to generate tension/excitement.
- There is always an audience, but they do not always join in the game.

Children could develop this activity further by devising a game show of their own, drawing from their understanding of the genre.

Identification of the genre of media texts is not a straightforward process, as is the case with print-based texts. Genres can be fluid and a particular text might demonstrate features of various genres. In addition, many media texts deliberately play with the concept of genre. The extent to which young children can identify when this is occurring, particularly in parodic texts, might be more limited than older children, but this should not prevent practitioners from drawing children's attention to this complexity where appropriate.

Representation

Media representations are framed by the producers of texts and taken up by readers in different ways. The way in which different media represent the world is shaped, amongst other things, by the producers' intentions and the perceived interests of the intended audience. It should not be assumed that young children cannot engage in critical review of representations in the media. As a number of researchers and educators have demonstrated, children of a very young age are able to engage in critical literacy practices (Comber and Simpson, 2001; Vasquez, 2004). There are many ways in which representation in the media could be approached. For example, exploring websites in groups, using an interactive whiteboard, can offer a fruitful means of examining the way in which gender and ethnicity are portrayed. The Bob the Builder website[1] offers much potential for critical analysis by children in the early years. In the *Digital Beginnings* study (Marsh et al., 2005), this was a very popular website with children, but what constructions of gender does it offer? On the page on which Bob appears in his 'mobile home'[2], he clutches a clipboard, ready for some serious work. Children can click on a television and telephone, which emit electronic sounds. However, when we move on to the caravan[3] of Wendy, Bob's business partner, she is pictured holding a bunch of flowers. Children can click on a bird and a kettle in her room, which emit high-pitched sounds. When the children click on Bob, he shouts a resounding 'Hello', whereas when Wendy is clicked upon, she merely

1 http://www.bobthebuilder.com/uk/index.html (accessed January 2008).

2 http://www.bobthebuilder.com/uk/all_you_need_to_know_about_bob_the_builder.htm (accessed January 2008).

3 http://www.bobthebuilder.com/uk/bob_the_builder_parents_homepage.htm (accessed January 2008).

sniffs her flowers. A careful review of this site with children would enable a range of gender stereotypes to be analysed. Similar analyses can be undertaken of a range of media texts, although this work should be approached in ways which encourage the children to generate the challenging questions regarding texts, rather than simply spotting the stereotypes drawn to their attention by practitioners.

Institution

A focus on institution involves exploring the way in which media texts are produced and distributed by various institutions, such as film companies, the newspaper industry, web companies and so on. In the early years, a productive approach to the area of media institutions would be to draw children's attention to the way in which some companies own or have influence over a large amount of media. So, for example, children in the Foundation Stage could identify the range of products developed by Disney, which includes films, magazines, toys, websites, holiday theme parks and so on. Children in primary classes could move on to investigate the range of internet products and sites owned by Google, which includes the search facility, Google Earth, Google Maps and Google Video, amongst other products. This development of understanding of the way in which some companies dominate global media will provide a platform for more detailed work in later years on the impact of this on media production and dissemination.

Audience

Work on media audiences involves asking children to identify for whom a particular text is produced and how it reaches its audiences. The first work on media audiences should involve children in reflecting on their own media choices. Discussions with children can focus on what television programmes, films, comics and magazines they like and why they like them. In later stages of media work this can lead to an analysis of how an audience has been identified and targeted, but in the earlier stages it will involve developing children's understanding that different texts are produced for different audiences. What is made for adults may not always appeal to children, and vice versa. Other activities could include showing children comics and magazines aimed at adults. Children can then be asked:

- Who is this written for?
- Would grown-ups or children want to read it?
- What makes you say that?

- What would want to make you read it?
- What kinds of television programmes/films, magazines do children like?
- What kinds of television programmes/films, magazines do your mum/dad/ grandparents like?

Whilst one of the aims of work on media literacy is to develop children's critical engagement with media, this should not be undertaken in a way which undermines the pleasure children experience as they engage with film, television, computer games and so on. It is possible to navigate this difficult tightrope if teachers are, firstly, knowledgeable about which texts children engage with outside of school and, secondly, willing to let children explore these pleasures in the space of the classroom (Marsh and Millard, 2000; 2005). In addition, as stated previously, analysis of media should always, where possible, be linked with production. It is in the design and production of texts that pupils have opportunities to draw upon their critical understanding of media language, genre, representation, institutions and audience.

Conclusion

The recent emphasis on the development of media literacy (Ofcom, 2004) has implications for schooling. If children are encountering texts in a wide range of media outside nurseries and schools, then it makes sense for them to be able to analyse, understand, respond to and produce texts using these media in nurseries and schools. No longer are paper and pencil the preferred modes of communication for many in society (Kress, 2003), including very young children. Examining the way in which these 'toddler netizens' (Luke, 1999) are navigating the worlds of technologically-mediated childhoods and ensuring that a curriculum is developed which is appropriate for their needs is a significant task for early years educators in the twenty-first century. The aim of this chapter has been to highlight practical approaches to the teaching and learning of media in early years settings and schools, and to raise some key questions about how future curricula and pedagogy in this area should be developed. There has been significant progress in recent years in relation to the recognition of media literacy as a central skill; it is now time to extend this work in order to ensure that schooling for our youngest children is appropriate for the digital age.

Suggestions for further reading 📖

British Film Institute (BFI) (2008) *Reframing Literacy*. London: British Film Institute.

Marsh, J. (ed.) (2005) *Popular Culture, New Media and Digital Literacy in Early Childhood*. London: RoutledgeFalmer.

Marsh, J., Brooks, G., Hughes, J., Ritchie, L., Roberts, S., and Wright, K. (2005) *Digital Beginnings: Young Children's Use of Popular Culture, Media and New Technologies*. Sheffield: University of Sheffield. Available online at http://www.digitalbeginnings. shef.ac.uk/ (accessed November 2005).

Resources

The BFI website and educational materials offer a range of support for work on film. See www.bfi.org.uk, which has details of *Starting Stories 1* and *2* (collections of especially commissioned short films for Key Stage 1), *Story Shorts 1* and *2* (collections of especially commissioned short films for Key Stage 2), and *Moving Shorts*, *Real Shorts* and *Screening Shorts 2* (collections of especially commissioned short films for secondary schools).

The *Look Again* teaching guide is available as a free download from the BFI website, www.bfi.org.uk/education/teaching/lookagain/pdf/bfi_edu_look-again_teaching-guide.pdf

Film Education has an extensive website which offers downloadable resources for work on film. See www.filmeducation.org.

Acknowledgements

I would like to thank Lynn Scott and the head teacher of Childwall Valley Primary School, Liverpool, for their permission to use Lynn's excellent work as illustrative material in this chapter. I am also grateful to Christine Bland of Birmingham Local Authority for her agreement for me to use data on children's writing from their action research projects. As usual, working with Peter Winter of Monteney Primary School was very rewarding and I am grateful to him for allowing me to share his work with others. Finally, I would like to thank Mark Reid at the British Film Institute (BFI) for his permission to use the case study material from the BFI Lead Practitioner Scheme for Moving Image Education in this chapter.

References

British Film Institute (BFI) (2002) *Story Shorts*. London: BFI.

British Film Institute (BFI) (2008) *Reframing Literacy*. London: BFI.

Buckingham, D. (2003) *Media Education: Literacy, Learning and Contemporary Culture*. Oxford: Polity.

Buckingham, D. (2004) *The Media Literacy of Children and Young People: A Review of the Research Literature*. London: Ofcom.

Buckingham, D., Grahame, J. and Sefton-Green, J. (1995) *Making Media: Practical Production in Media Education*. London: The English and Media Centre.

Burn, A. and Leach, J. (2004) 'ICTs and moving image literacy in English', in R. Andrews (ed.) *The Impact of ICTs on English 5–16*. London: RoutledgeFalmer. pp. 153–79.

Comber, B. and Simpson (eds) (2001) *Negotiating Critical Literacies in Classrooms*. Mahwah, NJ: Lawrence Erlbaum.

Department for Education and Skills (2007) *Early Years Foundation Stage*. Nottingham: DfES Publications. Available online at http://www.standards. dfes.gov.uk/eyfs/ (accessed May 2007).

Goodwyn, A. (2004) *English Teaching and the Moving Image*. London: RoutledgeFalmer.

Hall, N., Larson, J. and Marsh, J. (eds) (2003) *Handbook of Early Childhood Literacy*. London: Sage.

Kress, G. (2003) *Literacy in a New Media Age*. London: Routledge.

Lankshear, C. and Knobel, M. (2005) 'Digital literacies: policy, pedagogy and research considerations for education.' Plenary address, ITU Conference, Norway, 20 October. Available online at http://www.geocities.com/c.lankshear/Oslo.pdf (accessed November 2005).

Learmonth, J. and Sayer, M. (1996) *A Review of Good Practice in Media Education*. London: British Film Institute.

Luke, C. (1999) 'What next? Toddler netizens, Playstation thumb, techno-literacies', *Contemporary Issues in Early Childhood* 1 (1): 95–100.

Luke, A. and Luke, C. (2001) 'Adolescence lost/childhood regained: on early intervention and the emergence of the techno-subject', *Journal of Early Childhood Literacy* 1 (1): 91–120.

Marsh, J. (2002) 'The sound of silence: emergent technoliteracies and the early learning goals' Paper presented at the Annual Conference of the British Educational Research Association, University of Exeter, 12–14 September. Available online at http://www.leeds.ac.uk/educol/documents/00002584.htm (accessed May 2007).

Marsh, J. (2006) 'Emergent media literacy: digital animation in the early years', *Language and Education*, 20 (6): 493–506.

Marsh, J. and Bearne, E. (2008) *Moving Literacy On: Evaluation of the BFI Lead Practitioner Scheme for Moving Image Education*. Leicester: United Kingdom Literacy Association (UKLA).

Marsh, J., Brooks, G., Hughes, J., Ritchie, L., Roberts, S. and Wright, K. (2005) *Digital Beginnings: Young Children's Use of Popular Culture, Media and New Technologies*. Sheffield: University of Sheffield. Available online at http://www. digitalbeginnings.shef.ac.uk (accessed November 2005).

Marsh, J. and Millard, E. (2000) *Literacy and Popular Culture: Using Children's Culture in the Classroom.* London: Paul Chapman.

Marsh, J. and Millard, E. (eds) (2005) *Popular Literacies, Childhoods and Schooling.* London: Routledge.

Ofcom (2004) *Ofcom's Strategies and Priorities for the Promotion of Media Literacy: A Statement.* Available online at http://www.ofcom.org.uk/consult/condocs/ strategymedialit/ml_statement/strat_prior_statement.pdf (accessed March 2005).

Oldham, J. (1999) 'The book of the film: enhancing print literacy at KS3', *English in Education* 33 (1): 36–46.

Parker, D. (1999) 'You've read the book, now make the film: moving image media, print literacy and narrative', *English in Education* 33: 24–35

Parker, D. and Pearce, H. (2002) *Story Shorts: Using Films to Teach Literacy.* London: DfES Publications. Available online at http://www.standards.dfes.gov. uk/primary/features/literacy/659883/bfi_storyshorts.pdf (accessed May 2007).

Primary National Strategy/United Kingdom Literacy Association (PNS/UKLA) (2004) *Raising Boys' Achievement in Writing.* London: HMSO.

Reid, M., Burn, A. and Parker, D. (2002) *Evaluation Report of the BECTA Digital Video Pilot Project.* London: British Film Institute.

Sharp, D. (2006) 'Participatory culture production and the DIY internet: from theory to practice and back again', *Media International Australia Incorporating Culture and Policy* 118: 16–24.

Valentine, G., Marsh, J. and Pattie, C. (2005) *Children and Young People's Home Use of ICT for Educational Purposes: The Impact on Attainment at Key Stages 1–4.* London: HMSO.

Vasquez, V.M. (2004) *Negotiating Critical Literacies with Young Children.* Mahwah, NJ: Lawrence Erlbaum.

Family literacy: past and present

Viv Bird

Introduction

There has been increasing interest in family literacy over the last 20 years. Family literacy is seen as a way to encourage families to develop their children's early language skills, a critical component of healthy child development. Its role in engaging parents in their child's learning once they start formal education is widely recognised. Family literacy is also a legitimate route for many parents to develop their own skills in reading and writing, often leading to new qualifications and improving their chances of finding employment. Family literacy can be found in all sorts of settings, not just schools and early years centres, but also in libraries, family centres in prisons, travellers' sites and teenage parents' groups. Family literacy is therefore multifaceted and multipurpose and straddles a number of professional interests and policy areas, such as health (including mental health), early years' development, education, criminal justice, housing and social policy.

This chapter provides a brief explanation of the history and the research evidence around family literacy. It describes some of the key family literacy programmes, with a particular focus on ways family literacy can support families at risk of social exclusion. Two case studies are offered as illustrative examples.

Family literacy: definitions

The term 'family literacy' can cause some confusion. In an overview of family literacy in England, Hannon and Bird (2004) identified two meanings to the term 'family literacy'. Firstly, family literacy means literacy practices within families, and is influenced by the educational level of parents, social class and culture. Secondly, family literacy describes literacy programmes or activities that involve families. The concept of the use of a programme to change family literacy practices originated in the United States in the 1980s and became widespread in England in the 1990s.

Family literacy comes from two distinctive strands of education – early childhood development and adult literacy education – which were linked in the 1990s through family literacy programmes. Current theory around family literacy conceptualises it as a set of cognitive skills, or as social practices, or as a combination of the two. Most family literacy practitioners aim to impart short-term skills, but also long-term changes in families, relating, for example, to support for children's school education, improvements of adults' basic skills, employability and attitudes to lifelong learning.

Family literacy activity can be found anywhere where there are families. Surveys carried out by the National Literacy Trust in the late 1990s (Hannon and Bird, 2004: 31) painted a rich tapestry of hundreds of different family literacy initiatives taking place in a wide range of settings including schools, day nurseries, libraries, family centres, travellers' sites, churches and housing schemes. These programmes were defined broadly as those that aimed to work through parents to improve the reading and writing of their children as well as those that had the improvement of parents' literacy as their aim. Most programmes were in English but many were in other languages (Welsh, Bengali, Urdu, Punjabi and Turkish). Some involved parents in literacy-related activities such as making books or puppets. Others focused on parents with very young children through sharing books or storytelling. Some were informal and short-term, others led to the accreditation of parents. Family literacy was part of the educational landscape.

Research into family literacy

It is interesting to note that in the 1980s, research played an important role in establishing the foundations for parental involvement in their children's literacy development. The Haringey Reading Project investigated, over a two-year period, the effect when children aged six to eight in a disadvantaged part of London took reading books home. Their parents were encouraged to help their children by talking about stories, listening to their children read aloud and generally ensuring that reading books together was an enjoyable experience. Tizard et al. (1982) found that the programme produced significant reading test gains. A later study by Hannon et al. (1986) audio-taped children reading at home to their parents and also reading to their class teachers in school. They found that the great majority of parents – even those with limited literacy – were a help rather than a hindrance. These studies helped educators to value the parental contribution, but there was little exploration of the role of other family members (for example, grandparents and siblings), or what impact such programmes might have on the skills levels of the adults themselves.

The University of Sheffield's REAL Project developed a conceptual framework to help parents support their children's early literacy learning, known as the ORIM framework (Hannon, 1995). The acronym 'ORIM' stands for: Opportunities to read texts, attempt writing and to talk about literacy; Recognition of early literacy achievements; Interaction with more proficient literacy users; and a Model of what it is to use written language in everyday life. The ORIM framework has been used in a number of settings, notably, by the Peers Early Learning Partnership (PEEP), which runs weekly sessions in areas of disadvantage for families with very young children. Session leaders model different ways of sharing books with children, songs and rhymes are taught, and the contribution of everyday talk to children's development is emphasised. Evangelou and Sylva (2003) found that the children in the PEEP group made greater progress in their learning than those in the comparison group in their study in the areas of vocabulary, language comprehension, understanding about books and print and number concepts.

A significant breakthrough for family literacy in England came with government funding in 1993, via the Adult Literacy and Basic Skills Unit (ALBSU), for four family literacy demonstration programmes in areas of deprivation. Each programme, which was based on a model imported from the United States, consisted of three components: basic skills instruction for parents, early literacy education for young children aged 3–6 and parent-child activities. Each course lasted 96 hours over a 12-week period. The evaluation by Brooks et al. (1997) reported on positive changes in attitudes and literacy practices on the part of participating parents, which were maintained when they were re-interviewed six months later. The follow-up research showed that children in families participating in the programmes were holding their own, and that their educational prospects were better than they would have been without the programme. The impact on the parents was strongest in terms of providing a huge boost to their confidence. The programmes avoided an over-concentration on reading and genuinely focussed on talking and writing. It was noted that the parents benefitted from being able to move straight from a session to a shared activity with their children where they could try it out, and if necessary have the activity modelled by the teacher.

The success of the demonstration programmes led to national funding for the 96-hour family literacy programmes, targeted in areas of deprivation, and this became the 'dominant' delivery model for many years. Another aspect of the ALBSU initiative at that time was a small grants scheme to support innovation in family literacy. A wide range of community groups began to deliver family literacy, offering more flexible approaches, tailor-made to suit the needs of local families. For example, one project offered home-based provision for Muslim women who were recruited and taught by other women who spoke the same language. As the National Literacy Trust surveys indicated, a wide range of family literacy provision was developed, supported by a myriad separate funding streams. As a result, over the next five years, there were increasing concerns about the rigidity of the approved 'dominant' ALBSU model and whether this programme could provide appropriate support for all families, especially those with particular social or language needs.

This led, from 2004 onwards, to the Learning and Skills Council (LSC) funding for a broader range of funded courses within the Family Literacy, Language and Numeracy (FLLN) programmes, which sit within the umbrella of family programmes. Since 2004, LSC-funded FLLN programmes include taster courses, introductory programmes, short courses and intensive programmes (including the original 96-hour programme). Family programmes also contain a family learning strand aimed at helping parents and carers to be more able to support their children's learning and development, and with greater confidence. 'Wider family learning' as it is known, can lead to or complement more specific family literacy courses.

How family literacy supports social inclusion

The Literacy and Social Inclusion Project (2002–2005) was a Basic Skills Agency national support project delivered by the National Literacy Trust. Bird (2004) highlighted the policy challenges in getting 'hard-to-reach' families participating in family literacy programmes. The project examined the evidence for successful home and community literacy practices that engaged, motivated and improved the literacy skills of individuals at risk of social exclusion[1] in relation to five areas of investigation, including building parents' skills. In *Every Which Way We Can*, Bird and Akerman (2005a) developed the evidence for successful family literacy approaches within a wider social policy context, and proposed a model for building parental skills. In *Literacy and Social Inclusion: The Handbook*, Bird and Akerman (2005b) provided the rationale for a community literacy strategy and the steps for putting one into practice.

The research review identified two studies which further confirmed the importance of family literacy programmes. The US Harvard Home-School Study (Roach and Snow, 2000) had interviewed children since the age of three (they are now 21) and showed that the greatest predictor of their literacy development was support for literacy in the home; the areas of greatest impact were sharing books. In England, the EPPE research project (Sylva et al., 2003) confirmed that a high quality home-learning environment where parents are actively engaged in activities with children, promoted intellectual and social development in all children, over and above social class. These findings resonated with a UK government that, from 1997, was keen not only to raise educational attainment, but also to address social exclusion.

The Literacy and Social Inclusion project findings stressed the relationship between poor literacy, low self-esteem and low confidence, which is the reason why many parents do not volunteer to sign up for family literacy programmes. National surveys indicate that one in six adults has low levels of literacy and numeracy, but that few adults regard their reading, writing or maths as below average. This can make it hard to persuade these parents to take up learning opportunities, but supportive peers and working through trusted intermediaries can make a difference. Informal learning through taster sessions in non-threatening locations build parental confidence and, at the appropriate time, they can be encouraged to participate in more structured learning. As parents relax and become more comfortable in educational settings, they also involve their children in educational activities, read with them and take them to arts events or to the library.

---

1 The term 'at risk' is used to describe those who are at risk of social exclusion and who also have poor or underdeveloped literacy or language skills. These include high-risk groups such as children excluded from school, travellers, asylum seekers and problematic drug users.

Four key elements were identified during the course of the project as being critical to engaging those parents with little confidence and few skills:

1 Building relationships.
2 Meeting their needs and interests.
3 Providing book and reading experiences.
4 Working in partnership and using intermediaries.

Engagement is key. Many people find it easier to come forward to participate in a course on helping their child to read and write than to admit to difficulties with literacy themselves, but it is best to engage those hard-to-reach parents through activities that do not initially involve reading or writing. It is particularly important to recognise the literacy practices that are happening in homes, and to build bridges between what is happening there and with the early years setting or school. Pahl and Rowsell (2005) recognise that home and school literacy practices can be different, and stress the importance of drawing on individuals' own experiences and cultural identity to help them access mainstream language and literacy learning.

Even so, parents with low confidence and skills may find it hard to sign up for family literacy courses, especially if they feel that what they do already to help their children's literacy development is not recognised or valued. What works is to provide opportunities – in local centres, schools, community groups, anywhere where parents feel at ease – for parents to take part in taster sessions on subjects that interest them. It may take some time to engage parents at this stage, and it helps if there are also opportunities for them to 'drop back in', if they drop out for any reason.

The initial focus needs to be on building relationships, between the parent and the teacher or other professionals, and between learners themselves. This can happen in different ways and can take time. It may require home visits to persuade a parent to come along. Start with something that will interest them, is fun and provides opportunities for success. Parents report they feel 'comfortable', they 'enjoy' themselves and they have 'made friends'. What they are doing is building their self-confidence and their personal support networks in preparation for changes in their lives. Be patient; there may not be obvious 'learning outcomes' but these are important building blocks before learning takes place. In an exploratory study into community-focussed basic skills provision, Hannon et al. (2003) highlighted the importance in allowing time for development. This means spending time networking with community groups or organisations that can support or enhance provision, talking to parents or carers about what they would like to do, putting on taster sessions that reflect their interests.

Sessions might be related to their children's development, learning how to use computers, searching on the internet or money management (especially for parents of secondary-age children), or consist of practical activities such as crafts, baby massage, gardening projects or making story sacks. These approaches all provide informal opportunities for reading and writing. Once parents start to enjoy learning something new and they feel comfortable with the tutor and with others taking part, they are more likely to take up suggestions about how to help their children's developing literacy, and to try them out at home.

Connecting families to what is already known and experienced is recognised as good practice by teachers. Marsh (2005) found that children are familiar with, and become literate across a range of media that may include moving images and texts in a variety of forms. These include television, film and computer games, and children respond to these sources by talking, role playing, dancing and singing. Parents in Marsh's study were generally happy to encourage and join in this play, perhaps because they felt happy with television narratives, more so perhaps than with the picture books found in nurseries. Looking for ways to connect with popular culture (screen reads, text messaging, looking at on-screen social networks such as Facebook) may be a way to talk to less confident parents about language and literacy.

Where parents are English speakers of other languages (ESOL), it can help to provide multilingual tutors or volunteers who speak community languages, and use materials or texts in the relevant languages as well as English.

Story sacks are a popular, non-threatening way of encouraging parents and carers to start sharing stories with their children, especially those parents with little positive experience of books, or those with ESOL needs. A story sack is a large cloth bag containing a children's book with supporting materials to stimulate reading activities and make shared reading a memorable and enjoyable experience. The sack contains soft toys of the book's main characters, and props and scenery that parents and other adults can use with children to bring a book to life, even if the adult's reading skills are limited. The sack might include a non-fiction book on the same theme, an audio tape of the story, a language-based game and a short guide containing questions to ask, words to consider and other ways to extend the reading activity. Less confident parents may be happy to join a group that is making their own story sacks, and discuss ideas with them about how to get the best use of the sack's contents, and help with storytelling. In Cornwall, the Family Learning team coordinates and delivers the Bookstart scheme, and uses the Family Learning Bookstart Story Sacks courses to promote adult learning. These courses have the dual aim of, firstly, helping parents and carers to learn how to tell stories to their children and increase their enjoyment of books, and, secondly, to encourage these adults to think about their own skill development. The initial session focuses on 'reading with your child' and the developmental benefits to children and families. Subsequent sessions focus on using rhymes and storytelling to help children to develop speech and language skills. In parallel, the family learning tutor encourages the adults to evaluate their own skills levels and signposts them to other learning opportunities as appropriate.

The cultural sector offers opportunities for making family literacy sessions really exciting. These activities can help parents to get to know how to use local community resources such as libraries and museums. Most libraries run regular rhyme time sessions for families with very young children, and will be also keen to offer library visits, book loans or even a storytelling session to family literacy groups. Cultivating strong links with the local library will encourage parents to become members, and discover books that excite, entertain and inform. For instance, parents can get advice on how to capitialise on the Harry Potter phenomenon and find new authors that their children might like to read.

In the following section, I offer detailed case studies in order to illustrate how family literacy can be encouraged and promoted.

Case study 12.1   Creative family literacy in Rochdale

Rochdale is an industrial town in the north-west of England which has a significant ethnic minority population, mainly from Pakistan and Bangladesh. Since the 1980s, Rochdale local education authority has pioneered family literacy programmes to suit particular contexts and communities, retaining an essential vision of enabling parents and children, separately and together, to celebrate their talents and enjoy learning. One of the ways that this works is through the Partnership Education

Service, made up of teams who encourage and support parental involvement in improving the literacy of preschool and school-age children, particularly with families where English is a second language. A key aim is to encourage creative and practical learning and enjoyment, using different environments and projects with artists. The success of family learning in the authority has led to the development, in 2006, of an authority-wide literacy policy that embraces family and community literacy activity within a coherent approach to raising literacy standards from the early years, school-based literacy strategy through to adults' basic skills development.

Funding comes from a variety of sources and supports a manager along with a team of eight part-time multilingual workers, based in 13 primary and nursery schools. They promote home–school liaison and develop family learning courses in these and other schools, as well as early learning programmes in Sure Start projects for 0–4 year olds and their parents.

What goes on

Rochdale's family literacy programme encourages parents to spend time looking at how children learn and then try out practical activities with their own child. Some of the sessions take place outside the school. There is an oracy trail in the local park, an environmental-print walk in the community and a day trip to an interactive museum or aquarium. Three sessions are working with a local artist.

The course is taught, where appropriate, by multilingual tutors from the Partnership Education Service who speak community languages, and materials are produced in Urdu and Bengali as well as in English.

All courses take place once a week in the primary school, supported by a crèche. They are spread over the school year so that parents can be involved longer-term in the life of the school and take part in many other types of courses set up in response to parents' needs. These include craft workshops, learning English, making story sacks, using computers and passing the written driving test.

Holiday activity packs

In consultation with parents and teachers, the Partnership Education Service has produced an activity pack for use by children on extended holidays to Pakistan and Bangladesh. The pack enables family learning with early primary years children and can be personalised for each child

(Continued)

(Continued)

and school. It contains an introduction in Urdu and Bengali, and practical activities which value the culture and environment of the places visited. Topics include weather, local arts and crafts, transport, kites and rhymes. Literacy skills are used in a real context and for communication, and the open-ended curriculum encourages learners to follow their own interests.

Multilingual liaison workers from the Service help schools and families to work with the pack before and after the visit, building positive relationships between families, workers and schools, and encouraging partnership and feedback. The pack encourages family learning and enthusiasm for learning, and families feel that their heritage and languages are included and valued. Pakistan and Bangladesh are seen as contexts for learning rather than being 'underdeveloped', and the children have something unique to contribute to school on their return. Their diaries, photos and artefacts are brought in and used as resources, and an exhibition of photos is planned.

The pack has been judged a success based on the responses of families and teachers, and the observations of teachers and workers from the Service.

Case study 12.2   Sure Start Newington with Gypsyville – story and craft in libraries

This Sure Start local programme runs weekly story and craft sessions in two local libraries in Hull. Parents and children are encouraged to join in with the activities, and to join the library and borrow books. The local programme works with Bookstart to provide free book packs for children aged two and three-and-a-half (through local nursery schools), in addition to the book pack received by all babies at nine months. The project is the result of a strong partnership between Bookstart, Sure Start and local library staff.

What goes on

The library sessions last for an hour, and usually begin with storytelling from a big book. There is then a craft activity linked to the story – for example, making fish to go with Rainbow Fish, or an activity with fruit for Handa's Surprise. Finally, there is more storytelling and the opportunity for parents to join the library. The books used include those in languages other than English, and books of different sizes and containing different colours and textures to promote the inclusion of children with additional needs.

Engaging parents

The sessions are promoted to parents through the Sure Start local programme and also through the home visits at which the Sure Start Language Measure is carried out. Staff have found that these home visits, during which one of the Bookstart packs is also delivered, help to ease parents' worries about opening the door to officials. Parents who have attended more than one session at the library also seem to become more relaxed and willing to join in. Some parents are automatically choosing and using books with their children when they arrive at the sessions, when previously they would ask for toys or just sit and wait.

In another group run by the Sure Start local programme (a parent and toddler group), parents have gained enough confidence to take the storytelling part of the session themselves.

Looking ahead

Support for families is a strong feature of current government policy to address social exclusion, and additional money has been provided for family learning, including family literacy programmes. In December 2007, the government launched the Children's Plan, which aims to intensify the support it provides for parents, with earlier intervention and more joined-up services. There will be increased support for parents to move from welfare to work and a focus on improving childcare, and addressing the needs of hardest-to-reach families by tackling the causes and consequences of deep-seated social exclusion. Improved outreach services via Children's Centres, and more intensive support for the neediest families (piloted by a key worker approach) offer opportunities for more sustained and targeted family literacy work. Partnership with adult educators can help to target parents and carers with literacy needs at school-based information sessions for parents, or as part of extended school provision.

There are challenges ahead for those who work in the field. These include widening the appeal of family literacy programmes to fathers, professional development and evaluation. Attracting fathers onto family literacy programmes is problematic and specific approaches are required to engage them; for example, holding family literacy events at weekends, in sports centres or libraries, which are more likely to attract working dads.

As provision has expanded, there is a need for joint professional development among early years educators and adult educators. For example, early childhood educators are not trained or experienced in working with adults and, therefore, in understanding how to engage adults with previous negative experiences of schooling. Adult educators often find they need to know more about preschool development and the school curriculum. Higher-level courses are being developed for adult basic skills' teachers, courses which include family literacy modules, but funding for training is problematic, with no national body for family literacy to take on these issues. An urgent dialogue with the relevant government departments is needed to raise awareness of the benefits of family literacy and learning programmes, and to ensure that they are included in delivery plans for closing the gap in educational attainment, and meeting adults' skills needs. Funding is also required for more flexible approaches to attract harder-to-reach families.

The final concern is one of research and evaluation. What is needed is sustained research into basic issues; for example, there is still no clear evidence that combined family literacy programmes are more beneficial than separate programmes for adults and children, or the effect of programmes that combine family literacy with, for example, support for children's behaviour. Also, there is a need for longitudinal studies to show the effect of family literacy programmes, and to update the findings of the original ALBSU demonstration programmes.

But there are opportunities too. Continued government investment in the book-gifting programmes run by Booktrust across the UK means that there is a Bookstart offer linked to library joining schemes in every town and health clinic. These provide real opportunities for getting parents – dads too – really engaged from the very beginning in sharing and enjoying stories with their young children. These ensure that parents receive the message right from the start that reading with their children is important.

Throughout this chapter, I have stressed the importance of recognising the valuable role that family literacy practices have in the literacy development and achievement of children. There are many initiatives taking place that promote family literacy and there has never been a more exciting time for schools to become involved in this work. Teachers need to be aware of the schemes available so that they can promote them to families and ensure that families are in touch with the appropriate agencies. They also need to develop strategies themselves to involve parents in children's education. Unless they do so opportunities for developing effective partnerships may be lost.

Suggestions for further reading

For further details on the history of family literacy in England, and the development of family literacy in the United States, look at the Hannon and Bird chapter, and others, in *Handbook of Family Literacy* (2004) edited by Barbara Wasik. Mahwah and London: Lawrence Erlbaum.

Carol Taylor's article (2005), 'It's in the water here: the development of a community-focused literacy strategy', shows how family literacy can be part of a community-focused approach to improving area-wide literacy skills. The article is in a special issue on 'Family and Community Literacies' in *Literacy* 39 (2): 64–7, United Kingdom Literacy Association and Blackwell Publishing.

DfES (Department for Education and Skills) (2004) *Family Literacy, Language and Numeracy: A Guide for Policy Makers*. Nottingham: DfEs Publications.

References

Bird, V. (2004) *Literacy and Social Inclusion: The Policy Challenge*. London: National Literacy Trust.

Bird, V. and Akerman, R. (2005a) *Every Which Way We Can*. London: National Literacy Trust.

Bird, V. and Akerman, R. (2005b) *Literacy and Social Inclusion: The Handbook*. London: The Basic Skills Agency.

Brooks, G., Gorman, T., Harman, J., Hutchison, D., Kinder, K., Moor, H. and Wilkin, A. (1997) *The NFER Follow-up Study of the Basic Skills Agency's Family Literacy Demonstration Programmes*. London: The Basic Skills Agency.

Browne, E. (1995) *Handa's Surprise*. London: Walker Books.

Evangelou, M. and Sylva, K. (2003) *The Effects of the Peers Early Education Partnership (PEEP) on Children's Developmental Progress*. Oxford: Department for Educational Studies, University of Oxford.

Hannon, P. (1995) *Literacy, Home and School: Research and Practice in Teaching Literacy with Parents*. London: Falmer.

Hannon, P. and Bird, V. (2004) 'Family literacy in England: theory, practice, research and policy', in B.H. Wasik (ed.) *Handbook of Family Literacy*. Mahwah, NJ: Lawrence Erlbaum.

Hannon, P., Jackson, A. and Weinburger, J. (1986) 'Parents' and teachers' strategies in hearing young children read', *Research Papers in Education* 1 (1) 6–25.

Hannon, P., Pahl, K., Bird, V., Taylor, C. and Birch, C. (2003) *Community-focused Provision in Adult Literacy, Numeracy and Language: An Exploratory Study*. London: National Research and Development Centre.

Marsh, J. (2005) 'Digikids: young children, popular culture and media', in N. Yelland (ed.) *Contemporary Issues in Early Childhood*. Buckingham: Open University Press.

Pahl, K. and Rowsell, J. (2005) *Literacy and Education: The New Literacy Studies in the Classroom*. London: Paul Chapman.

Pfister, M. (2000) *The Rainbow Fish*. Zurich: Nord-Sud Verlag.

Roach, K.A. and Snow, C.E. (2000) 'What predicts 4th grade reading comprehension?' in C. Snow (Chair) 'Predicting 4th grade reading comprehension in a low-income population: the critical importance of social precursors from home and school during early childhood'. Symposium conducted at the annual meeting of the American Educational Research Association, New Orleans, LA. Available online at http://gseweb.harvard.edu/~pild/RouchAERA2000.pdf

Sylva, K., Melhuish, E., Sammons, P., Siraj-Blatchford, I., Taggart, B. and Elliott, K. (2003) *The Effective Provision of Pre-School Education (EPPE): Findings from the Pre-school Period*. London: Institute of Education.

Tizard, J., Schofield, W.N. and Hewison, J. (1982) 'Collaboration between teachers and parents in assisting children's reading', *British Journal of Educational Psychology* 52: 1–15.

13

Going fishing: observing, assessing and planning for literacy development in young children

Fran Paffard

Our nets determine what we catch. (Eliot Eisner, 1996)

Hana was a British born four-year-old of a Moroccan family. Her first language was Arabic. Silent for the first few weeks in the nursery, she quickly blossomed into an animated if ungrammatical communicator in English. Hana loved to talk and in particular loved the tape recorder, set up in a corner of the class with blank tapes for children to record their own thoughts and stories. She spent long periods of time hunched breathily over it, composing her latest story. Invariably they would begin with her own personal story convention, 'Once upon a little tiny time,' then there would be a pause and she would continue in a coaxing voice, 'Are you sitting in a comfortably? Then I will tell you this *really* good story' and off she would go again.

The Ringling Tingling Man was one of her later creations, and as with many of her stories, his tale was never completed. It was enough for Hana to have created him and unleashed him into the world:

> the Ringling Tingling man was good and nice to children and he never smack them even when they are very, very naughty ...

Thinking about Hana now, I find myself wondering how her literacy skills would be judged against the current forms of assessment that are commonly used in early years education. She left nursery a confident teller of tales, but encouragement to write produced howls of 'I can't doooo it'. She had only recently begun to draw representational pictures and was far too eager to talk to be regarded as a good listener. Orally inventive and an idiosyncratic composer of story forms, Hana was as yet unimpressed by the transcription and decoding of print. She wrote her name recognisably to us but it was scattered over all four corners of the paper. Above all, remembering Hana brings home to me the pernicious fiction of the 'normal child' against whom all our children are to be measured.

In this chapter, I want to look at the importance of observation and assessment in supporting and planning for young children's developing literacy. The chapter begins with a glimpse of the development of an individual child, Hana – unless we keep the child at the centre of our thinking, we shall soon be led astray. With her and every other unique child in mind, I shall then go on to look at what effective practices in assessing and planning for young children's literacy might involve.

Underlying principles

One of the key principles of early years education is that we start from where the child is, and that careful observation and assessment is fundamental to this process. The cycle, therefore, of observation, assessment and planning begins with that gradual accumulation of knowledge of the child through observation, samples of work, and a respectful gathering together of other views from parents, practitioners, previous settings and the child herself. As Drummond points out, 'the key issues in assessment are moral and philosophical, not organisational and pedagogical' (Drummond 1993: 12). Assessment and planning in the early years must be firmly based on the principles of early years education, focussing on what the child *can* do and is interested in, and building on this.

If we view children as active constructors of their world, then we need a literacy curriculum that engages and motivates them in developing literacy, and gives them an active role in assessing their own progress. If we believe that children learn best through play and through interaction, then we need to be planning and providing a wide range of opportunities for literacy in these contexts, and to be observing and assessing their progress as an integral part of the day. If we believe that their learning is not compartmentalised, then we should be alert to their literacy development occurring as part of a holistic learning process and be aware that each child's route into learning is unique. We need to respect the rights of children to explore and learn in the here-and-now, and not regard either their literacy or our assessments as boxes to be ticked, or merely preparation for later.

A widely accepted view is that literacy is simply about learning to read and write. But the reality is more complex. Literacy takes place within the context of all learning; it is a part of a symbolic system that has at its heart all the richness of oral communication, without which the written word has no meaning. Whitehead emphasises the holistic nature of children's learning and argues powerfully for a broad conception of literacy:

> Early education must build on a range of literacies including symbolising and representing meanings through non-verbal communication skills, gesture, movement, dance, music, listening, talking, drawing, painting, modelling, building, story-telling, poetry-sharing, scientific and mathematical investigations, rituals and religious celebrations.
> (Whitehead, 1990: 192)

Literacy in this light is a rich carousel of representation, through which children gain entry into a diverse world of forms for communicating meaning, expressing thoughts and feelings, and creating new ways of seeing the world. Immediately, it becomes apparent that this complex interpretation of literacy will not be amenable to simple tests of children's progress, nor can it be planned for in any rigid schematic way.

How we view the purposes of literacy will also decree a lot about the means we use to get there and how we will judge our steps along the way. Do we want children who solely have the necessary reading and writing skills in order to function in the workplace? Or do we want children whose lives are transformed by the power of literacy, children who will be talkers, readers and writers for life?

Whilst assessment must aim to be as objective as possible, the complex learning processes of young children make this a formidable task. Assessment is a judgement not a measurement; as Drummond helpfully reminds us, 'Assessment is essentially provisional, partial, tentative, exploratory and, inevitably, incomplete' (Drummond, 1993: 14). There is enormous pressure on schools and on teachers in the current educational culture of league tables and results to produce easily quantifiable assessments, but as Kelly (1992) points out:

> Accuracy of assessment is related inversely to the complexity and the sophistication of what is being assessed. And since education is a highly complicated and sophisticated process, assessment can be regarded as measurement only in the remotest of metaphorical senses.
> (Kelly, 1992: 4)

Assessment is inevitably subjective whether we like it or not. Our notions of childhood and our values are culturally determined. A seven-year-old in a British school who cannot read will almost certainly be causing concern; the same child in Denmark will only just be starting out on specific literacy learning. As Wyse and Styles (2007) recently argued, the current obsession with phonics as the prime means of teaching reading is contradicted by most research evidence, and ignores the individuality of the child. Our present education system seems set on teaching all reception-age children to learn decontextualised (high frequency) words, and to know all the sounds and letters of the alphabet, regardless of their interest or ability to do so. However, comparisons with Hungary and Denmark show clearly that children acquire these skills with ease a couple of years later.

Neuroscience brain research also adds daily to our understanding of young children's development (Gopnik et al., 2001). It has demonstrated, for example, the difference in development of the language centres in the brain between boys and girls, and the relatively late development of boys' vocabulary. We also know that all children, and boys in particular, need to develop their gross motor skills, wheeling large circles with their arms, before they are able to develop the fine motor skills needed to form the tight loops of handwriting.

Our view of literacy needs to be critically examined rather than accepted unquestioningly. As Tobin et al., (1989) so fascinatingly demonstrate, our values affect our curriculum and our judgments of children:

> In China the emphasis in language development is on enunciation, diction, memorization, and self-confidence in speaking and performing [...] Language in Japan – at least the kind of language teachers teach children – is viewed less as a tool for self-expression than as a medium for expressing group solidarity and shared purpose. Americans, in contrast, view words as the key to promoting individuality, autonomy, problem solving, friendship and cognitive development in children. In America children are taught the rules and conventions of self-expression and free speech. (Tobin, Wu and Davidson, 1989: 102–103)

The salutary lesson here is to be aware (and critical) of the value systems in which we operate.

Also important to consider is the polycultural society in which we live and the conflicting views this can give to children's own conceptions of literacy. As Gregory has so revealingly documented, the different forms and purposes of literacy bilingual children meet at home and at school can mean that schools often fail to build on the understandings and experiences that children bring from home (Gregory, 1996). Kenner (2000) has given some inspiring examples of ways of bringing children's home literacies into the classroom, such as using Turkish karaoke videos in the classroom and encouraging parents to write letters to far-off families, thus using the different scripts and languages of children's home lives for real purposes in school.

In England, there are now very specific, prescribed expectations for young children in their acquisition of literacy, through the Early Years Foundation Stage, the National Literacy Strategy and the National Curriculum. Although each aims to support children's development of literacy, there is an underlying problem. The narrower a target for children is, the more achievable it is, thus it is far easier to demonstrate clearly that a child can 'link sounds to letters, naming and sounding the letters of the alphabet' than that he or she can 'use talk to organise, sequence and clarify thinking, ideas, feelings and events' (DfES, 2007). At a time when teachers are increasingly pressured to prove their effectiveness, these easily quantifiable targets are in danger of edging out meaningful assessments of children's progress.

Within this context, then, how can the early years practitioner positively approach literacy? If we are to defend children's rights to be assessed and planned for in such a way that their literacy, their understanding and their self-esteem will be supported, then we need to be clear about the practical ways in which this can be achieved. Having dealt briefly with the wider question of why assess children's literacy, let us look more closely at the practicalities of implementing effective literacy assessment and planning in early years settings.

How should we observe, assess and plan?

With all the pressures on the early years professional practitioner it is hardly surprising that many educators feel that they have no time to stop, observe and reflect on the learning going on. Yet without this, everything that we do is of dubious value. Drummond (1993) argues for beginning that familiar cycle of early education practice: plan, do, observe, record, plan at a different point. We waste much of our energies on hopeful, often misdirected, planning. If we start with observing, analysing and reflecting on children's learning, the curriculum we offer children is likely to be a far better match to their individual and corporate concerns.

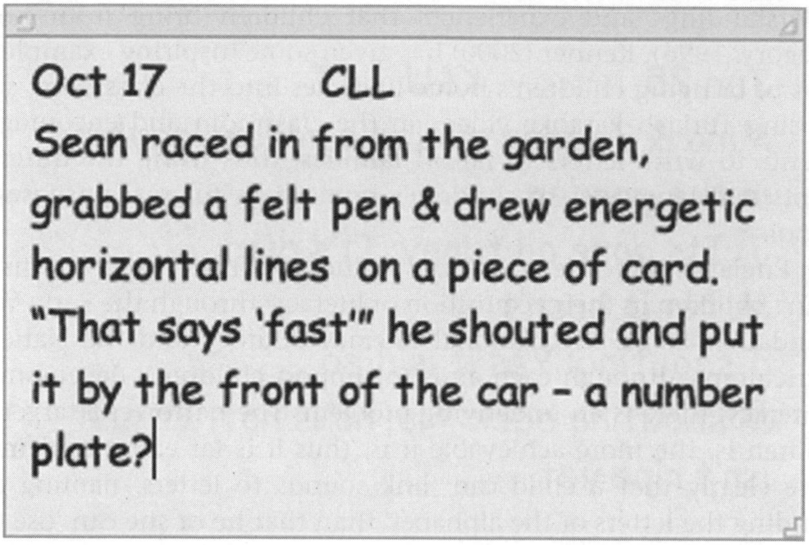

> Oct 17   CLL
> Sean raced in from the garden,
> grabbed a felt pen & drew energetic
> horizontal lines on a piece of card.
> "That says 'fast'" he shouted and put
> it by the front of the car – a number
> plate?|

Figure 13.1   Observational notes

Drummond (1993) frames the process of assessment as having three stages; collecting evidence, making judgments and from this there are outcomes. Observation provides valuable evidence that must then be carefully analysed and the judgements made from this go to inform the outcomes. Observation can be free or focussed, providing full narrative descriptions to be analysed later, or looking for particular aspects of learning – each has its place. Observation doesn't need to be (and often cannot be) removed from the life of the class or setting. Often the richest observations come while participating with children in an activity, frequently at a tangent to the subject in hand. 'See this', said Murat (3 years 11 months), holding up his bread at the lunch table, 'it's a triangle'. Taking a bite, he continues, 'Now it's an "L" shape, and now it's a number "1"!'

In recent years, early years teams have evolved increasingly efficient ways of recording these valuable but fleeting snippets of learning. Every practitioner develops his or her own preferred method of capturing these moments of 'significant achievement' (Hutchin, 2000). Some use pocket notebooks, many now use Post-it® notes and address labels so that moments such as these can be scribbled down, then transferred at the end of the day or week (examples can be seen in Figures 13.1 and 13.2).

Many early years settings have folders or clipboards pinned up in different areas so that interesting goings on can be jotted down there to be collated later. These fragments may seem small, but they are the

> Jun 25   K&U, LCT
> Mina & Jayden found a yellow ladybird
> in the garden.
> J: Its gone all funny. It's died
> M. No it hasn't
> J shouting: Yes it is died
> M shouting back: No, no is not. It just
> isn't ripe yet.

Figure 13.2 Observational notes

stuff of learning, and, importantly, in a staff team they can be reflected on and analysed later.

Interactions

Some of the most important assessments we do as early years practitioners never make it onto paper. The initial response to, 'Look what I can do', 'Come and see our garage' or 'It's gone all soggy' are the most crucial to the child. As Gura (1996) points out, 'evaluative praise' can have the opposite effect to the one intended. Comments such as 'That's lovely, dear' or 'I like the colour' can lead to over-dependence on adult authority judgements, and undermine independent thought and children's trust in themselves. Instead, descriptive or informational comments focussing on attributes of work or the processes involved, and discussions with children about their own intentions and meanings will provide children with a context for seriously assessing and celebrating their own work. To display interest to a child without committing yourself to a particular aspect of their learning is one of the surest ways of getting children to reveal their innermost thoughts. One of the most powerful words that can be uttered to a child is a gently interested 'mmmm?'.

We should also be wary of our own responses to children's perceptions of reality: 'My mum teaches me to write, at school I just play'.

As professionals, such conceptions of learning are deeply threatening to us, but it is the child's understandings, and their families, that we need to work with, not deny, if we are to support his or her learning. Discussions with children and parents about the learning going on can lead to a real collaboration in the learning process, in which everyone feels involved and valued.

One of the most potent strategies for a team (however small) is the review at the end of the day. This can be 10 to 15 minutes when staff sit down, collate and share observations, interpret their findings and use them as the base for planning, both for individual children and for the curriculum. One nursery school noticed a large number of children interested in enveloping and enclosing (Athey, 1990), and decided to extend this across their provision. The team incorporated Eve Sutton's picture book *My Cat Likes to Hide in Boxes* as a theme, but also provided hidey-holes in the garden, construction that covered things up, wrapping up materials in the workshop, and different-sized cats for different-sized boxes. This use of the real evidence of what children do know and are interested in to inform the planning generated a powerful match of curriculum with children's interests and a focus that lasted productively for several weeks.

Sampling

Observations are one form of evidence, but it is important to collect a range of forms of evidence to build up a holistic picture of children's abilities. Most nurseries and schools now keep folders with regular samples of children's work, but these also need to be meaningful examples of children's own work, not merely samples of adult-directed tasks or all work collected on a single day. There is also a danger here that sampling may focus on the end product, and that some children will produce reams of drawings and writing which are easy to store, while others will be immersed in huge constructions, wild dramatic play or other forms of representation equally valid but far harder to preserve. Photographs are powerful tools here, and while they cannot capture the full experience, they can, with notes, record an important moment. Recording talk, whether it is taped or a scribbled transcription, is very revealing; the actual words children use, demonstrating their oral skills and their thinking, are very powerful indicators of a child's progress. For every sample of children's thinking, the context in which it takes place is important; a piece of paper with two scribbles on will tell us little on its own, but the accompanying note – '2:10:97, Belal came straight in and wrote this from right to left and said, "That's my Koran writing, I do it at my house". First time I've seen him writing' – adds considerably to our knowledge of his growing biliteracy.

Profiles

From this collection of samples, observations, conversations and photos, significant evidence can be selected to form a profile. This is a cumulative, developmental record charting children's progress over time. Increasingly, early years settings are involving children and families in this process, so that the child is consulted on what pictures, photos and observations are included, often sticking them in themselves. These treasured books can then be kept accessible and provide a focus for children, staff and parents to read, discuss and reflect on them.

In recent years, the Learning Stories pioneered in New Zealand by Margaret Carr (2001) have begun to influence assessment practices in the UK. Her learning stories are firmly rooted in the context of the New Zealand curriculum 'Te Whaariki' but draw powerfully on the work of Susan Isaacs and Mary Jane Drummond. She argues that assessment should be charted against a few broad learning dispositions rather than a plethora of narrow skills and knowledge, and that these should provide an ongoing narrative picture of the child, and a framework for discussion between practitioners, parents and children. The stories themselves are pieces of narrative observation that are then analysed against the dispositions of belonging, well-being, exploration, communication and contribution. In the UK, practitioners have welcomed the 'story' approach to children's learning in its emphasis on the uniqueness of each child, and the support it gives to a developmental approach to assessment and learning. In many settings, this is translating into the reflective use of narrative observations, development of profile books, parental involvement, and dialogue with children and families about their learning. Fortune Park Children's Centre, in Islington, London, uses their profile books as a shared document between home and school, with parents and children adding in photos, drawings and comments alongside those from staff. Maria, a busy Foundation Stage coordinator of a three-form entry school works with her team each week making narrative observations (learning stories) on the three or four children per class that are her focus children for that week. These are then discussed with staff alongside other assessments and shared with parents as the children become the focus for planning the following week.

Who should be involved

It is an awesome responsibility to sit in judgement on another human being and it is one that should be shared. It is both a truism and a fact, that has yet to be truly recognised in practice, that parents and carers are their children's first teachers. Children do not arrive in early years settings in a vacuum, but have a wealth and diversity of experience behind them. Records from playgroup or other settings, admissions forms, settling-in forms, and the first parent and child conferences can all provide valuable information on which to build. Parents can and should be active collaborators both in supporting and assessing children's literacy development, using a flexible range of structures: PACT schemes, home–school books with room for comments, regular conferences, parents reading, writing and talking in class.

Where possible, observation and assessment should also be shared between a key worker with prime responsibility for keeping a child's records, alongside a team who will all feed in their own observations and analysis, committed to collaborating, remaining flexible and receptive to sharing views and information. The aim for a complete view of the child is far more likely to be realised by this counterbalancing of different views, than by supposedly objective tick lists or tests. This is especially true when those views represent different training, as is the case with teachers and nursery nurses, and different types of relationships with the child, as with parents and staff. Here, I am proposing both a more arduous and more fulfilling task than the brief standardised assessments of checklists and tests. In this light, all the concerned adults are acting as action researchers, viewing and reviewing their understandings in a spirit of passionate enquiry. This demands highly knowledgeable, deeply reflective practitioners able to perceive individual threads of learning amongst the densely woven fabric of children's play. Such practitioners need to hold in their heads the many possible interpretations of children's play, to intervene (or not) in just such a way as their intimate knowledge of the child tells them will best support and extend the learning going on.

Self-assessment

Recent research on self-esteem (Goleman, 1995; Roberts, 1995) has clarified the extent to which the child's own emotions and dispositions affect their learning, and their involvement in the process of evaluating their learning is increasingly being shown to be crucial to their success (Gura, 1996). Stephen (5 years 4 months) who repeatedly tore up his work, saying (as his older brother Mark said), 'It's rubbish, it's just scribble', was amazed to see Mark's own samples of writing from nursery onwards, each struggle valued and preserved. Stephen was encouraged to try again and Mark became the competent writer sharing his skills.

We need to 'let children into the secret' (Hutchin, 1996: 16) of their own learning and engage them in an ongoing dialogue that takes their interests and their own view of their learning seriously. Involving children in self-assessment shares the power with them and by encouraging reflection and metacognition enables them to gain greater understanding of the processes of learning (Eisner, 1996; Gardner, 1993). Just as a bilingual child may have a greater understanding of how language works by their ability to understand more than one language, so too all children can benefit from thinking about their own thought processes, and about the things that have helped them learn. Equally, we need to recognise the power of their community of peers. Trying to write his name on his picture, Justin (4 years 2 months) said despairingly, 'I can't do S. I can do sharks but not S.' 'Yeah' said his friend Ross (4 years 4 months) consolingly, 'You just never know which way they're going to go'.

What should be observed

In terms of even the simplest interpretation of literacy, the adult needs to understand and recognise children's development of mark-making, iconic and symbolic representations, and support their access to culturally set forms of symbols and calligraphic skills (see Chapter, 7 this volume). Early years practitioners need a wide range of subject knowledge about child development and literacy development to fully recognise and support children's learning. We need to understand and support children's specific development in phonic, grapho-phonic, syntactic, semantic and bibliographic knowledge, and to be prepared to find them in unexpected places.

Anna (4 years 6 months) hasn't spoken much since her mother died, but every day she constructs her funfair in the block play and carefully re-enacts her day out there. Her play reworks and reviews her understanding of a symbolic system in a way which will transfer as a skill to her reworking of written language, but it also fulfils her own deep need as adult-led activities would not. Shane (3 years 7 months) spends most of his time out of doors circling, wheeling and diving, perfecting on a grand scale those movements which provide the foundation of the circles and curves needed for letter formation. Shakil (4 years 3 months) is endlessly caught up in a cycle of violent role play as Duplo cars crash and people die, his whirling scenarios are the patchwork pieces of later dramatic compositions. Jade's (4 years 10 months) insistence on singing, 'Stinky winky bum bum' is not only a cheeky piece of insubordination, but also a piece of phonic wordplay, more fun and more informative than is to be found in all the text-books and reading schemes. Gulcan (1 year 2 months), who repeatedly pulls down the photo book of babies from the shelf and babbles to it as she turns the pages, already knows lots about how books work and sees reading as a worthwhile activity. Each of these children is engaged in a 'literacy activity' worth observing, analysing and acting on within the context of their individual development and need.

Literacy development, as we have seen, cannot be confined to for-mal instruction in reading and writing, but occurs spontaneously within many different contexts. What we choose to see as significant in the development of literacy depends on a deep understanding of the many processes involved. Riley (1996) suggests that the emer-gence of literacy into conventional forms is an interactive process combining meaning-making and code-breaking strategies, both of which need to be recognised and supported. Latifah (3 years 4 months), sweeping her hand through the fingerprint and saying, 'Look a rainbow, like in Rainbow room' is both using symbols to rep-resent her world and linking them with other symbolic knowledge. Matthew (4 years), excitedly recounting the fight he witnessed outside the pub, is extending his oral skills and struggling to put his experience into narrative form. Harry (4 years 3 months), looking at the Halifax logo and saying, 'That's in my name' is beginning to focus on envi-ronmental print and to recognise individual features. Saida (4 years 1 month), laughing because her friend Billy's name sounds like the Punjabi name for 'cat', has discovered homophones. Zoe (4 years 10 months), scribbling urgently on scrumpled pieces of paper and stuffing them into envelopes, is 'paying the bills' and demonstrating her knowledge of the purposes of writing. Dominic (4 years 8 months), painstakingly copying 'Crayola washable felt pens' onto a piece of paper, is extending his repertoire of mastered words; he knows now that there is a right way to write and is intent on achieving it. If we look only for narrow achievements, the easily observable and the superficial, then we miss the deep learning going on underneath.

Athey's research (1990), that highlighted the complexities of chil-dren's learning through absorption in schematic patterns of behaviour, has given us a new light to shine on children developing literacy. Not only are the graphic forms of writing first experimented with in action and across different media, but more fundamentally we can key into a deep level of interest in the interactions, the stories and the provision we offer them. Damien (4 years 4 months), engrossed in exploring a horizontal schema, loved producing lines of writing on the computer, and would spend hours writing letters on very long thin pieces of paper. He was interested in the directionality of print on the page, and the stories he loved were *The Line Up Book, The Elephant and the Bad Baby* and *The Enormous Turnip*, each with their long horizontal lines.

Where should children be observed?

Everything we know about young children's learning tells us that the child reveals his or her greatest knowledge and skills during child-initiated activities, and, in particular, during play. It is important to remember the distortions that can occur if we try to assess children in a test environment, and when tests they are given don't make sense to them. As Donaldson's (1978) famous revision of Piaget's work demonstrated, a task that children were unable to do in a vacuum, they performed with ease when it was presented to them in a way that made 'human sense'.

Thus, the child's abilities should be observed and analysed during the everyday good practice of the early years setting, alone and in groups, outside and inside, remembering that learning takes place during lunchtime, by the coat pegs and in the toilets. Hall and Robinson (2003) have demonstrated how confidently children take on literate behaviour, in particular given a variety of provision as part of imaginative play. Nor should it be forgotten that the setting is only one part of the child's life and that important information and experiences from home will add greatly to our understanding. Jimmy (4 years) proudly wrote the Chinese character for water, that he had learnt at community school that week, on all his pictures.

When should children be assessed?

Essentially, assessment must be a continuing record of the child's progress, constantly reviewing and updating the shared understanding of his or her learning. Regular, informal discussion with children and parents makes this a part of everyday life. Termly or yearly formal parent conferences allow a deeper, more solid review of progress to take place. Observation itself needs to pick up on spontaneous happenings of note, but can also be more organised to track a particular child over time or to survey the use of a particular area.

As with where we assess, it is important to look at children at different times; children reveal their knowledge in different ways and leaping to conclusions may lead us to seriously underestimate the child. Children who are silent when they arrive, or at group time, may be vociferous at lunchtime or when playing outside. Knowledge of how children are in the home can check our assumptions made about them in school. Jordan (4 years 2 months), a sociable and energetic constructor at school, was an only child who peopled his home world with imaginary friends and by storytelling extraordinary adventures.

Ideally, a balance needs to be struck between maintaining frequent observations, making sure that quiet or self-sufficient children don't slip through the net, allowing time for dense narrative descriptions that can be unpicked at leisure, and noting the particular significant moments (Hutchin, 1996) which mark a change or progression in the child's thinking.

Planning for language and literacy development

If observation and assessment are woven into the fabric of the curriculum as I have suggested, then planning becomes a more logical, meaningful and less arduous process for all concerned. Planning for literacy should be building on a rich existing basis, including: knowledge of the individual child, their interests, progress and learning styles, and a learning environment that encourages a rich diversity of language and literacy opportunities. Children need routines that are supportive, and adults with secure subject knowledge and a store of strategies to develop children's burgeoning imagination and abilities. Most of all, children need to have good reasons for developing their language and literacies, both for purpose and for pleasure.

The environment needs to be planned to provide opportunities for listening and talking, and reading and writing across a whole range of purposes and genres. Interesting and well-resourced role play areas, furniture arranged to encourage collaboration, exciting writing areas and cosy reading corners inside and out will promote learning. Outside spaces need areas for chalking, clipboards with pens attached, easels that can be used for mark-making, notices, scoreboards, waiting lists, etc. and role play set ups that give children real reasons to write (Hall and Robinson, 2003).

Structures and routines can be seen as opportunities for developing communication and literacy; self-registration systems, relaxed chatty lunchtimes, a careful balance of child-initiated and adult-directed activities, and a timetable that allows children freedom to explore at length and in depth are all ways to enhance learning opportunities for children. Nurseries and schools as institutions can easily develop routines that run counter to children's learning (sitting quietly, lining up in silence, taking hours over the register), but alert practitioners are quick to see the potential for learning and for empowering children by involving them in routines. One nursery school engaged two helpers every day to take around the 'big book' and record which adults wanted tea or coffee, a reception teacher encouraged children to write up their name on the waiting list for the bikes, and again for the computer. Another nursery has a 'tidy-up inspector' who, armed with a clipboard, checks and makes notes on the tidiness of each area.

Planning for language and literacy needs to be within the context of the whole curriculum, all areas of learning intersect and the aim should be to encourage 24-hour literacy, not a 'literacy hour'. Long-term planning for language and literacy should use official curricula, such as the Early Years Foundation Stage in England, as its launching pad, and there is no need for other laborious documentation. Schemes of work and long-term commitment to certain repeated topics are more likely to stifle creativity than be a useful structure for planning. The long-term aim for the practitioner is to encourage each child to develop her or his language and literacies in their own unique way, and to leave the Foundation Stage excited and enthusiastic about their learning.

Long-term planning for literacy can be enhanced by an agreed list of core books and rhymes that provide a store of high-quality texts that children will get to know well during their time in the setting. These texts can be developed with multiple copies and big books, with story sacks, story props and puppets to extend children's experiences. Core books and their props provide a strong basis for all children to develop confidence in their literacy but the visual support, clear illustrations and repetitive texts are particularly supportive for bilingual children and for some children with special educational needs.

Medium-term planning should not be detailed or rigid. The purpose of such planning is most of all to plan for excitement, to think ahead about broad themes, trips out, role play areas; rich experiences that will provide a launch pad for children's learning but that may require forward planning and organising. It may include a rough plan ahead by week, so that a whole team can be aware of key books, major events and experiences.

... no plan written weeks in advance can include a group's interest in a spider's web or a particular child's interest in transporting small objects in a favourite blue bucket, yet it is these interests which may lead to some powerful learning. Plans should therefore be flexible enough to adapt to circumstances. (DfES, 2007: 12)

Short-term planning is the key to effective practice, using the accumulated knowledge of practitioners and parents to plan learning experiences that will really match and challenge children's development. In practice, this is generally a weekly plan based on a review of the past week and of particular children. An example of a planning format can be seen in Figure 13.3. Confident practitioners will often leave sections of the planning free towards the end of the week in the expectation that plenty of possibilities will arise from the children's own ideas.

In a reception unit, Sam and Cameron spent Tuesday racing around being Batman and Robin; their slightly exasperated nursery nurse suggested that they designed and made costumes. By Thursday, this suggestion had spread like wildfire and all over their reception unit costumes were being designed and made, materials explored, stories told and roles negotiated. The responsive reception team were quick to capitalise on the learning potential and planned focus activities were abandoned in favour of this tidal wave of excitement. Some settings are increasingly planning from individual children; for example, taking four children a week, reviewing their current learning and interests and planning both focus and independent activities specifically with them in mind. In this system each child is planned for in depth every half-term, and, of course, activities planned always engage plenty of other children too.

These plans should both extend children's interests and abilities, and aim to engage them in areas of learning that they are not accessing. Wilf, whose reading and wild dramatic play far outstripped his mark-making abilities, was chosen to be one of a group of boys writing a superhero story scribed by the teacher. The story construction extended his compositional abilities, reading it out to the class celebrated and extended his reading fluency, and for the first time he chose to illustrate a page of the book alongside his friends and began to draw and develop his mark-making skills.

Planning for children up to three

The development of integrated centres and children's centres has prompted a critical look at our existing planning systems. A weekly

PSE	Communication, language and literacy	Problem-solving, reasoning and numeracy	Knowledge and understanding	Physical	Creative	
Themes, visits, core texts	Focus activity Staff Children Learning intentions	Focus activity Staff Children Learning intentions	Shared area Focus activity	Outdoor Focus activity	Independent activities	Group times	Other
Monday						
Tuesday						
Wednesday						
Thursday						
Friday						
Focus children	Children to observe			Outings, visits, events		Messages, homework

Figure 13.3   Example of a weekly planner

plan often does not fit the lightning pace of change in a toddler's interests. The younger the child, the more flexible and focussed around the individual child the planning needs to be.

Farina's (20 months old) energetic exploration of her food at lunchtime prompted her key worker to provide cornflour and finger paint for her to explore over the next few days, encouraging her burgeoning mark-making. Ten months old Hussein's key worker, Diane, spent much of the afternoon responding with eye contact, smiles and echoing to his sudden burst of joyful vocalising. Practitioners at a north London Children's Centre use a simple planning format with each child's name on a sheet of A4 pinned to the wall; one side has observations and the other planning ideas. Staff jot straight onto the sheet or stick on Post-® it notes. There is no time for formal planning meetings, but staff sit with the children at the end of each day, look at the sheets, discuss what has happened alongside the children and plan for the following day. They are thus reflecting and responding in intimate detail to the individual development of each child.

Summative records and transitions

There are points in a child's progress at which a summary of their achievements needs to be made; for example, when the child moves from one setting to another. For the harassed teacher receiving 30 reports at once, formative assessments are too detailed and need to be synthesised to be helpful. Summative assessments that track the individual child's progress are more likely to give a true picture of the individual child, and a more helpful starting point for furthering their development. These records should draw on the accumulated evidence and knowledge of all those involved with the child; they should be precise about what the child can do, their skills and their conceptual development, but also focus on their interests and their attitudes towards literacy, since these will be crucial in fostering their development. Systems that include brief samples of children's work and observations alongside the summative comments give a stronger 'snapshot' of the individual child than comments alone. In these summaries, too, children can have their voices heard. One reception practitioner has a learning wall with photos of every child, and alongside each photo a statement and a plan; for example, 'I can hop on one foot across the playground', 'I want to bake a strawberry cake' (see Figure 13.4) and so on.

As the year progresses, these personal targets are achieved and reviewed, and unsurprisingly every child can read most of this display.

Figure 13.4   The learning wall

These summative records too have their place in planning for the child, whenever there is point of transition. From home to nursery, nursery to reception or reception to Year 1, it is crucial that those receiving these carefully prepared summative records take them seriously and use them as a foundation for future planning.

Conclusion

In this chapter, I have proposed that observation, assessment and planning of young children's literacy need to reflect both the principles of early years education and a broad interpretation of literacy. Assessment should, therefore, be positive, celebrating children's achievements and valuing their struggles and mistakes. It should be formative, concerned with process as well as product, with meaning-making as well as code-breaking. It should take place as an integral part of the child's daily experiences, based firmly on careful observation and analysis, and should include all the significant people, most importantly the children themselves. Planning based on this dense knowledge of the child can then be effective, exciting and remain flexible and able to respond quickly to change and development.

Above all, effective assessment and planning must be helpful to the child; assessment that does not support the child's development is at best a waste of precious time and at worst can damage children's self-esteem and, thus, their capacity to learn. If instead assessment can help us tune into the child's experiences, understandings, expectations and enthusiasms, then we can more effectively plan for and support their development of a powerful range of literacies for life.

It has not been my aim in this chapter to provide a template for assessing and planning for literacy; instead I have put forward principles and some strategies. Developmental assessments require thinking practitioners who will draw from a range of sources to create forms and methods rooted in thoughtful practice, tailored to their needs and always open to change. Meaningful planning should be broad in its reach but focussed in its support of individual children. Creative planning for literacy should leave a memory with the child, and be the springboard for learning, not a straitjacket. To finish where I began with Hana, I am reminded of those occasions when she did tell a story to the end, thoughtfully self-assessing. Again there would be some husky breathing, then she would say 'Did you enjoy that my story? – Quite good really ...'.

Suggestions for further reading 📖

Godwin, D. and Perkins, M. (2002) *Teaching Language and Literacy in the Early Years*. London: David Fulton.

Hutchin, V. (2007) *Supporting Every Child's Learning across the Early Years Foundation Stage*. London: Hodder Murray.

Whitehead, M. (2004) *Language and Literacy in the Early Years*. Third edition. London: Paul Chapman.

References

Athey, C. (1990) *Extending Thought in Young Children*. London: Paul Chapman.
Carr, M. (2001) *Assessment in Early Childhood Settings: Learning Stories*. London: Paul Chapman.
DfES (2007) *Statutory Framework for the Early Years Foundation Stage*. Nottingham: DfES Publications.
Donaldson, M. (1978) *Children's Minds*. Glasgow: Fontana.
Drummond, M.J. (1993) *Assessing Children's Learning*. London: David Fulton.
Eisner, E. (1996) *Cognition and Curriculum Reconsidered*. London: Paul Chapman.
Gardner, H. (1993) *The Unschooled Mind*. London: Fontana.
Goleman, D. (1995) *Emotional Intelligence*. London: Bloomsbury.
Gopnik, A., Meltzoff, A. and Kuhl, P. (2001) *How Babies Think*. London: Phoenix.
Gregory, E. (1996) *Making Sense of a New World*, London: Paul Chapman.

Gura, P. (1996) 'What I want for Cinderella: self-esteem and self-assessment', *Early Education* Summer: 3–5.

Hall, N. and Robinson, A. (2003) *Exploring Writing and Play in the Early Years.* London: David Fulton.

Hutchin, V. (1996) *Tracking Significant Achievement: The Early Years.* London: Hodder and Stoughton.

Kelly, A.V. (1992) 'Concepts of assessment: an overview', in G. Blenkin and A.V. Kelly (eds) *Assessment in Early childhood Education.* London: Paul Chapman.

Kenner, C. (2000) *Home Pages.* Stoke-on-Trent: Trentham.

Lewis, J. (2006) *The Enormous Turnip.* London: Ladybird.

Riley, J. (1996) *The Teaching of Reading: The Development of Literacy in the Early Years of School.* London: Sage.

Roberts, R. (1995) *Self-esteem and Successful Early Learning.* London: Hodder and Stoughton.

Russo, M. (1986) *The Line Up Book.* New York: Greenwillow.

Sutton, E. (1978) *My Cat Likes to Hide in Boxes.* Illustrated by Lynley Dodd. Harmondsworth: Puffin.

Tobin, D., Wu, D. and Davidson, D. (1989) *Preschool in Three Cultures.* New Haven: Yale University Press.

Vipont, E. (1971) *The Elephant and the Bad Baby.* Harmondsworth: Puffin.

Whitehead, M. (1990) *Language and Literacy in the Early Years.* London: Paul Chapman.

Wyse, D. and Styles, M. (2007) 'Synthetic phonics and the teaching of reading: the debate surrounding England's "Rose Report"', *Literacy* 41 (1): 35–42.

Index

Added to a page number 'f' denotes a figure and 't' denotes a table.